WILLIE

By

Willie Kell

© 2003 by Willie Kell. All rights reserved.

No part of this book may be reproduced, stored in a
retrieval system, or transmitted by any means, electronic,
mechanical, photocopying, recording, or otherwise, without
written permission from the author.

ISBN: 1-4107-0370-3 (e-book)
ISBN: 1-4107-0371-1 (Paperback)

Library of Congress Control Number: 2002096475

This book is printed on acid free paper.

Printed in the United States of America
Bloomington, IN

Edited – Barbara Storey

1stBooks - rev. 04/01/03

Contents

Book One: The Medicine Man 1
Book Two: The Pioneers—Dad, Maw, Old John, and Mary 15
Book Three: When Mother Died 32
Book Four: Pal, The Wonder Dog 55
Book Five: Life, On Maw's Old Farm 65
Book Six: When Maw Died 91
Book Seven: My Life With Daddy and Mary 105
Book Eight: Out On My Own—At 14 118
Book Nine: The Innkeepers 125
Book Ten: Learning About Girls and Other Things 132
Book Eleven: I'm In the Army Now 140
Book Twelve: Love, Marriage, and Irene 152
Book Thirteen: Being a Medicine Man, Like Daddy 162
Book Fourteen: The Derby 171
Book Fifteen: God Bless Our Borrowed Tent 179
Book Sixteen: This Old House 186
Book Seventeen: Billy Was Born 200
Book Eighteen: The Gambler 203
Book Nineteen: June 1953—Our Patti and Shakespeare 210
Book Twenty: The Executioners 214
Book Twenty-one: One Night of Cheatin' 217
Book Twenty-two: The Great Betrayal 224
Book Twenty-three: The Big Race 230
Book Twenty-four: Jimmy, From Whence He Came 236
Book Twenty-five: Our Own Farm 238
Book Twenty-six: The Cardboard Guitars 243
Book Twenty-seven: The Race Announcer 245
Book Twenty-eight: Irene and her Racehorses 249

Book Twenty-nine: The Creamcheeze Good-Time Band 258
Book Thirty: Cutting Records, National TV, The Forum 261
Book Thirty-one: Record Deal With MCA, World's Largest 264
Book Thirty-two: The Wedding by The Willow —and Other Interesting Things 266
Book Thirty-three: Sometimes It's Hell 270
Book Thirty-four: Cutting The MCA Album and Cutting Irene Loose 273
Book Thirty-five: Good Night, Irene—I'll See You in My Dreams 276
Book Thirty-six: The Cousins 278
Book Thirty-seven: Guitar Pickin', Songwritin' Son of a Gun 280
Book Thirty-eight: Nashville, New Orleans, and Texas 283
Book Thirty-nine: I'm Published 286
Book Forty: Pitching Songs In Nashville and Loving Her 293
Book Forty-one: The Serpent of Florida 297
Book Forty-two: The Life and Songs Of Stephen Foster 301
Book Forty-three: Beautiful Stoney Keppel 306
Book Forty-four: Jesus, Fanny Crosby, and Me 310
Book Forty-five: Billy's Last Song 312
Book Forty-six: Billy's Gone, Who's Going to Sing His Songs? 317
Book Forty-seven: Playing The Big Stage 319
Book Forty-eight: The Big One That Got Away— 324
Book Forty-nine: Willie Kell Presents "HANK WILLIAMS—HIS LIFE AND HIS SONGS" At The Port Charlotte Cultural Center Theatre, Florida 327
Book Fifty: Time's Winding Down—Still Living on Dreams 330

Introduction Page (1st)

'Willie'

The true story of a child growing up during the Great Depression, then the War.

The son of a horse trading, old-time medicine man. When Willie's mother died he went to live on "Grandmaw's" farm, was educated in a one room school.

Summer nights, was bath time back at the creek with the bullfrogs.

He tells the heart-wrenching story of a boy and his dog "Pal".

Willie grew up to follow in his Daddy's footsteps, selling they're home-cooked wonder medicine for a time.

Then later became a famous harness race announcer, on TV and radio.

He tells of world- renowned drivers he has known and of the big race he won with a two hundred-dollar horse.

He talks of his times among his horse & buggy Amish friends.

His acquaintance with some of Hollywood's biggest movie stars.

A close encounter with Murder and the Hangman!

Willie's children grew up to become well-known entertainers, making several recordings and television appearances.

Willie himself became a Nashville songwriter and recording artist and there was the million-dollar song!

An amazing story of an impoverished childhood, the tragedies and triumphs, his travels through Canadian winters and across the sunny southern U.S.A.

His is a life of love, lust, heartbreak and self-made success.

You will laugh, you will cry and you will surely be entertained as he spins his incredible story!

Discography

Albums on C-disk and cassette

The Life and Songs of Stephen Foster
Narration of Stephen Foster's life along with his best songs

Beautiful Stoney Keppel
Original songs and a couple of classics

Jesus His Life on Earth
Narration of the life of Jesus along with tribute to Fanny Crosby
And 10 of Willie's gospel songs

Willie Kell in Nashville
original songs

Willie Kell back in Nashville
original songs

Songs of Love and Life
original songs

Songs are property of Old John Records—williekell.net

I dedicate this book to those who have touched my life in some special way and gave me a reason to write it.

Willie

Book One: The Medicine Man

Being born on a warm August morning under the stars of Leo, in a place nestled along the shore of beautiful Georgian Bay in southern Ontario, has, I suppose, in no small way played a part in my love for the winds of summer. I guess the melodic sounds of splashing water washing onto the rocky shores still sing in my mind, like some romantic song. Through the years I have borrowed from those sounds in creating my music.

I began to travel an interesting and entertaining pathway of time at just ten days old. When the day came for Mother and I to go home from the hospital where I was born, Daddy came, along with my older brothers and sisters, and took us to the big three-ring circus that was playing in our town. I sometimes wonder if that first look at the world outside left me with a yearning and a special love for show business and the people who are a part of this wonderful, gypsy way of life. Although I don't remember the sound of the ringmaster with his golden voice, introducing the acts, or the roar of the lions, tigers and elephants, or the cracking of the lion-tamer's whip, being just ten days old, and I can't recall the smell of the sawdust scattered on the ground under the big top, but I believe—in some kind of fairy-tale way—that wonderful circus day has influenced and led me on the interesting, winding pathways that I have walked.

My first recollection of life in this world, as I look back into the rearview mirror of time, is being an observant and sometimes imaginative little boy at the tender age of three, living in that pretty town in a little white house covered with a mixture of plaster and cement called roughcast. There were four rather small rooms in the house and eight people living there, Daddy, Mother, and us six children. I was the second youngest. Our baby sister Elizabeth was only a few months old. That was the fall of 1929, just at the time of the big stock market crash. The "roaring twenties" were down to their last whimper, and for most of the next decade we struggled through a cruel and merciless economic depression that engulfed the world as we knew it. Those years were known as the dirty thirties.

Daddy had bought the place for five hundred dollars by trading a horse in on it. It had a small barn, a garden, and there was a gully running between our place and the neighbours'. Daddy made arrangements for the garbage men to dump the ashes, cinders, and dry garbage in the ravine, to fill it up. There would be bottles, cans, and all kinds of interesting things among that garbage. They would bring it on certain days of the week in big wagons pulled by giant teams of horses. It was something to look forward to. This was also a great place to play. Fred—the neighbour boy next door—and I would spend hours in that gully finding all kinds of treasures.

Our house had no electricity, at first. Daddy had that put in the next year after we moved there. But we did have running water that came out of one tap over the kitchen sink. Besides the kitchen, there was a front room and two bedrooms upstairs. Mother did all the cooking on a wood-burning cookstove, both summer and winter. We had a table, an assortment of chairs, and a sideboard cupboard for the dishes. There was a trapdoor leading to the basement, where the vegetables and preserves were kept. It was cool in the basement; the milk sat on a ledge at the bottom of the stairs.

Willie

In the front room we had a small coal-burning stove and a large dining room table with matching chairs and buffet. There was a pullout couch, where my two older brothers and I slept. Our two older sisters slept together in one room upstairs, and our baby sister slept in Daddy and Mother's room. Although it may have been a bit crowded, and tempers would flare up from time to time, I would say that, for the most part, we got along real well. There was a lot of happiness in that little home.

We had no modern facilities, but a half-decent outhouse in back with two large holes, as I remember. I was *always* afraid of falling in, and it seemed a long way to the bottom, especially just after it was cleaned out. Our toilet paper was part of a catalogue hung by bindertwine on the inside of the door. The cracks between the old, dried-out pine boards were big enough so you could see what was going on outside in the daytime. After dark, one of my brothers or sisters would light the coal-oil lantern and come out with me. It was always kind of scary in that little back house at night, with those giant shadows dancing on the walls. My sister, Florence, would tell me ghostly stories, and in the eerie stillness of the night there would seem to be strange noises. The outhouse left a lasting impression on my mind, and to this very day, I am rather uneasy alone in the quiet darkness. And although I have never seen a real-live ghost, perhaps there have been times when they have seen me.

There was another intriguing thing about that old toilet out back. Every once in a while, when those mountains beneath the holes would get up near the top, a big wooden-wheeled wagon would come in the night, pulled by what seemed to me, as a child, a ghostly team of horses. This wagon was like a big wooden box with a top on it; there was a smoky old lantern that hung on the side, along with a couple of shovels. Then there were

Willie Kell

two strange men sitting up front on the seat of that wagon; one was white and one was black. They would drive this big old wagon around to the back and clean out the toilet. We called them scavengers. Even though we knew better, we pulled back the curtains to gawk at them. We could hear the clanging of their shovels as they worked out there by the light of their smoky old lantern. When the job was finished, they backed the team around and drove the old wagon out into the night. The next morning you could see the marks of the wagon wheels and the footprints of the horseshoes in the driveway, and once again the back house was cleaned out.

There were two years between each of the first four children in our family. Then six years between Jim and me, and then two years and nine months after I was born, Elizabeth came along. Florence was the oldest, then Birdell, then Arnold, Jim was next, then me and Elizabeth. The three oldest all had nicknames, and I will refer to them always by those: Florence was Toots, Birdell was Sweet, Arnold was Son. Everyone knew them by these names, which stayed with them through life. For a time, I was Dodger.

Mother was rather a frail woman—five foot two inches, weighing about ninety-five pounds—with dark hair and a pretty smile. She had developed rheumatic fever in her teens and it left her with a heart ailment that plagued her for life. And life wasn't that easy for Mother, having to cook over the old wood cookstove for six kids. She washed our clothes by hand—heating the water in a boiler on the stove and using old-fashioned bar soap, she then scrubbed them on a washboard. Mother was very artistic, and an expert seamstress. She made most of our clothes, even our coats, out of old clothes folks gave her. She was a good, God-fearing, beautiful human being.

Willie

Daddy was a handsome, talented, very bright man who stood about five foot eight, of slight build but with broad shoulders and strong hands and arms. He was born in a farmhouse in Perth County, Ontario. Although he only weighed in at two pounds when he was born, and almost died when he was operated on for appendicitis when he was seventeen (they operated three times before they got it right), he went on to become a tough man. But the effects of that operation left him with a bad heart that bothered him from time to time. And his hair turned grey early in life as a result of all the ether he was given during the operations. Daddy was born with a nice smile and had a great gift with words. Both of these attributes contributed to his success as a salesman and made him endearing to the opposite sex.

It was about the time when we moved into that little white house that he started selling patent medicine. He got the recipe for this medicine from a friend on a horse trade. This friend had stolen it from a medicine man who had travelled around for years selling it. That medicine man had stolen it from an old doctor. Although it had an interesting and questionable past, this same medicine was quite a good product.

It was made from a combination of herbal extracts, glycerine, magnesium sulphate, potassium nitrate, oil of wintergreen, Barbados aloes, and a generous mount of H_2O. Mother or Daddy made the stuff on that old cookstove in a big granite kettle. The ingredients were slowly stirred in with a wooden spoon. After it was cooked, it was left to cool. Then this kettle of medicine was set on the kitchen table and brought up to volume with water. Next thing was to dip it out of the kettle with a pitcher and fill the bottles. At first they were 12-ounce bottles but years later the size was reduced to 8 ounces. Mostly they were used bottles, which meant they had to be washed and boiled. When the bottles were filled, they

Willie Kell

had to be corked. Daddy would press the corks in against the corner of the table. Next the corks were dipped into a brownish-red bee's-wax mixture that sealed them. Later on, plastic caps were used. Each bottle was labelled and then wrapped in newspaper. The aroma of the medicine hung around for a day or two, floating throughout the little house. Mother came up with the name Ton-A-Lax, and that's the way it was patented.

In the winter Daddy went selling it with a horse and cutter. He would drive out in the country or to a village, sometimes staying with the farmers or village folk for a night or two. He would put his horse in their barn, have supper and breakfast with the folks, trading them a bottle of medicine for his keep. If he was lucky, he might come home in a day or two with a bit of money, and often he traded medicine for vegetables, butter, eggs, or meat. After all, there were eight hungry mouths to feed at our house. Sometimes he would put five or six bottles in his overcoat pockets and walk around town, selling it from door to door.

When the springtime came and the roads were open for cars, he would load up a case of forty-eight bottles, head out in the Model T Ford, and go selling this great wonder medicine for several miles around in the country. Those days, the label read, "Famous Indian blood purifier and rheumatism remedy." As time went on, all of these beautiful accolades had to be removed from the labels. Little by little, through the years and through government regulations, the words were finally reduced to just the name and directions.

Ton-A-Lax was priced at a dollar twenty-five a bottle, but Daddy would encourage his customers to buy what he called "a treatment." A treatment was ten bottles for ten dollars. He explained that, although they were only paying for eight bottles, they were getting ten.

Willie

After all, they didn't get that old arthritis in a day and it would take awhile to get it out of the system. Sometimes he gave them a bargain, five bottles for five dollars, or he would give an extra bottle or two for his meals and overnight lodging. Those days, a hotel room was about seventy-five cents.

The people out on the road were always happy to have him stay, not only for the extra bottle of medicine, but because Daddy was such a talented, personable man. He told stories about wolves, bears, people, and places most of those folks had hardly heard of before; he sang songs, and he entertained them. When they asked questions, Daddy had the answers. Often he was about the only entertainment they had, and he brought them news from the outside world. A lot of the country folks those days didn't get a daily newspaper and they couldn't get around as well. Many drove a horse and buggy. If they *did* have a car and could afford to drive it, more than likely it was a Model T Ford, for it was known as 'the poor man's car." There were fifteen million of them sold. In the winter, when the weather was cold, it sometimes took a lot of cranking and coaxing to get those old Fords started. Those days, you wouldn't find a radio out in the country among the farm people, either. They started getting those battery radios along about the early to mid-1930's, and some even had telephones, the big old crank-type attached to the wall. There was often a dozen or more on one line. Everybody knew their neighbour's ring. That way they kept up with the local gossip, but often had to rely on a salesman or someone from outside the community for other news.

Without a doubt, Daddy was the world's greatest salesman. He had learned his craft well, and at an early age. In his time, he had sold just about anything that could be sold door to door, from cooking pots to chamber pots, bedsprings, mattresses, liniments, and medicine. With anything that he sold, he soon became an expert. He studied the subject well. He could answer all questions and explain every detail. He could tell the folks how this great wonder medicine removed the poison from the human system. How it took the uric acid out of the bloodstream and the kidneys and cured people with gout, arthritic, and rheumatic conditions. Oh, it helped people with neuralgia, nervous conditions, eczema, and was a good tonic and laxative, as its name suggested. It wasn't bad to take, perhaps a little bitter.

Daddy had such a wonderful memory. He could read an article in the newspaper or in a magazine and put that together with the things people out on the road would tell him about a certain condition, and he was soon able to explain the various organs and functions of the human body, and how this famous Indian medicine helped nature to heal some of the afflictions that came upon mankind. Mostly, if he sold the medicine to a new customer, that person would be satisfied with the results and tell a friend or a relative, who might have a similar complaint, and soon Daddy would have another customer. The product was very good, and did just about what it was supposed to do in most cases. Although some would complain, say it was worthless, and want their money back, few—if any—ever got it. Daddy always said that money was too hard to come by to go giving it away. Yes, that old folk remedy of Daddy's was a blessing to many people. There were some that claimed to be cured or greatly helped who had suffered with various ailments, some threw away their canes and crutches—people who had doctored for years, old folks with rheumatic and arthritic conditions, children with eczema and poor appetite.

Although Daddy had sold just about everything before he started selling medicine, after he began selling Ton-A-Lax, he never did sell anything else door to door

Willie

for the rest of his life. He never really made any money at it, just enough to keep body and soul together (sometimes barely) in those old depression days.

He had gone to public school for five years, but only attended about half the time, though he was quite smart at school. He was out selling pots and pans door to door when he was just a young boy, when other kids were in school. He was driving around with a horse and democrat (small wagon), peddling his wares, getting his education on the job. By the time he was fourteen he was earning a living and had become an expert horseman and horse trader. Although he was of slight build, he had those big shoulders and strong hands, and could handle himself quite well in a fight, if need be. But the trauma of the appendicitis operation took its toll on his heart, and he never had a lot of ambition.

When he was finally strong enough after the operation, he started out on the road with a horse and rig, doing the only thing he knew how to do—peddle those pots and pans and trade horses along the way. If he met someone who had a horse that had kicked the buggy to pieces, Daddy would trade for that horse and get some money difference. Maybe the horse he traded had a worse fault; maybe it didn't. He could handle horses others couldn't. If the horse was lame or had the heaves, he knew how to deal with it. He could doctor up a horse and make it better lots of times, then trade it to someone else. It was along about this time he got the nickname "Doc," and throughout his life many of his friends and acquaintances called him that. This was long before he became a medicine man. Daddy was what folks called a horse-gypsy. If he got a horse that was getting old, maybe a little grey over the eyes, he had a remedy for that. If it was a black horse, shoe polish rubbed in those grey spots made the horse look a lot younger. If it was a bay or chestnut, he made up a

Willie Kell

mixture of potash crystals and water, then skillfully painted it over those grey hairs. He used to say, if people dye their hair to look younger, why not make the poor horse look younger? After the horse was sold or traded and the colour wore off, folks might be a bit disappointed, but by that time they probably liked the horse well enough they didn't mind the few grey hairs. It was something like turning back the speedometer on a car, which is quite common these days.

One day Daddy's gypsy travels brought him to that pretty town along the shores of Georgian Bay, where the splashing waters wash up onto the shore and sing romantic songs to those who can hear them. Mother lived there with her family. Her mother kept a cow and sold milk to the neighbours around. Mother played the organ in church on Sundays and the piano in a sheet-music store during the week. It was a time before the gramophone became popular, and if someone wanted to hear a song or play and sing a tune, they bought the song in sheet-music form. Mother would play the song, sometimes singing along, and if the person liked it, they would buy it. Daddy was a good singer, so when he came into the store to hear some music, he and Mother sang together. Then he invited her for a buggy ride after work. Then, as time went on, they sang, went for buggy rides, and fell in love. They sang Stephen Foster's great songs: "Swanee River," "Oh, Susannah," and "Beautiful Dreamer." Daddy would tell stories he had heard about Foster, the talented songwriter: how he had died at just thirty-seven years of age with but thirty-eight cents to his name, how his wonderful songs had found a way to touch the hearts of people.

Well, Daddy's gypsy ways wouldn't allow him to hang around one town too long. Even if that town was the prettiest and the biggest he had ever seen. And even if he was in love with Florence, that beautiful girl in the

Willie

music store. The only thing to do was to take that sweet girl with him. Her mother wouldn't hear tell of Florence marrying that handsome, horse-trading gypsy, so they drove off with a horse and buggy in the night, eloped, and were married in the historic town of Penetanguishene on Friday, the 13th of September 1913. They had no home and drifted from town to town, staying in hotels and boarding houses while Daddy peddled his wares, traded horses, played cards, and sometimes drank too much whiskey. They were living in a small apartment above a store, on the main street of the town of Hanover, when their first child, Florence (later to become Toots), was born on November 8 1914. Soon after this they moved to Owen Sound, the big town on the shore where the rest of us first saw the light of day. This was back in 1914, the year the first big war started. There were more horses on the roads those days than cars. So horse-trading was a pretty good business to be in, especially if you were good at it, like Daddy was.

One day when he was out trading, he made a deal for a covered wagon with high wooden wheels and steel rims, and a gate on the back for easier loading. When the gate was closed, there was a spring clip on either side of it to hold it tightly in place. This model also came equipped with a hand brake on the side. When applied, a small block of wood pressed against the back wheels, to hold the wheels from turning. This kept the wagon under control while going down steep hills. In the good weather, Daddy travelled around with that covered wagon and carried a tent along to sleep in at nights. He would have a team of horses hitched to the wagon and lead a few more behind, trying to make a living. He was something like a mobile used-horse dealer.

There were times when Mother and the kids went along on these summer trips. That was before my time.

Willie Kell

It must have been fun setting up camp, pitching the tent, and lighting the campfire. The kids had to find wood so that Mother could cook supper over the open fire, and everybody would be hungry after the day's dusty travels. Often there would be other horse-trading gypsies around, and several would congregate together. They would sing, tell stories, play cards, and many a horse trade would take place among them. And although sometimes these travelling gypsies could be perhaps a little careless in telling the truth with the folks out on the road, among themselves they were mostly honest. They even had their own language; I learned a few words from Daddy. I remember that *rajee gajee* was an ordinary, not very smart, perhaps potential customer, while *cajee gajee* was a policeman, and horse was *gry*. By using this language, they could talk without being understood by outsiders.

Mother, being the artistic, good-living person she was—not to mention rather quiet—was never really fond of this gypsy way of life, but she loved Daddy so much, and wanted to be with him. Sometimes it was just as well, 'cause he needed someone to watch over him. Mother never was good with horses; they were either stepping on her toes or doing something, and she was rather timid of the big brutes. Although there was one horse Mother could handle and drive, Old Jim, so Daddy kept him around for years. He was a good-sized standardbred gelding. They said he knew more than some people, and though not handsome, he had a special character about him. Old Jim also had a serious ailment called the heaves. It's a respiratory ailment, making it difficult to breathe—something like asthma in humans. There is no cure for the heaves, but Daddy knew how to take care of it. Dampen all hay and feed oat-bran mashes, mixing in a little molasses, baking soda, and mustard. Keep the animal away from all dust and dry

Willie

straw; make their bed with wood-shavings. Old Jim thrived on this special care, and was a useful horse, great for peddling bedsprings and mattresses. He would jog along the country roads doing about ten miles per hour at the trotting gait. When you needed some speed, old Jim would swing over to the pacing gait, and could really tramp right along. A pacer moves both legs on one side of the body in the same direction, while the trotter is diagonally gaited. Of course, the old horse couldn't go fast very far because of the heaves. He didn't look like he had any speed, so Daddy won quite a few bets with him, racing against some local hotshot. They say he was never beaten for a city block. Old Jim even took on the great racehorse, Billy Bishop, named after the World War I fighter pilot hero, who was also born and raised there in that town by the shore. This same horse, Billy Bishop, was no slouch, winning big races in Canada and the U.S.A., but on that Saturday morning, in the cold of winter, hitched to a cutter, old Jim did beat that famous horse fair and square down the main street, when they raced for a city block.

When he would go along on the road with the other horses and the covered wagon and someone would come along to the camp with their fastest road horse, Daddy would casually say. "We may have something around here to race, have a little fun. What say I hitch up that old brown horse tied to the wagon wheel, and just to make it interesting, why don't we bet $5.00?" Well, Daddy picked up quite a few $5.00 bets with Old Jim.

One day, out on the road, somebody took a liking to the old horse and Daddy traded him away. It seems he forgot to tell the man about the heaves; it was just a day or two and the man came back with the poor old horse. He was wheezing, coughing, and heaving terribly. Daddy traded the man something else, and Old Jim was

Willie Kell

back home again, where he got his regular good care and soon was feeling fine.

Daddy and Mother
Book 1 "The Medicine Man"

Willie

Book Two: The Pioneers—Dad, Maw, Old John, and Mary

It was a year or so after the first world war, and my paternal grandparents, along with their younger son, Jock (Daddy's younger brother), bought a farm about seven miles out of town. It was in Keppel Township, back on a winding side road. Jock had spent three years fighting the Germans over on the battlefields of Europe. The Soldiers' Settlement Department allowed that he could buy a farm and they would help with the finances. Jock knew little about farming, but Dad—being raised on a farm—had some experience, so they became partners.

Well, it wasn't *much* of a farm—100 acres of the stoniest land in the world. There was an old frame house, covered with cedar shingles. It was said to be the very house where Keppel Township's first non-native child was born. There was a good-sized barn, and a drilled well near the house, with the coldest, hardest water you ever drank or tried to wash in. There was a cute little outhouse in back with a million summertime spiders in it, and an occasional good-sized snake would slide in under the door to rest out of the hot afternoon sun. This, of course, was always a great conversation piece if company had to go in a hurry.

The old house had a big kitchen, a front parlour, and a bedroom off the parlour. There were two bedrooms upstairs in the front part of the house, and there was another set of stairs leading up from the

Willie Kell

kitchen to a big room that was Dad and Maw's bedroom. It had one window that looked out over the back woodshed into the fields and pastures, where there were stone fences and stone piles everywhere.

Jock had always lived with his parents, except for the time he was away in the army. He was the youngest in their family of four children, and Maw spoiled him. After he came back from the war, she spoiled him even more. When he got out of the army, he met a lady from Toronto, and before long they were married. Aunt Mabel was well educated and had a good job in Toronto before they were married, but I guess she thought it would be a change, moving up to that old farm and being a farmer's wife. It turned out they were a terrible match as man and wife. Jock hadn't got through grade school (although he was clever), he had an awkward way about him, and he couldn't look dressed up if he was wearing a tuxedo. This, along with being spoiled by his mother and having a stubborn, moody way, made it difficult to reason with him, even though he was good-hearted and handsome. Aunt Mabel, being independent all of her life, making her own way in the big city and having a fighting spirit, was not that easy to get along with either. This combination—along with living with Maw and Dad under that old farmhouse roof with not one modern facility—was a minefield waiting to be walked on.

The marriage soon ended in a divorce. Aunt Mabel went back to Toronto and got a good government job, but in just a few years she took sick and died.

In the meantime, back on the farm, Dad, Maw, and Jock worked away trying to pay for that stony old place and get some livestock around. Well, it wasn't long before they had a herd of cows; just about every breed you could find and almost all the colours of the rainbow.

Willie

They soon had 100 pigs, a team of horses, sheep, goats, chickens, ducks, and geese running all over the place. The team was a pair of half-bloods, Doc and Tom, frisky as 2 year olds. Those horses worked the land and pulled the democrat to town or any other place they went. It was all the transportation they had. These people, with the hearts and souls of pioneers, picked the stones from the fields with their hands and built stone fences, so they could work the land. Everything was done the hard way. For the six months they kept the livestock in the barn out of the winter storms, they pumped all the water they drank by hand, with a cold, old iron-handle pump. The water ran downhill through a hollowed-out cedar rail to the trough in the yard. There was a windmill, but it didn't work, and nobody bothered to find out that it would only cost 75 cents to have it fixed until after they had pumped that water for several years.

But they made money and they didn't spend it; they found a way of getting along. Dad had a talent for buying what others didn't want and buying it cheap. He would buy a cow that would kick the milk pail over and teach that cow a lesson, 'cause he could kick as hard as the cow could. If a cow jumped the fences, they had a rig called a "poke a leather strap" around the cow's neck, with a big stick attached to it in front. Sometimes they would get a sucker—a cow that sucked another cow. Some do—they wanted the milk in the pail. Some cows would suck themselves, but they didn't suck long when Dad got them. He would put a little halter on the cow with nails sticking out from the nose-band; this changed her mind real fast. Yes, they had a whole farm full of misfits, but they made money with those misfits.

They milked the cows by hand, then separated the cream from the milk with a hand separator; the cream came out one spout and the skim milk came out another. They sold the cream to the creamery in town, which

Willie Kell

brought in cash every week. The creamery manufactured butter and other dairy products from it. They fed the skim milk to the calves and pigs and also got buttermilk from the creamery for nothing to feed to the pigs. The pigs loved it, especially with some stale bread they got from the bakery, also for nothing. Yes, they got bread, cakes, biscuits, and all kinds of goodies from the bakeries. Maw used it on the table if it wasn't too stale and mouldy. Those cakes were delicious, but most of them went to the pigs and calves. Another thing they did was collect garbage from the restaurants; there was everything in that stuff, the pigs enjoyed it. Dad would bring a load of it home every week when he took the cream to town with the team of horses and the democrat. It must have been something to see: this fat man with the team hitched to that old wagon, loaded down with garbage, buttermilk, big burlap bags filled with bread, cakes, and other gooey things, and of course the week's supply of groceries, heading out of town on that long trip home to the farm, with a million flies tagging along behind.

In the warm weather, the pigs were kept in the apple orchard. They slept in the shade of the trees and ate the fruit that fell on the ground. Come to think of it, those pigs had it pretty good. The fences were never up to much; somebody had to keep an eye out that they didn't get on the road. Although, there weren't many cars to run over them back on that old side road.

Often on a Sunday, Daddy and Mother would hitch up a horse, load the kids in the buggy, and go out to the farm for the day. Sometimes, when Daddy was away with the covered wagon on the road, Mother would take the kids, drive "Old Jim" out to the farm, and spend the day with Maw. It was always a good time at the farm: Maw would make a nice meal, and there would be

Willie

something to bring home. Perhaps some vegetables from the garden, or butter, eggs, and milk from the cows, and often meat from a pig or steer that Dad had butchered.

Dad was a strong, rugged man. He weighed about 250 pounds in his younger days, stood 5 foot 11, could kick his foot up over his head and outrun most people half his age, though he didn't run from anyone. He wore an 18-inch collar on his shirts, and one day when he and Maw went into a store to buy him a shirt, the clerk measured his neck to find out his size. When he saw that it was 18 inches around, he said. "We don't sell horse collars in here." Dad didn't think it was funny.

Dad had learned to survive from a young age, through necessity. Both he and Maw were born and raised in Perth County, Ontario, in the Listowel area, and their children were born and brought up there, too. They moved to Owen Sound after their oldest daughter, Birdell, had married and moved to Toronto, about 1908. By the time they moved to the farm, most of Dad's wild ways were over—no more drinking, no more cigars, and hardly a fistfight anymore. By that time he was about 55 years old and had mellowed with the years, although he had been quite a man in his time.

His father, John Kell, had come out from Yorkshire, England on a sailing ship in the mid 1800s and had carved a couple of farms out of the Queen's Bush in Perth County, on what is now Highway 86. At that time, the Queen (Queen Victoria) would give an Englishman 100 acres of land. Of course, the land was bush, but if he cleared the land and built a dwelling, the land was his. At that time, Canada belonged to England, and these brave men and women we call pioneers were a proud part of our Canadian history. Without these rugged settlers, our country would be a much different place today.

Willie Kell

After Old John cleared some land and built a small log dwelling—as was his arrangement with the Queen—he went to work in the city of Toronto, taking care of horses. His wages were $12.00 a month and one new pair of boots every year. He stayed at that job for four years, although he did get up to the farm a few times in that four years, taking a stagecoach part of the way but walking miles of the long road by himself. One time he found squatters in his little cabin. They had been living there for some time, but old John chased them off, locked the place up, and went back to his job in the city.

When the four years had passed and he had saved enough money, he moved to his farm, married a bride, Mary, and went on with his life. This time, he built a good-sized log house with 4 bedrooms, cleared the land, built a good barn for his livestock, and prospered. They had four children—two boys and two girls. Dad (Arnold) was the only one of the four to reach adulthood. He was born August 2nd 1863 in that log house that John built. On July 30th 1868, Mary died at just 32 years of age, but she had lived long enough to see her oldest child, Annie, die almost 10 years earlier, when that little girl was less than 3 years old. Young Arnold was looking forward to his fifth birthday when his mother died on that hot July day, there in the log house.

John never married again. He struggled along on the farm and tried to raise the children. But scarcely six weeks after Mary died, he would bury their baby boy—named John, after his father—in a tiny grave above his mother. By that time, John also owned another 50-acre farm a mile or more up the road toward Listowel, and had built a nice brick house for his retirement at the edge of town. But Old John would bury another child—Mary Jane, in April 1877, she was only 15—then be dead himself a couple of weeks before Christmas 1879. Yes, on a cold December day, at just 17 years of age,

Willie

young Arnold would see his father, the last of his family, laid to rest in Woodlawn Cemetery a few miles west of town, and be on his own to face what must have seemed a very cruel and lonely world.

At just 17, young Arnold was the lone survivor and the sole heir to the properties and anything else his father had left behind. He often told me that he never expected to live very long; he had watched his mother, father, and siblings all die young, and he knew that he had to be next. It was just a matter of time. So young Arnold started living as much and as fast as time would allow, 'cause he figured time was running out on him. He started a wild way of life—drinking hard liquor, smoking cigars, trading horses with anybody that wanted to trade, and fighting anyone who tried to stand in his pathway. He became real friendly with the Beaton family that lived up the road a ways toward town. Old Man Beaton was a Scottish immigrant who had migrated to Idaho in the northwest U.S.A., where he got hold of a dying silver mine. I guess when things started going bad there, he moved to Ontario, Canada. There were three girls and a boy in the family. The boy's name was Peter; Daddy named me after him (my second name). Well, I guess old Pete was quite a fellow, an excellent judge of horseflesh, good whiskey, and pretty women. It was just natural for young Arnold to fall in with the Beatons. He and old Pete had wonderful times together. I reckon that Pete helped Dad spend some of old John's hard-earned money.

Now, not only did Dad like Pete, but he took a shine to Pete's good-looking sister, Isabelle. She was just in her mid teens, fair complexion, blue eyes, and skinny legs. I guess old Pete's sister had her eye on Arnold, too, for it wasn't long until she was married to him at just sweet 16. Arnold was about 22 at the time.

Willie Kell

Their first years together were difficult; Maw was so young, and Dad's wild ways led to problems they didn't know how to deal with. Things went from bad to terrible, until they finally lost the last of Old John's farms. But not before they managed to have four children: two girls and two boys. There was Birdell; Maw found the name in a book she had read, and they always called her Birdie. Then there was Elizabeth (Lizzie), another Arnold (my Daddy), and Jock, who was christened John after his paternal grandfather. But Old Man Beaton, Scottish as he was, gave them $5.00 if they would call him Jock. Birdie was the oldest and Jock the baby, Daddy was the second youngest.

It wasn't long after Jock was born, in 1892, that the farm was gone and they moved into town. Dad got into the butcher business, and started selling pots and pans door to door as a sideline. He kept on trading horses and tried to make a living. It could have been about this time that he stopped looking over his shoulder for the angel of death, after he had lost all of his father's money and properties. I guess he could hardly believe that he was still living, but he was—just a whole lot poorer than he should have been. Maw learned to be a good manager, and Dad started changing his ways. They were a fine-looking couple when they would dress up on a Sunday to go to the Pentecostal church. Maw was ever a lady, born and bred, and a proud one. Dad never liked getting dressed up, but come Sunday morning, Maw would make sure he had on his suit, best shirt, and tie, and off they would go to church. Dad was always opinionated and outspoken, but honest and fair. One Sunday, the pious pastor was comparing the stubbornness of humans with that of pigs in his sermon. He went on to say that you could have a field of corn—ripe, delicious, and ready to eat—and you could have a herd of pigs, hungry pigs, and you could try and get those hungry pigs into

Willie

that cornfield. But if those pigs didn't *want* to go into that cornfield, all heaven wouldn't get them in. Dad stood up right then and in his strong, manly voice, said, "Yes, brother, and if you did get them in, all hell wouldn't fetch em out." Maw was embarrassed, but the congregation loved it. That was Dad Kell: a wise man, something of a philosopher who had wonderful sayings that I'll never forget. He used to say, "a man's word is his bond, and if a man's word is no good, neither is the man."

Back around the turn of the century and later, Listowel was quite a hockey town. The legendary Bill "Cyclone" Taylor was growing up there about that time. He went on to become one of the greatest players to ever lace on a pair of skates and is in the Hockey Hall of Fame. When the Maitland River would freeze over in the winter, young boys learned to skate and play hockey on it. The river ran under the stores for a block or two, and it was a wonderful place to skate, like an indoor arena. Daddy learned to skate there, like Cyclone Taylor did. Dad was quite interested in hockey, like most of the local people. And when Listowel made the playoffs one year, probably about 1907, a young part-time referee from Toronto stayed with the Kells when he came to town to officiate. His name was Arthur Anglin. Arthur was a cartoonist with Canada's largest newspaper, the *Toronto Star*. And just like something from a Hollywood movie, Listowel won the championship that year, and the young referee from the big city fell in love with the pretty girl in that small town. Well, it wasn't *really* something from a Hollywood movie. Movies had hardly been heard of in that part of the world back then. The young cartoonist would come from time to time and visit, and Birdie would be waiting for him at the station. She was always so excited to see her handsome Arthur step down from the train. Soon they were married, and Aunt Birdie moved to Toronto. They had two beautiful children, a boy and a girl: Arnold—yes, another Arnold—and Marian.

Arthur Anglin came from a fine, well-to-do family. The Anglins were diamond merchants, good stock with wealth and class. A cousin, Margaret Anglin, was a well-known actress, and one of Arthur's uncles was a Supreme Court judge. Arthur's father had accumulated a considerable amount of money and property before he died, and Mrs. Anglin continued the good life as a widow, travelling and trying to spend some of that money. She had a fine collection of jewellery, furniture, and houses. One time, when she was returning from a trip to the States, she was detained at the border, the Peace Bridge at Buffalo, because they suspected the old girl of smuggling diamonds into Canada. It seems she was loaded down with precious rocks. She had to call her lawyer in Toronto and have the matter cleared up before they would let her cross into Canada.

Arthur was a local celebrity and loved to celebrate. As time went on, he spent huge amounts at the racetrack and drank quarts of whiskey. One night when he was returning home after a night out with his friends, he gave the taxi driver a $100.00 bill for a tip. The honest cab driver came to Aunt Birdie's door the next day with the $100.00 bill in his hand and said, "Mr. Anglin gave me this for a tip last night, and I don't think he was quite sober at the time, so I'm returning it to you." Aunt Birdie told the cabby to keep it; she said he would only give it to someone else the next night.

One night, Arthur didn't come home in a taxi. As a matter of fact, he didn't come home in anything—he just didn't come home. He disappeared, vanished, no good-bye, no nothing; he was gone. He left Aunt Birdie and the children with very little except for a few pieces

Willie

of fine furniture, a couple of diamond rings, and a broken heart. No one ever heard of him again, although years later it was rumoured that he lived for a time in British Columbia.

Aunt Birdie and the children moved in with her sister Lizzie and Uncle Bill Barber, who by this time were also married, had two children, and were living in Toronto. Birdie had to get a job to support her and the children, but it wasn't long until she was unable to work. She developed a blood clot in her leg and had to be in bed. Finally, she had to take her children and go live at the farm with Dad and Maw. She and the children went by train from Toronto to Owen Sound on a hot August day. Dad met them at the station with the team and democrat. There was that poor sick woman with those children, riding out to the farm. Seven long miles over rough roads in the hot summer sun after riding the train from Toronto. What an experience for those kids, coming to the farm way back on that winding side road past miles of stone fences. There was no electricity, no bathroom, not even water on tap; you had to fetch it in a pail from the pump out in the yard. Maw was waiting when they got there, and she put poor Aunt Birdie to bed in the downstairs room off the parlour. The trip had been hard on her. The old doctor came out to see her a time or two, but there was little to be done. The poor soul died there in that bed and left her two beautiful children orphans. Arnold was 12 when his mother died and Marian was 8. Dad bought a plot at Greenwood Cemetery in Owen Sound and she was laid to rest there. Maw told Aunt Birdie that she would take care of the children and send them to school, if the good Lord spared her, and so she did.

Dad and Arnold never did hit it off that well. The boy was quite intelligent, but perhaps a little disoriented having to live and work on that farm. Dad still had a temper, and by this time hated the name Anglin. Anything the kid would do that displeased Dad, he would liken him to his no-good son-of-a-bitch of a father. On the other hand, they saw Marian as being like her mother, their beautiful Birdie. Dad and Maw revered Birdie; to them she was a saint, and losing her like that in her early 30s must have torn their hearts half out. So, Marian's life out on the farm, though not all that wonderful, was much better than the life poor Arnold had to live.

The Anglin kids were artistic; not cut out for life on the farm, but they made the best of it. After all, what else could they do? It was either the farm or an orphanage. They didn't have much choice.

Arnold was a born actor, like his famous cousin—a clown, an entertainer. I suppose he took on these different characters to hide from the real world, and to disguise his true life and the hard blows it had dealt him. Those blows were sometimes quite real—from a willow switch, handed out by the hard hand of Dad.

In the summer, when school was out, things would be a little better for the Anglins, 'cause that's when Daddy and Mother would take our family out to the farm. Sometimes the kids would stay there for a week or two. Often in the summer Aunt Lizzie and Uncle Bill would come and bring their kids, another Arnold and Isabelle (named after Maw), and spend some time at the farm.

You will notice by now that there are five Arnolds: Dad, Daddy, Arnold Anglin, Aunt Lizzie's Arnold Barber (they called him Bud), and then there was our Son. Lizzie and Bill moved to Toronto after they were married. Uncle Bill was a barber—a Barber by name

Willie

and a barber by trade. The Barbers always seemed to have nice clothes and a fancy car.

There were a lot of good times on the farm when everyone would get together, often on a Sunday or some special occasion. Maw would cook wonderful meals, and they would talk about all kinds of things. There were great stories and interesting experiences told around the big kitchen table or in the parlour. Aunt Lizzie was a good talker and storyteller, and would tell stories about her interesting city friends. Uncle Bill told stories he heard in the barbershop in downtown Toronto. Daddy had great stories of life out on the road. Dad and Maw would tell what was happening in the neighbourhood, and Jock had interesting things to tell about his great adventures overseas. Mother was a good listener, but still had her say; then she had her children to watch over and talk to.

After dinner the kids would go outside and play. Arnold Anglin, being the oldest, would teach them to dance. They would also sing and act. Arnold found them old clothes to dress up in and they had great times, often out on the upstairs barn floor. He was such a character, and the other kids loved him. He had lost his top teeth early in life, and one time, while fooling around, his false teeth fell out into the manure. So what did he do? Just what any other clown would do—he went to a nearby cow, squirted some warm milk on the teeth to wash them off, and then stuck them back in his mouth. What an act! What fun! The kids loved it.

The hens ran all over the barn, upstairs and downstairs, and laid eggs in the cow mangers, behind doors, up in the haymow, or wherever they could find a place to hide them. It was the kids' job to find these eggs, but they could never find them all. Sometimes there would be a nest of baby chicks peeping out from under an old clucking hen; she wouldn't be all that

Willie Kell

happy at being discovered. Sometimes Arnold would open an egg and eat it right out of the shell.

Other times they would find a nest of rotten eggs. One warm summer day—not a Sunday, it was just a day—my sisters, Toots and Sweet, were spending a little time at the farm. All the kids were up in the hay mow, looking for eggs. Dad was in town with the team and democrat. The kids found a nest of real rotten eggs. Now, there was an opening, about a foot square, up near the peak of the barn, and on that warm summer day it looked quite inviting for an egg-throwing contest. Most of the eggs missed their mark, and the smelly, yellow mess ran down the inside of the barn-boards. However, some did find their way through that little opening at the peak of the barn, and when someone got a bull's-eye, there was a great cheer for the successful thrower. It was so much fun, especially for Toots and Sweet. But it wasn't so funny when Dad came driving into the yard and one of those rotten eggs landed right on his best hat, and the gooey, yellow, rotten egg ran down his fat face. Dad didn't think it was one bit funny, and poor Arnold got hell again.

One day Dad bought a big straight-back Clydesdale gelding for $2.00. He was blind in one eye and homelier than a hillbilly's hound-dog, and although he was only 7 years old, he was slower than a Mississippi mule. But the big horse was honest and reliable and strong as a yoke of oxen. Old Donald was sentenced to a life of hard labour on the farm, and soon became a part of the scene. They even got a mate for him, a little brown mare they called Minnie, and they were quite a team. There was *only* 500 pounds difference in their weight, and they were horses of different colours. Dad had paid $8.00 for Minnie, so the total cost of that team was a whopping $10.00, and with a couple of dollars worth of harness on them, this

Willie

pair of misfits worked the farm for the next 10 years or more.

By this time, Jock was doing most of the farming. Now, if you could have seen this Mutt and Jeff team of horses with the old, scrappy harness on them, hitched to the wobbly, wooden-wheeled wagon, with steel rims always threatening to fall off in the hot, dry summer weather—it was something like a Laurel and Hardy movie. Jock would drive up to the watering trough in the yard between the house and the barn. He never was much of a teamster; he was also left-handed, awkward, and bowlegged. He wore overalls that always seemed a size or two bigger than they should have been, a straw hat hung on his head, and a homemade cigarette sticking out from the side of his mouth. He was never really interested in farming, always appeared preoccupied. I suppose he often wondered what he was doing on that stony old farm in the first place. But right then he would be busy slowly dipping pails of water out of the watering trough and pouring it over those old wagon wheels—to swell the wood in them so the steel rims would stay on long enough to carry another load of what ever it was he was hauling at the time.

As they prospered, there seemed to be more bickering among them on the farm, Maw and Jock on one side and Dad on the other. They had bought the farm in 1920, and added another 40 acres of flats and stone pasture a few years later, so now they had 140 acres of the stoniest land in the world. But less than ten years had gone by and the place was paid for, they had about twenty-five milk cows, some young cattle, lots of pigs, all those chickens, geese, and goats, some old horse-drawn implements, and of course that $10.00 team of horses. And by now they had a nice nest egg of savings in the bank for a rainy day. They hadn't spent much money in those ten years, but they had finally got the stable cemented and they did at last spend the seventy-five cents to get the windmill fixed, to pump the water into the new cement trough.

Dad had always done the business, banked the money, and paid the bills, and there were no questions asked ... until one day early in the 1930s. Jock took a load of fat hogs to market, and when he deposited the fifty dollar cheque he had got for them, he asked the teller, "How much have we got in there now?" She looked it up and told him, "$50.79." No, she had not made a mistake: Dad had gone in and taken the money out—over $3000.00—and not told anyone.

They made an agreement that Maw would own the farm, everything that was there, and leave it to Jock when she died. Dad would keep the money. At that time, a year or two into the Depression, the farm wouldn't be worth the $3000.00. Dad kept a horse to drive and his old buggy, but he was finished with the farm, though he lived there most of the time and would help milk the cows. Often he would peel the potatoes and help Maw get meals ready. He bought another farm a few miles away for $900.00, a hundred acres with a nice log house and a barn. He called it the ranch, and he would go there and hang out sometimes.

The Anglin kids were grown by then and had left the farm. Arnold got a job on the big ships and sailed around the world several times. He married a girl from Quebec, and when their sailing days were over, they lived in a suburb of Montreal. But he died mysteriously, murdered at the time of the FLQ uprising. The police were on strike and no one was ever brought to trial for it. Marian was married in the early thirties; sadly though, her husband took sick and had to be confined to a mental hospital for the rest of his life. They had one boy named Arthur, after Marian's father.

Willie

John, Mary and children
About 1860

Dad Kell

Book Three: When Mother Died

The early thirties brought many changes into all of our lives: the depression was at its worst, and everyone on our street was on city relief except for us and a rich old fellow up the road. That man spent the winters in California, and we spent the winters wondering if we were going to make it until spring. With city relief, the man of the house had to work for the city a couple of days a week—shovelling snow, cleaning streets, or whatever jobs they had. For this, the city administration gave money to these poor folks to buy the bare necessities of life. Many a hard-working man was on that old relief, 'cause they just couldn't find a job. Men were working for their meals, some were lucky enough to find work cutting wood all day for 75 cents or a dollar. It was hard times, for sure!

By now we had a Model T Ford coupe, with canvas top and a place to put things in back, like a trunk. We could, on occasion, prop the lid open and get a couple of the kids in there. It was a 1927 model; Daddy bought it in late 1930 for $30.00. Sometimes on a Sunday we could all somehow crowd into that little car and head for the farm.

Looking back, I remember Daddy having quite a few friends come to the house. There was Jimmy Barber (not related to Bill), originally from Listowel; he had been a drinking buddy of Uncle Pete Beaton, and I guess he and old Pete had some great times together. Jimmy told some good stories about Uncle Pete. Seems that Pete had

Willie

a job as a horse buyer for a big outfit in Indiana, but one time he came home to Listowel for a holiday and hung around 'til all of his money was gone. The people he worked for in Indiana sent him the money for train fare to get him back, and he spent that, too. Finally they sent him a one-way ticket and he went back to Indiana, got married, and settled down. He lived his life and never came back to Listowel. Old Pete was buried in Indiana.

Jimmy Barber was in the bedspring business. He had a small, portable hand machine that wound the wire into six-inch cone-shaped springs. When these springs were wired together, you had a bedspring. This was before the invention of the spring-filled mattress. Jimmy sold these springs door to door for most of his life, and got Daddy into the business. Many a spring set was put together at our house, and then Daddy would go out selling them, sometimes with old Jimmy. In all the years Jimmy was on the road, he never did learn to drive a car, but peddled his springs with a horse and democrat or buggy. When Daddy started driving cars in the mid 20s, Jimmy would sometimes go along; the springs were kind of awkward and had to be tied on somehow. It would be quite a thing to see someone going down the road with these springs tied onto a buggy or a Model T Ford. Jimmy never did get to trust those darned automobiles. Often, on a steep hill, he would get out and walk. This must have been fun for anyone driving the car. Sometimes he would take springs along when Daddy sold medicine.

He was a binge drinker and would sometimes get drunk and get into fights, though he wasn't much of a fighter. He had a habit of saying in his conversation, "between you and I." One time, when he was sporting a black eye from one of his drinking bouts, he used this expression, and Toots—not all that fond of him—would

Willie Kell

say, "between you and I and my black eye." Old Jimmy wasn't amused.

He was single, had no home, and lived at boarding houses and hotels. He was always dressed nice—suit, tie, and a vest with a gold watch and chain. I think it would have been about 1934 when he died. He was out drinking with some of his buddies, got into some bad swamp whiskey, and it killed him. He was buried in a pauper's grave. I don't know where his gold watch and chain ever got to; I guess either his whiskey-drinking buddies or the undertaker got it.

Then there was another Jimmy, Jimmy Sharpe; he was from a well-to-do family, fine people who had a lot of property and were well respected. Jimmy Sharpe ran a livery stable in town. Daddy used to hang around there quite a bit in his horse-trading days, looking for deals, and playing cards. A livery stable was like a horse taxi mostly; the customers rented a horse and rig and did their own driving.

This Jimmy was always inclined to get into some kind of trouble or be involved in crooked deals, trouble with the law. In his first brush with the wrong side of the law, he was about 20 years old and held up a store in Detroit. Even though his family spent money on a good lawyer, he did some time in jail for this silly little venture. As time went on, Jimmy Sharpe sold the livery stable, moved to Toronto, and started selling cars. It was a time when the livery business was dying out because those darn automobiles were taking over. For the most part, Daddy lost contact with Jimmy for several years.

Another one of Daddy's friends was a little man named Gordon Eager. He was from a farming family out in the country a few miles, but he became interested in harness-racing horses, standardbreds. He got into

Willie

breeding, training, and driving them, though he was never very successful at it. In those times, a lot of people weren't very successful because there just wasn't the money around. However, Daddy named him "Pop," after the famous American harness-racing trainer and driver, the legendary Pop Geers—the silent man from Tennessee who had driven many world champions in his day. That Pop, the real Pop Geers, sad to say, was killed in a harness-racing accident.

Daddy's friend, Pop Eager, raised horses and collie dogs on his farm and, like a lot of people in those times, found that trying to make a living was a struggle. One day Daddy and Son were out to Pop's farm and came home with this cute, cuddly collie pup; Pop had given him to Son. Well, it wasn't very long and our whole family fell in love with Pal. Time soon went by, and in just a little while this cute, cuddly pup became a good-sized dog. He was dark brown with white legs and markings on his face and chest. Pal was very clever and seemed to learn things quickly. Daddy bought Son a good secondhand harness for him, and Pal became a great sled dog. He knew all the commands and Son taught him to trot like a horse. He had a little halter for Pal with a ring on each side where he attached the reins, or lines, to guide the dog. Another one of our friends, a blacksmith, made a set of shafts with a whiffletree, and it would attach to either the wagon or sleigh, depending on the season. Soon Pal showed signs of being a special dog. Son drove him all over, even out to the farm or to Pop's farm, or downtown for groceries. Everybody was impressed with Son's dog; he was the pride of our whole family. He watched over us, and we always felt that harm couldn't come to us as long as Pal was around, even if Daddy was away.

However there was one person who *didn't* like our Pal, a man who lived up the street a block or so. He used

Willie Kell

to ride by on his bicycle, and when Pal was a pup, the man would kick at him when the dog barked. The poor man had a terrible stutter, and between him kicking and stuttering at the dog and Pal barking at him, their relationship deteriorated. It was an ongoing battle between them.

Son would hitch up Pal and drive him all over town, just about any place he wanted to go. The only place he didn't take him was to school. He made a little garden harrow—nailed some small boards together, then drove spikes and bolts through them—and would hitch Pal to this harrow and work up the garden or drive him up and down between the rows to loosen the soil. Yes, Pal was a wonder dog, a friend, a part of our family. Wherever Son took him, people were always amazed at this horse-like dog. Everybody loved Pal, except that stuttering man.

I had started school by this time, kindergarten. I never really liked it that much then, and was, for the most part, even less impressed with school as time went on. Except for a couple of subjects—literature and memory work—I found school very boring; perhaps a good place to meet girls.

Mother's poor heart bothered her more as the years went by; she had to rest quite a lot. I can remember the doctor coming to see her from time to time. Mother had three sisters and a brother, all married. Uncle Tom Crighton, Aunt Alice, and Aunt Matilda lived in Pontiac, Michigan; Auntie Mae and her husband and family lived in the border city of Sarnia, on Davis Street. My maternal grandparents lived just a couple of blocks from them on the same street. We had a bunch of cousins on Mother's side of the family that we saw once in a while, and even in the depression they seemed to be

Willie

prosperous. They, like Mother, had all been born in Canada, but had moved to the States and done pretty well. Herb Lawson, Aunt Alice's husband, and Saul Dell, Aunt Matilda's husband, were contractors.

John Crighton, Mother's father, was a fine, talented man. He stood 6 feet tall with a slim build. He played the violin, was a great photographer, and even developed his own pictures. He trained dogs to do all kinds of tricks, and had a shoe-repair business in Sarnia. One time he fell and injured his back and hip, and when I knew him he was quite bent over.

Grandpa Crighton's ancestors migrated to Canada and the U.S.A. from Scotland, they were direct descendants of Mary Queen of Scots.

More has been written about this reigning monarch than any other in history. She has been seen as a romantic icon, a woman who followed her heart, known for her tolerance. She was born in Scotland in December 1542, the time of King Henry V111, was crowned Queen of Scotland before she was a year old. Married at 15, her short life was turbulent indeed. She was imprisoned and finally beheaded. Her cousin Queen Elizabeth signed her death warrant. However her tomb in Westminster Abbey is the most elaborate of all the royal tombs. Her son King James translated the bible.

Grandma was a small, kind of a squatty woman; her maiden name was Jones. Her father was Arthur "Goatie" Jones, an interesting character. Grandma's mother, Granny Jones had wonderful stories to tell. Granny was of British Aristocracy, known then as "Lady Louise" until she fell in love with Arthur. They were married in England then sailed for Canada, they're first child was born at sea. Of course her family of aristocrats disowned her for marrying a commoner. However Granny and "Goatie' lived happily ever after.

Willie Kell

In the summer of 1932, one of Mother's sisters and her husband came to our place while they were visiting in the area. When it was time to go back home, they invited Mother, little Elizabeth, and me to go with them to Sarnia to visit Mother's people for a while. Lord knows she needed a holiday. I don't remember much about that trip to Sarnia, but I remember being there at Grandma's house on Davis Street. It was a big frame house with a veranda running from the kitchen door around to the front door in a kind of a quarter circle. It seemed always shady out on the veranda, and there were chairs to sit on. There was a nice yard out back with trees and a little garden. Grandma kept a few hens; they would lay eggs for them, and if she had some left over she gave them to Auntie Mae. She could always use a few extra eggs, for she had eight kids to feed. Grandma had a couple of canaries, one in the kitchen and one in the front room, and they were always singing, it seemed. One thing they had in that house was an inside bathroom, flush toilet, even store-bought toilet paper hung on a roll. What wonderful inventions!

I remember Grandpa being a quiet person. He would sit in a big chair and listen to the radio and read a lot; sometimes he would say something or have a little joke. I liked him, and spent quite a bit of time in the front room with that old man. He had a good sense of humour. Daddy told me a story about the old man selling a pup from his famous trick dog, Peggy. The man that he sold it to expected this pup to be able to do all the tricks its mother could do, but try as he might, the pup couldn't learn even one trick. When the man came back complaining to Grandpa about this dumb dog, Grandpa reminded the man that there is one important thing in training an animal: the trainer must know more than the animal if he is going to teach it anything. The man didn't come back complaining to Grandpa again.

Willie

Auntie Mae and Uncle Milton lived up the street a block or so from Grandma's house, and I used to spend some time up there playing with their kids. They lived in a big old frame house, too, and there was a golf course right behind it; we used to go and find golf balls. There was an old shack in the backyard and we spent time out there. It was fun being with all those kids.

As time went on, Mother's health grew worse and soon I was staying at Auntie Mae's place all the time. When September came, I started back to school with their kids. Auntie Mae belonged to what seemed to me a strange kind of religion. The women wore black stockings and didn't curl their hair; they had it done up in a bun at the back of their heads, or sometimes it hung down in braids. I remember them having meetings, praying and singing—it was all kind of strange to me, 'cause back home we didn't go to church, and about the only time I had heard the Lord's name, somebody was taking it in vain. Oh, I guess I had been to Sunday school a few times with the other kids, but I didn't know much about religion. I sure knew a bunch of cuss words, though.

You never heard a single cuss word in Auntie Mae's house, not until I got there. I had quite a few bad words in my vocabulary, and out playing with these cousins, from time to time I guess I would utter some of these profanities. When my pious-tongued cousins told Auntie Mae about this, I almost lost my happy home. "Where did you ever learn to swear like that?" Auntie Mae asked me in front of all these kids. I told her I learned it from Son.

Oh, how terrible the truth was! I had always been bad for swearing; Daddy thought it was cute. One time, out at the farm, we were all sitting around Maw's big kitchen table; it was Dad's birthday, and Aunt Lizzie and Uncle Bill and their kids were there from Toronto.

Willie Kell

When the old man blew out the candles on the cake, I hollered out over the crowd, "How old are you, Dad?" He answered, "Sixty-six." That must have seemed a lot to me, cause I said, loudly, "Sixty-six—Holy Jesus!" It would be my birthday the very next day; I would be three.

Everybody thought it was so cute—everybody but Mother. She didn't like me to swear. I remember one time her threatening to wash my mouth out with Sunlight soap; she had her hand on my head and the soap half in my mouth before I promised to quit—but I didn't. They say that one time a religious man came to our door. And when he said something to me, I answered with one of my favourite profanities. Mother said, "Little boy, if you are going to talk that way, you will have to go home; we can't have you talking like that around this house." "Home?" I said. "Where the hell do you think I am now; this *is* my home, Mother." It must have been very embarrassing for her.

It was just about the end of October that year when Daddy and the other kids came to Sarnia, to see Mother and take Elizabeth and me home. They came with Toots' boyfriend, who had an almost new 1931 Model A Ford sedan. It was a fancy car—plush cushions, gearshift on the floor, a deluxe model. He had bought it for about $500.00. George was real proud of that car, and Daddy asked him to take them to Sarnia. It would have been a long trip in our old Model T coupe.

When it was time to head out for home, Toots stayed behind with Mother. She needed her there; Mother was in bed most of the time by now, and when Daddy and us kids kissed her good-bye as we left for the long drive home, we didn't realise then it would be the last time we would see her alive. She was dying with heart problems, and I guess she knew. Her ankles were swollen so badly

Willie

and she was weak, but God bless her, she didn't complain, though it must have hurt her so to say good-bye.

It was kind of late when we got away from Sarnia. I can remember going through the towns at night on the way home; they were all lit up because it was Halloween and the kids were out doing their trick or treat. It was no trick or treat for us; we were sad, having to leave Mother and Toots behind in Sarnia on that Halloween night in 1932.

It was two weeks and two days later, on November 16th, that Mother died. She was just 40, but her frail body would not allow her to reach her forty-first birthday, less than three weeks away on December 4th. It was noon hour and we were having something to eat in Mother's little kitchen when a neighbour lady came to the door with the terrible news. Toots had phoned the neighbour; we had no phone. It was a sad and heartbreaking time, but none of us there could ever have imagined that the news the neighbour brought us would bring so many changes into our lives. That it would tear our family apart, cause so much pain and anguish, and leave all of our lives in disarray. Jimmy Barber had some kind words and tried to comfort us, said he knew what it was like as he had lost his mother when he was just a boy. Well, he might have tried to be kind, but on that dismal November day, at the very worst time in the most devastating depression in memory, anything anyone said was little comfort to us. It seemed the world was closing in on us. Mother was gone.

Daddy had no money; he still owed a couple of hundred dollars on the little house, and couldn't even find the money to pay the taxes. Daddy went out to the farm, to Dad, and borrowed the money for Mother's funeral. There would be a place to bury her in one of those graves beside Aunt Birdie, in old Greenwood

Willie Kell

Cemetery. There would still be four graves left after Mother was buried.

Old Mr. Fulton, the undertaker, went with the hearse to Sarnia to get Mother's body and bring her home. Toots came with her. The undertaker brought her back to the funeral parlour and put her in a little greyish-blue casket. Daddy took Elizabeth and I to see her. I remember him holding us up to look at her lying there in that coffin. She looked like she was sleeping, and I have always remembered that angelic look on her face, but little did I realize what a loss it was. I was just too young at 6 years old.

The day of the funeral, Elizabeth and I stayed with a kind neighbour lady down the street, and after the funeral, some folks stopped by our house before heading out of town. They said it was the biggest funeral ever held at that funeral home. It seemed this quiet, beautiful lady who had been our mother was not only loved and respected by her children and family, but by many others as well. As Aunt Lizzie and Uncle Bill were leaving to go back to Toronto, Daddy said. "The best two in the family are gone," meaning Mother and Aunt Birdie. Maw always said that the good die young.

At the time of Mother's death, Daddy was 42, Toots was 18 (her birthday had been the week before), Sweet was 16, Son had turned 14 in September, Jim was 12, I was 6, and our little Elizabeth just 3. It was pretty quiet and sad around our place after the funeral, and in the days and weeks that followed. Daddy had to get out on the road, to try and get some money to put food on the table. Trouble was, nobody *had* any money, for medicine or anything else. Farmers couldn't afford to drive their cars; many cars sat in garages or outside, up on blocks to keep the tires from rotting. They drove a horse and buggy, walked, or went with the neighbour, if they were

Willie

lucky enough to have a neighbour that had transportation. Many went begging for food for their family.

The roads were full of hoboes looking for handouts. They rode the rails, the freight trains, and slept in boxcars. These so-called knights of the road went from town to town, often eating out of garbage cans or whatever someone gave them. In the winter, hundreds were found dead, frozen to death in those cold old boxcars or in some back alley. It was sure enough hard times, back in them hungry thirties, but there wasn't the crime we have today, and folks helped their neighbors.

The great songs of Jimmy Rogers told sad stories of some who died in those boxcars, like his song, "Hobo Bill's Last Ride." Jimmy Rogers himself had been a brakeman on the railroad, and knew firsthand the hardships of these men. When Jimmy developed tuberculosis and was too sick to railroad, he picked up his old guitar and wrote and recorded the experiences he had seen and turned them into songs. Jimmy died in his early thirties, just six months and ten days after Mother died, on Friday, May 26, 1933. He was in New York City recording his last songs. Too sick to even play his guitar, Jimmy's last recording date was two days before he died. They put his body in the baggage coach on a train bound for home—Meridian, Mississippi—where he was buried.

Daddy befriended many a hobo down on their luck; picked them up, gave them rides, and although he didn't have much himself, would buy shoe laces or something they were selling to help them along life's hard road. Daddy got that soft heart for the downtrodden honest enough, for many a hobo would stop at Maw and Dad's home for a good meal and a place to rest for the night.

One time a prisoner had escaped from the jail in town; I don't know the nature of his crime, but his

Willie Kell

picture was in the local newspaper and folks were warned to watch out for him. Well, this escaped prisoner came to the farm. Maw was there by herself, I guess Dad was in town. Jock may have been back in the fields at the time. The man asked Maw for something to eat, so she cooked him something, packed him a lunch, and after thanking her, the man was on his way. There was no talk of him escaping jail or that he was running from the law, but Maw recognised him from the picture in the paper. They just talked small talk about the weather and how the crops were. He ate down what Maw cooked for him, took the bag of lunch she made up for him, said thanks, and was gone. I never really heard if they caught the man or what happened to him. There was little said about it; nobody knew except the family.

Yes, there was many a sad story back in that old depression, and there were many stories of kindness and folks helping one another. People seemed to rally to the needs of those less fortunate than themselves. I can well remember a famous hobo friend of Daddy's; his name was Alex McDonald. He at one time traded horses out on the road, but after his wife died, he started to hobo. It became a way of life for him. Daddy proudly introduced "Old Alex" to me when we met him in a small town where Daddy was selling medicine and Alex was looking for a handout on the street. Alex was dressed so shabbily, and even had an overcoat on in the summer. I remember thinking how the poor fellow smelled; seemed like he could sure use a nice, soapy bath.

No, it was not a good time to try and make a living selling medicine or anything else. As Daddy used to say, the poor folks had no money and the rich didn't spend theirs, not with door peddlers. Although Daddy never had a lot of ambition, he tried to keep that old Model T on the road, always bringing home a bit of money, some butter, eggs, or whatever he could get. I remember one farmer owed him $5.00, but he just didn't have the money, so he gave him a pair of pigs. Daddy brought them home in the back of that little car. He gave one to Maw and had the other one made into sausage, ham, and other goodies. We lived on pork that winter.

Toots had passed her grade 12 (in those days they called it the 4th form) and got a job as a bookkeeper for a fellow that sold and fixed typewriters. Her wages were $5.00 a week, when she got paid; sometimes when the guy had no money and couldn't pay her, she had to come home empty-handed. Sweet had to quit school, stay home, look after the house and take care of little Elizabeth, and send the rest of us to school.

All the family excelled in school except for me. They were mostly at the top of their class. The local paper used to print the honour roll each month from the schools. The Kell children were always at or near the top; one month all four of the oldest kids were first in their respective classes. That was before I started, and it's a good thing for them that it was, for surely I would have ruined their perfect record. Although, when Elizabeth came along, she would have been right up there with them. She became an excellent student.

As that terrible year of 1932 was coming to a close, Daddy was preparing us for a bleak Christmas. Santa Claus wouldn't be happening this year; if he ever really did come other years before that, I don't know, don't remember. I'm sure Mother would see to it that we got something, 'cause if she was able, she would make us something. I don't recall a Christmas before that one, but I well remember Christmas 1932; it was sad without Mother.

Daddy, Elizabeth, and I went out to the farm to spend Christmas with them. I think Toots spent Christmas at her boyfriend's place. His mother was

Willie Kell

from England. Her husband George's father had been killed in the first world war and she lived on a war widow's pension. Really, she had it pretty good, a government cheque coming in every month. It wasn't a whole lot, but more than some able-bodied men were earning in those times. I think one or two others in the family went there that Christmas Day. She was a kind soul and quick to help someone in need, though it wouldn't be like a Kell to go begging.

We had a good dinner at Maw's table, as usual, though I don't remember getting any kind of present. Maw gave us an orange, and that was a treat for Elizabeth and me. I do remember that Mary Parson and her mother were there. They lived up the road a mile or so in a log house on a stony old 50-acre farm. Mrs. Parson was a neighbour to Maw and visited her from time to time. Her husband had left her and gone to live in the bush up north somewhere. She survived by milking a couple of cows, making a bit of butter and selling it, selling a few eggs and a couple of calves once a year. It was no way to get rich, but I guess she lived somehow, like many more.

Mary would celebrate her 25th birthday in a few weeks, and was a good-looking young woman—black hair, brown eyes, shapely body, and nice legs. She was 18 years younger than Daddy and 18 years older than me. But for all the difference in their ages, she seemed to like Daddy and, looking back, she was making a play for him that Christmas Day at Maw's farm. They talked quite a bit, and I can remember them in Maw's front room sitting next to one another, all smiles. Daddy didn't look as sad about the way things were going at Christmas, as he had told me they were going to be before we went out to Maw's farm that day. I could see that he liked this woman, and even though I was only 6 at the time, it bothered me.

Willie

Well, it wasn't long into the new year before this Mary showed up at our house one night after supper. It seemed that the fellow who brought her there had a flat tire soon after they arrived and spent the next couple of hours out in the January cold fixing that darned tire. He had to take the tube out and patch it and fill it up with air with a hand pump. There was this poor fellow, out in our driveway, very little light, fixing that tire in the cold, while Mary was in the house sitting on Daddy's knee and having a wonderful time. We learned later that it was Mary's car—a green Model T Ford hard-top coupe. This same Mary had flattened the tire or let the air out on purpose. There she was in the warm house, teasing around with Daddy, while her poor boyfriend was out there in the cold fixing the tire. Well, he wasn't her boyfriend for long; Daddy was. The girls, Toots and Sweet, saw what was going on that night of the flat tire and were not very happy with it.

As time went on there was a lot less happiness in our home because of this Mary Parson. Toots and Sweet didn't like the situation at all, and soon let Daddy know that they were not happy with his new love affair so soon after Mother had died. But this love affair between them kept getting more intense as the days and nights went by, and soon she was spending more time at our house, sitting on Daddy's knee, wiggling around as though she had a grasshopper in her pants. Mary had a job working at a hotel downtown in the dining room and kitchen, and she would bring goodies to the house. She'd bring cakes, pies, cookies, and all kinds of things to eat, stuff that was left over or things she would steal from the place.

I guess that we ate pretty good that winter, what with the pig meat, the garden vegetables, milk and eggs Maw would give us, and what Mary would scrounge from the hotel. Sometimes Mary brought goodies and hid them to take out to her mother and her brother and his family, who lived with the old lady out on the little farm. One time the girls found this hiding place and we ate the stuff. There was hell to pay! She ranted and raved, cursed and swore. Oh, there was a lot of tension between Mary and our family. The tension got worse when the girls discovered she had stolen some things that had belonged to Mother. Little things she had left for us—a child's quilt that Mother had partly finished for Elizabeth, and some other things that meant a lot to us. Mary took them from us.

It wasn't long before Mary moved right into our house and slept in Mother's bed. Daddy would walk down and meet her at the hotel and walk her to our house when she was off work.

It was an interesting time in our lives. Daddy was doing alright; he had this good-looking young woman living with him, feeding his sexual appetite, then getting cake and cookies for dessert. Toots bought a real nice Westinghouse radio with a big clock on it, it stood about four feet high. We could get all kinds of good programs on that thing. We got Amos & Andy, and on Saturday nights we heard the Grand Ole Opry all the way from Nashville, Tennessee. Oh, what a wonderful invention, this radio. Folks talking and singing songs over that radio from hundreds of miles away, and we could hear every word right there in our little house.

We kept warm on those cold nights burning wood in the kitchen stove and coke in the little front room heater stove. Coke was what was left over after they had taken the gas out of the coal, and it made a good heat and would burn slowly all night long. Son used to fetch it on the sleigh with Pal, a couple of bags at a time. He would hitch up the dog to the little sleigh and drive down to the gashouse, over the 10th Street bridge and along the harbour. The stuff cost 10 cents for a burlap sack full, the same price Daddy paid for a package of fine-cut

Willie

tobacco to roll his cigarettes. It was more than 2 miles down to the gashouse and back, and often a cold ride, especially if there was a northeast wind blowing out of Georgian Bay across the harbour. Son would dress warm and Pal had on his collie winter coat, and pulling that sleigh, sometimes over bare pavement, ice, and snow, he kept plenty warm. Son would get off the sleigh and walk alongside when they came to some bare pavement and he would walk up the long winding 10th Street hill. When they got back to the easy going, he would sit on the bags of coke and Pal would trot right along like a little horse. Son wanted to be a racehorse driver like Pop Eager.

The winter seemed to move along. I don't remember if it was a real cold winter—the winters up near the lakes are always cold enough—but I know there was a lot of snow around. Toots went to work for the typewriter man every morning, Son went to high school, Jim and I went to public school down below the hill, about three-quarters of a mile, and Sweet stayed home and did the house work and looked after Elizabeth. Mary went to work at the hotel, and Daddy had a little bay horse that he drove, hitched to the cutter, to sell a bit of medicine.

I remember one morning when I got to my class room at school, my hands were paining me awful; they had got real cold coming to school and when they started to thaw out, it hurt bad. Though I was always taught not to be a baby and cry, to be tough, I don't ever remember crying much about anything. That morning I did cry in school and told the teacher how my hands hurt me so, but Miss Lang, who by this time had taught a few generations, announced to the class that, "Willie's mother died a while back and now people make a baby out of him." Well, I knew I had lost my mother, but if anybody was making a baby out of me, they hadn't told

Willie Kell

me about it. Daddy was busy taking care of Mary, Toots had her boyfriend and her job, Son had Pal, and Jim helped Sweet with the housework when he wasn't going to school. Mary was taking care of a little girl about the age of Elizabeth. It seemed like she was planning to adopt this little girl, and she would bring her to our house quite a lot. I remember Daddy making a fuss over this kid, holding her on his knee, trying to please Mary. He really had enough to do looking after the kids that he had brought into the world, they needed him badly now that Mother was gone. But Mary would bring that kid to our house and sometimes she and Daddy would be playing with the little girl and Elizabeth, and I would be craving his attention and time. But Mary liked that; she was terribly jealous herself, and if she could hurt us children and take Daddy's love away from us it seemed to make her happy. No, where that school teacher ever got it in her head that anyone was making a baby out of me that cold winter, I'll never know.

Sometimes, when Mary wasn't there, Daddy would hold Elizabeth and me on his knee and sing to us. That was a good feeling, that rare time when someone would hold us in loving arms and say kind words or sing to us. But it happened very little once Mother had died. There were lots of times when Mother was living, Daddy would tell me stories of how we would go camping, just the two of us, and cook our meals over a camp fire, away up north. There would be wolves and bears up there, but they wouldn't get us. We were going to have a wonderful time, living in a tent in the bush. I just loved his beautiful stories and believed them. Sometimes he would get down on the floor on his hands and knees and pretend that he was a horse. I would get on his back and ride him and he would buck and snort like a bucking bronco. We had a wonderful time together, but that was another time, things had changed, the good times were

Willie

gone. Since Mary came into our lives, I felt like an orphan, and I'm sure my little sister Elizabeth felt about the same.

Daddy always was close to Son. Son liked horses and wanted to be out at Pop Eager's farm, or out at Maw's place. Growing up, when Mother was living, Son went with Daddy to different places. Jim, on the other hand, was closer to Mother. He and Daddy were never buddies. Jim was very gentle in nature and seemed to take after Mother. When she died, it was an awful blow to him; he was only 12 at the time, a terrible time to lose a mother. I don't think he ever really got over it. There was no one to take her place—certainly not Daddy, not with Mary on the scene.

It was getting close to spring, and at last that first long winter after Mother was in her grave was coming to an end. The snow was almost gone, but for the stubborn last drifts that had gathered along fences and places where it was shaded from the March sun.

One day when I got home from school, there was a big brown Hudson sedan car in our driveway. I had never remembered seeing a car as fancy as this one at our place before; even Uncle Bill's Pontiac sedan, or Uncle Herb Lawson's Buick wasn't as big and sleek as this car. I remember thinking that it looked like something that big gangster from Chicago, Al Capone, would be driving—maybe he was visiting us. With all the strange happenings at our house those last few months, I wouldn't have been surprised at anything. When I opened the kitchen door and walked in, Sweet was there as usual, and I could hear loud talking and laughter coming from the front room. I went to the door separating the kitchen and front room and looked in. There were several strange men in there with Daddy. I recognized one of them as Daddy's old buddy Jimmy Sharpe, the fellow that used to have the livery stable in

Willie Kell

town. He had moved to Toronto to run a used car business. Then there was a big, loud-mouthed fellow they called the "Mulligan Farmer"; he had a pocket full of money, $10.00 bills, and he was showing it all around. Jimmy and the farmer had on fancy clothes, dark suits, and those black Mafia-looking hats on their heads. There were a couple of other guys, locals—they were dressed ordinary. Then there was Andy; they called him Andy Gump after a fellow in the funny papers. Andy had a protruding nose and little ears that seemed to stick straight out. He didn't have fancy clothes; turned out that he was the driver. Took these fellows around, kept the Hudson running and looking shiny, and did errands. Jimmy and the farmer were in town on some kind of shady business and might have been trying to get Daddy involved in it, but Daddy would never get involved in anything that might put him in jail—never!

I think they hung around town for a couple of weeks, and were staying at a hotel, but they spent time at our place every day; sometimes they would come at night. They smoked cigarettes and big cigars, and they had whiskey too, and gave Daddy drinks. The girls were worried that he would start to drink again. I had never seen him take a drink, he had been on the wagon for a few years, but they say at one time he drank quite a lot.

One evening, Daddy and Mary and Andy the driver came home around supper- time. They were kind of leading Jimmy Sharpe, Daddy on one side of him and somebody on the other side, I think it was Mary. He had his dark suit on and that "Mafia hat" and dark sunglasses. They had been out to a bootleggers and drinking some kind of homemade swamp whiskey, and Jimmy drank too much of it and went blind. Jimmy was a big, tall fellow—tall, dark, and handsome—and seeing him with that long black overcoat on and the black hat and dark glasses, being led in and put to bed on our

Willie

couch, was a sight that a boy of six would not soon forget. I remember wondering how we would get that big fellow off that couch so we could pull it out when it was time for bed. That's where us three boys slept. He looked real sick and I could tell that they were worried about him. What if he died on our couch? Where would we sleep?

After an hour or so he started to come around. They gave him some tea or something hot to drink, got him up off our bed, and Andy took him away. He must have still been blind, 'cause they were leading him around. They led him out to the car and put him in the back seat. I watched out the window. This was all very intriguing to me, another strange chapter unfolding in the volume of bizarre happenings in my life from the time Mother, Elizabeth, and I went to Sarnia the summer before. Oh, no, Miss Lang, there was nobody making a baby out of me that night. I can't remember anyone noticing that I was even there.

Well, it was only a day or two after Jimmy Sharpe took the blind spell they loaded up in the Hudson sedan, said their good-byes, and left for the big city. By this time he could see pretty well, but he was still wearing the dark glasses. The "Mulligan Farmer" (his real name was Wilshire), like Jimmy, always had a hard time keeping out of trouble. Years later he hanged himself while doing time in Stony Mountain Prison.

It was real quiet around our place for a few days after they left. The girls were happy to see the last of them! Now we could get back to just eight people living in that little house, back to the fighting between Mary and the girls. It seems Son was friendly with Daddy and Mary and they treated him better. Jim stuck with the girls. Little Elizabeth and I were in some kind of no man's land, but the girls took care of us and so did the

Willie Kell

boys. I don't remember having anything to do with Mary; I think she mostly ignored Elizabeth and me.

Soon some of Mother's early flowers were peeking out along the south side of the house, where they were sheltered from the chilly breath of winter that still lingered. She loved her flowers and had planted some by the house. I remember that she liked pansies, and I never see them that I don't think of her. But she didn't want any at her funeral, said she enjoyed her flowers while she lived, and asked that no one bring flowers when she died. Her wishes were granted, for the most part. However, some kind soul did bring a small bouquet, and it was placed on her grave.

As the last of the windy winter storms came and went and the rains of April washed away what was left of the ice and snow, May of 1933 at last brought back the warm welcome sunshine that had been missing in our lives since before Mother died.

Book Four: Pal, The Wonder Dog

Late in May, Daddy got some seeds, potatoes, and other things to plant in the garden and the big kids helped to put them in. It wouldn't be the same now without Mother; she had a green thumb and things just seemed to grow for her. When the garden came up, the kids hoed it and pulled out the weeds. I had to help, and the big kids would yell at me if I pulled out something I wasn't supposed to. Son had Pal working, too, hitched to that little harrow he had made for him, pulling it up and down between the rows. One day Son had Jim driving Pal hitched to the harrow. It was not something Jim liked to do; he didn't care that much about Pal. After all, he was Son's dog, and though he didn't dislike him, driving a dog or a horse never really appealed to him. His soft hands and long fingers were meant to play a piano, and that's what he wanted to do. He always said that horses were smelly; guess he was right. Some of us rather like the smell of horses, and some don't. However, this day Son talked or bossed him into it, while he stood back and supervised the situation. Daddy was away, as he often was, so I guess Son thought he was in charge.

There was a big common kind of field behind our place and beyond the common was 10th Street, which led to the main road west out of town. Now who do you think was riding his bicycle, heading home with a bag of potatoes on the handlebars; sure enough, it was that poor stuttering neighbour. He mostly went right past our place on 11th Street, but I suppose with the potatoes

Willie Kell

on the handlebars, he thought he had better avoid Pal by going around on the other street. Well, that was a big mistake, 'cause Pal saw him—he just happened to be heading that way going along those harrows in the garden. With Jim driving him and not being much of a reins man, the situation was soon out of control. Pal took off after that man like some kind of racehorse, and Jim was no match for him. Pal ran across that commons like a devil dog from hell, growling and barking, the harrow bouncing along like some kind of toy behind him. He caught that man by the pant leg and pulled him off the bicycle onto the pavement, potatoes flying all over the road. Cars were honking their horns and stopping. Son and Jim ran after the dog and I ran as fast as my legs would take me. The man didn't get hurt, thank God—a few scratches and scrapes when he landed on the pavement. It could have been a lot worse, and the boys and I felt bad about it. Son gathered up Pal and the harrow, Jim and I helped the man find his potatoes. He was sure stuttering now, in a very loud voice. Someone once said if you get a real bad scare it can cure the hiccups, but it sure didn't cure that poor man's stuttering.

When school got out at the end of June, we got our report cards, I didn't pass into the next class; I failed. Those days, you either passed or failed. If you failed, it meant another year in the same class. In other words, you kept at it until you got it right. I was disappointed that I didn't pass, hated the thought of an extra year in school; next year I would work harder. That past year in school had been strange for me, starting my term in Sarnia, being there for two months, then changing to another school. The time away from school when Mother died and all the turmoil in our house I guess contributed to my dismal school year. I have often

Willie

thought that maybe that year I failed in school taught me a lesson in life—that when things get tough, you have to get tough, too, and try harder.

That summer, Son and I spent quite a lot of time out at Maw's farm. We helped with chores and Son worked in the fields. I used to help Maw, bringing in chips and chunks of wood to get the fire going for cooking the meals and doing down jars of fruit for the winter. There was a small cellar under the front bedroom. In the warm weather we could get down there from the outside. You had to bend your head to walk in that cellar if you were grown up—I guess it was made for little boys like me. Maw used to keep the cream, the meat, the butter and things down there because it was cool. There were stones piled around for a wall and she kept them whitewashed. In the winter you got down through a trap door; there were no windows in that little cellar and you had to light a lantern to see what you were doing. I kind of liked going and getting things out of the cellar for Maw, it was weird down there.

Sometimes brother Jim would come out for a day or two, but he wasn't very interested in the farm and mostly stayed in town. He liked being with the girls. On Sundays he went to church and got friendly with young people there. It was about that time that he started taking piano lessons. Daddy was on the road or away with Mary and that other little girl, and the bad feelings kept getting worse, with Daddy and Mary on one side and the girls on the other.

When September came around it was back to that old school, same class, but I got to know new kids, 'cause the ones from the year before were in the next class. This time school went better; I got off to a good start, and though I never enjoyed it very much, I learned a little more and found the work easier than it was the year before. But I was always happy when Saturday came. I

Willie Kell

often went over to play with my friend next door, who was a year or so older than me, but we got along well together. Fred had a wagon, a tricycle, and lots of nice toys; I guess 'cause he was an only child his folks could afford to buy him all that stuff. I can't remember having any toys. But with six in the family, we had each other, and we could talk, laugh, and sing—we didn't need as many toys. One day we were playing in Fred's yard with his nice toys and Pal was with us, and who should come riding in on his bicycle but the stuttering man from up the street. Pal bit him again; he didn't hurt him, very much, but he did bite him, and this time Pal was in deep trouble. The man went to the police, laid a complaint, and now Daddy and Son would have to get a lawyer and appear in court. The case came up a little while before Christmas.

Daddy hired a young lawyer to defend Pal. He didn't really hire him—he made a deal with him. It would be $5.00 if he won the case, nothing if he lost. Toots had gone to school with this young man and recommended him, but I think Pal deserved better. He needed a real criminal lawyer if he was going to beat this rap. When the day for the trial came, Daddy, Son, and the young lawyer went to court. Then the poor stuttering man got up to tell the judge what had happened and, being rather nervous about the whole thing, it made him stutter all the more. The young lawyer kind of snickered at the stuttering man, and the judge wasn't amused at this.

Daddy had told the lawyer that it was his job to make the judge believe it was the man who bit the dog. But whatever the young lawyer told that judge, it didn't work, because when all the evidence was presented, even after it was explained that this great dog Pal was trying to protect our family, that our mother had died and our father had to be away a quite a lot trying to make a

Willie

living for his family, that the stuttering man had kicked and stuttered at Pal from the time he was a pup, it didn't matter. Even after all of this, the stern old judge looked down over the top of his glasses at Son and said, "GUILTY! This dog has to be destroyed—he's got to die!" The judge gave us about a week to have our beloved Pal put down. "How could he do that?" we asked when Daddy and Son came home from court that cold windy day and told us the sad news. It wasn't a very happy time around our house, but Pal was going to have to die. They would gas him to death at the police station downtown.

Daddy came up with a great idea; it would be a little risky, but it just might work. Anything that could save our Pal would be worth the risk. At the time, they had a useless part collie dog at the farm that belonged to Dad. Daddy's idea was to take Pal out to the farm, bring the other dog in, and have the innocent, useless dog put to death. After all, he wasn't much good and they were planning on getting rid of him somehow; this would be a good way. We could leave Pal out at the farm for a while, maybe a year, until the heat died down. Then bring him back home and this time make sure he didn't get near that stuttering man.

Well, Son sure liked the idea, so the very next night, a Saturday, just after dark and when there was a good blanket of snow on the ground, Son hitched Pal to the sleigh for the long seven-mile drive to the farm. When he drove in at the farm, old Tom the farm dog came out barking to greet them and let Maw know they had company. Old Tom was a big yellow collie, a good cattle dog; they'd had him from the time he was a pup. But Dad and the useless dog were over at the ranch, so Pal and Son had more miles to travel the next morning. Son told Maw and Jock the sad news about Pal having to die, and then he and Pal bedded down for the night. The

Willie Kell

next morning, after Maw fixed the boy and his dog some breakfast to eat, they were on their way to the ranch to see Dad. When they got to the ranch, the brown-yellow dog came out to greet them; of course, he didn't know their reason for being there. That Son had planned on leading him back to town behind the sleigh, taking him to the police station to have him killed, then driving Pal back out to the farm and leaving him there.

Dad was happy to see Son and Pal; he was alone there at the ranch and way back on that side road he hardly ever saw anybody. He would often go over there and stay for a week or so when they would have a disagreement at the farm.

Son pulled the harness off of Pal and they both went on into the house. When he had given the dog some water to drink after their trip, Pal was soon sound asleep beside Dad's big box stove. It was a good time to tell Dad what they were there for. Son explained what Daddy had in mind—the exchange of the dogs, have his worthless mutt put down to save our beloved Pal. Dad took a deep breath, squinted one eye, and said, "Son, we can't do that. The judge didn't sentence this worthless dog to die, it's *your* dog that has to pay the price. I won't be a part of that kind of a deal. If the authorities ever found out, we would all be in trouble." Dad told him, "No, Son, I can't help you this time. Take your dog and do what has to be done." Son couldn't argue with Dad, and the old man helped him see that life can be cruel at times, but we have to face it, we can't run away from it.

Son and Pal rested there at the ranch awhile and Dad fixed them something to eat. Then Son put the harness on Pal and started out on that sad 10-mile journey back to town. He had a lot to think about, riding along there on that lonesome old road that cold December day just before Christmas. When they got

Willie

back to town just after dark, Son told us what Dad had said, that he wouldn't change dogs and Pal had to die.

I guess it was the next morning Son drove Pal down to the police station. It would be their last ride together. Yes, this great wonder dog who had just completed a round trip of 20 miles pulling Son on that sleigh through the December cold to try and save his life, was about to die in the gas chamber. That poor dog didn't think he had done any wrong when he bit that man, but now a boy and his faithful dog would have to part forever.

Son took Pal's harness off and patted down his brown winter coat, then walked into the police station, Pal was right behind him. The policeman there had heard all about this awful dog and was waiting for them, and in his official policeman's voice told Son to have a seat, it wouldn't take long. The man put a leash on Pal's collar. Pal licked his hand and looked at him with his big, friendly brown eyes, then looked at Son and seemed to say, "We have a new friend." The policeman remarked, "He don't seem that vicious," and then he led Pal in through a door. The old dog turned and looked at Son as if to say, "Aren't you coming with us?"

Well, it wasn't long until the man came out, carrying Pal's lifeless body, and he put him in a burlap sack, like a potato bag. His body was still warm. Son and the policeman put Pal on the sleigh, there with his harness; he said so long to the man who had just killed his dog and started for home. It would be Son's time to give Pal a ride. Son pulled the sleigh, with his faithful dog on it, up the winding hill to home. When he got home with Pal, everybody was crying. The next day Daddy and Son took Pal out to the farm, still in the burlap sack. Son dug a hole in the orchard and buried Pal, with his harness, below the frozen ground. We would never see his kind again; he was surely a wonder dog. We all missed him

Willie Kell

terribly, but it must have torn Son's heart out to see his dog, his Pal, have to die like that.

Christmas 1933 was another bleak one, although it doesn't burn in my memory like the one the year before. Santa Claus couldn't find us, and there was lots of tension in our house. Mary and the girls hardly spoke. If they did, it was to shout at one another.

That second winter after Mother died seemed to crawl by, but finally spring came. Mother's early spring flowers were starting to peek through the ground again, although there weren't as many that year. I guess nobody looked after them like she did. The winter after Christmas had been for the most part uneventful, except of course for the tension and animosity between Mary and the girls. Daddy stuck up for Mary against his family; it was them against us. Jimmy Sharpe came along in the spring one day and showed up at our house. He and Daddy took a trip to Toronto, and took Elizabeth with them. She was four years old. That day was the last time Daddy would see his six children together.

They took her to Aunt Lizzie's place on Quebec Avenue; they lived in a nice brick house. Daddy made arrangements for Aunt Lizzie to keep Elizabeth, the little girl who was named after her. Lizzie's daughter, Isabelle, who was fourteen at the time, was to take Elizabeth for an ice cream cone while Daddy and Jimmy Sharpe left. It was a sneaky thing to do, but he knew the little girl would cry to go with her daddy, I guess he knew it was wrong, what he was doing, giving up his own little child to be with Mary, but he couldn't face her and watch her cry. So, while little Elizabeth was eating an ice cream cone, Daddy and Jimmy Sharpe were driving towards home without her.

Willie

When he did get home, he told us that Elizabeth was going to stay with Aunt Lizzie for a while, and how she would be happy there. But I missed her so much, and wished that I could see her. What was going to happen to us next; now our baby sister was taken away from us. So many things had come to hurt us, and I was beginning to see that life had a lot of ups and downs, and lately it had been mostly downs. Elizabeth stayed at Aunt Lizzie's place for the next couple of years, and I don't think Daddy got to see her more than once or twice in that time.

Spring would soon turn into summer. The days were getting longer and summer holidays were just around the bend. Daddy started talking about the farm, preparing me for even more changes in our lives. "How would you like to live out on the farm with Maw? It would be a good life out there. When school starts in the fall, you can go to a country school—you'll like that," he said. "Son would be with you; he likes the farm, he can drive the horses, you would have a wonderful time," he kept telling me.

When the last day of school came, I got my report card and that year I managed to pass. I was quite happy about that, since I was smart enough by this time to realise that if I was ever going to get school behind me, I would have to pass—the sooner, the better. It was only a few days later that Son and I moved out to the farm, as Daddy had planned. Brother Jim went to live with Grandma and Grandpa Crichton in Sarnia; I think Grandma sent him a train ticket to go. Toots and Sweet stayed in our house, and by now Dad was there quite a lot. Toots, being cut from the same cloth as Dad, was making it pretty rough for Daddy and Mary by now. She and Sweet had gone to the Children's Aid Society and complained about things that were happening. Daddy knew what was going on, he had it all planned.

Willie Kell

With Elizabeth at Lizzie's, Jim at Grandma Crichton's, and Son and me out at Maw's farm, he and Mary would just blow away in the warm summer breeze—they were free. So they loaded their clothes, the medicine pot, the wooden spoon, and a few personal belongings into that Model T Ford roadster and took off to places unknown—unknown to us, anyway. It was just over a year and a half after Mother died, and now her little home was broken up. Daddy had not kept his promise to her, to take care of the children. Yes, Mother's children were now scattered like the leaves in autumn, blown around by the cruel winds of change.

Maw and Daddy
Book 4 "Pal the Wonder Dog"

Book Five: Life, On Maw's Old Farm

It must have been difficult for the girls. Toots was only earning $5.00 a week; I think she ate at her boyfriend's place sometimes. By now Sweet had a nice boyfriend, too. His name was Len Wilson, and he came from a big, good-living family of hard-working people. He had a job at the local table factory, and George, Toot's boyfriend, worked at a big printing place. Both of these boys were steady workers and they were fortunate to have a job. Though they didn't earn much money, those days it didn't cost much to live. A loaf of bread was ten cents and a quart of milk about the same. I remember Daddy telling of buying three pounds of steak in the village store in Shallow Lake for a quarter! Toots' $5.00 would go a long way toward keeping food on the table. Sweet went to her boyfriend's place for supper often; Len's mother was a good cook. They had eight kids around their table, and wouldn't mind one more.

While things were changing for us kids, they were also changing for Daddy and Mary. They lived mostly in a tent, cooking over an open fire and making the Ton-A-Lax there on the campfire, then Daddy would drive around trying to sell it. They were living up along the east side of Georgian Bay in the Muskoka, Penetanguishene, Coldwater area, travelling around, living, loving, and fighting. Mary was very jealous, and she wouldn't hear tell of him taking a drink, either. He had to change his ways, and he was finding that out the hard way. She had a real bad temper, I remember that from her living at our house, especially the time us kids

Willie Kell

ate her cakes and cookies—she about flipped her biscuits then.

Out on the farm, things seemed to drag along. They had a 1927 Model T Ford touring car by now, and Daddy had taught Jock to drive it. This model had a canvas top and originally had see-through side curtains, but they had been ripped off by the time they bought it. So we just had the open sides; guess it had been quite the car when it was new. Jock, being a bit awkward, never got to be a good driver, but he managed to get along and was happy to finally have a car. He would hold the steering wheel with both hands, and they seldom went further than the 7 miles to town in the thing. Out on the highway, he would rip it along about 25 miles an hour. If you ever said anything about what was going on along the road, he'd say, "I can't look, I'm driving this damn car." Anyway, that Model T was a lot faster and better than that slow old team of horses.

Old Donald and Minnie had a new teamster now; Son was doing most of the work. Jock had developed a kidney problem and couldn't do much for quite a while, and he was in bed a lot. That summer of 1934 they hired a young man named Wilson Graham, a big, strong, handsome fellow. It was fun to have him around; he sang, he laughed, and he made our lives happier. For a while we had two hired men; the other fellow was an old sailor who used to tell us all kinds of stories about the sea. His name was Billy Marshall. Son and the two hired hands did all of the work in the fields. My job was to pump them a cold half pail of water and take it to them when they came up to the barn with a load of hay, then lead old Donald when he was hitched to the rope that pulled the big bundles of hay in to the haymow. If they were staying back in the fields to work, they would take water with them and leave it in a shady place under a coil of hay or by a stone pile.

Willie

Haying was a slow process. First they hitched that tired old team of horses to a mower. It was a two-wheel apparatus with a long knife that stuck out from the side of it and glided along the ground. The knife went back and forth and was powered by the turning of the wheels, and it left the hay in rows. The driver sat on a steel seat and drove the team pulling this implement up and down the field until the job was finished. The next thing was to rake it into piles or bigger rows; this rake was also pulled by the team of horses. When the rake was full of hay, the driver pressed a lever with his foot and it dumped the hay. Then you would have long rows—windrows they called them—piled up two or three feet high, depending on how good the crop was. Then came the hard work that could soon raise blisters on soft, city-folk hands that were not used to the job. With pitch fork in hand, the idea was to pile this sometimes weedy, thistly hay into piles, or coils as they called them, like little stacks, rounded at the top so the water would run off if it rained. The coils would stay there for a couple of days if the weather was good and sunny, then it would be ready to haul up to the barn. Farmers prayed real hard for dry weather at this stage of the operation, 'cause if it rained on this hay it would not be as good quality. The cows and horses wouldn't like it as well. Now, if it rained a lot on this hay, it could be ruined, and you might have to burn it. The saying goes, "make hay while the sun shines."

Bringing the hay into the barn was another hard job. After the dew had dried off, you hitched the team to the hay wagon—we had the wagon with the high wooden wheels and steel rims. We had a big hayrack flat bottom, with some two by fours and boards bolted on so the hay wouldn't fall off the ends. The horses would stop when the driver told them to; there would be one man on the high, wobbly wagon and one or two pitching on these little piles or coils of hay with pitch forks. The man on the wagon moved the hay around and built the load. When they had a load on, about 10 feet high, the pitching men would climb up onto the wagon and sit in the hay; when they were all on, it was time to take it up to the barn. There was a steep hill, and a gangway up into the upstairs of the barn; the old team had to take a run at it to pull this huge load of hay onto the plank floor up over top of the stable. They unhitched old Donald and led him out, and he was hitched to a whiffletree that was attached to a huge rope. The rope ran through pulleys and was attached to a vicious-looking two-pronged thing called a fork that had a lever and a trip rope on it. My job was to lead the old horse about a hundred feet, or until the man on the wagon working this apparatus hollered. Each lift or bundle was one quarter of the load, four bundles to a load. Old Donald would pull these big bundles of hay up to the peak of the barn, which to me as a small boy looked a long way up. There was a steel track way up there, and this ugly-looking hay fork slammed into it and attached itself to the track. It would slide along this track, hanging onto that huge bundle of hay; the hay would be swaying back and forth as it rode along the track. When it got to where they wanted it, they would holler at me to stop old Donald, then the man on the wagon—often young Son—would pull this trip rope with a jerk and the bundle of hay would go crashing down into the mow. There would be one or two men in the mow levelling the hay with forks. They kept bringing this hay until the mow would be full to the top, but the cattle and horses would eat every last bite of it during the long six months they had to be in the barn, when the weather was cold and the ground was covered with snow. It smelled so good, that new-mowed hay; it left a sweet aroma that seemed to be floating all over the neighbourhood at that

Willie

haying time of year, 'cause most of the neighbours were taking in their hay, too, the very same way.

When we weren't haying, there would be mangles or turnips to hoe, and of course the never-ending chores. I had to fetch wood and chips to keep the fire going so that Maw could cook the meals, heat water, and put down the preserves for winter—peaches, pears, and the like. In the cool weather Maw baked bread, cakes, scones, and other things to feed us. Another little chore I had to do was bring water in, to fill the reservoir on the back of the stove and to keep water in the pail for cooking and drinking.

In the summer, after the cows were milked, it was my job to herd these hungry critters on the side of the road, to let them eat the grass there. The grass soon burned out among those stones in the back pasture, in the heat of the summer sun. There weren't many cars on that old side road those days, and the cows could wander all over the road. I had to keep an eye on them. Often I took them out towards the main road, but before they would reach the highway, I'd go ahead of them and turn them back. It was about a mile and a quarter to the highway; they would eat on the way out and the way back. There was a time or two when I fell sound asleep under the shade of a big old tree and the cows got a way out on that highway. I would wake up from my dreams and there wouldn't be a cow in sight, so I would run as fast as I could, and there they would be, all over the highway. Cars would be honking their horns at them, and I would round them up and get them headed back onto the side-road, out of harm's way. It reminded me of the nursery rhyme, "Little Boy Blue, come blow your horn, the sheep in the meadow, the cows in the corn." When I got to the pasture gate on the way back, I chased them in and headed across the fields to the house, and by then it would be dinnertime. I could tell the time by

Willie Kell

my shadow and the sun; by then, Maw would have dinner ready.

When it was time to come for dinner, Maw hung a white towel on the clothesline and banged on a part of an old plough that clanged like a bell. If the men were in the field while I was herding the cows, I would get to the house about the same time as they did.

I kind of liked herding those cows on that old side road—gave me time to think, sing, talk to myself, maybe write a poem and dream about a different kind of world.

When we would come into the house at noon, the big table in the kitchen would be loaded with a hot meal that Maw had cooked for us. But first we had to wash up, and I hated that. Being the youngest, I was always the last to wash. We had this little basin that sat on a small table in the corner of the kitchen, behind the stove by the door. You had to dip the water out of the reservoir with this dipper that we also drank out of. "Don't drip the water all over the floor, hold your hand under the dipper," Maw would say in a scolding voice. Then we washed with some old kind of miserable Sunlight soap. Washing my face was awful! We all had the same washcloth, and I hated having to use that same old rag, so I didn't use it very much. When Maw would see this, she would take that rag, rub soap on it, and wash me. She would hold one hand on my head and just about rub the skin off me, rub it all over my mouth after everybody else washing with it. *Yukk!* To this very day, I never use a washrag to wash, just splash nice clean water on my face with my own clean hands.

Drying was just as terrible. Maw made towels out of old flour and sugar sacks, thin as tissue paper, and by the time I got to it, the thing was soaking wet. She sewed these bags together like a belt a few feet long. It hung from a roller on the back of the kitchen door. After a couple of hired hands, Son, Jock, and Dad drying on this

Willie

so-called towel, it was hard to find a little corner for me to dry on. There wasn't one inch of that flimsy rag that wasn't wetter than my face and hands.

As that summer ran on, Wilson Graham, our hired man, was getting kind of homesick. He wanted to go see his mother, who lived about 25 miles away on a little farm. Jock was feeling much better by this time; although he couldn't work in the hay, he helped with the chores, took Maw to town to do the shopping and take the cream in to the creamery. As Wilson Graham talked more about wanting to go see his mother and mentioned that his good-looking female cousin was staying with her, Jock became more interested. Wilson didn't have a car. He was a restless soul, though he had faithfully promised that he would stay and work until the hay was in. After all, they were paying him top wages—$1.50 a day and his board.

Well, it was decided that, on a certain Sunday, we'd get the chores done and get in that old Model T Ford and go see Wilson's mother. Maw knew Mrs. Graham when they lived up the road a mile or so; she was a widow then, trying to raise her family. At that time she kept house for George Wilson. One day when she called him for dinner and he didn't answer, she went out to the barn and found him with a rope around his neck, hanging from a beam. He had killed himself. Sometime after that she got married again and moved away.

Finally the big day was here, the day we were going on this long trip. I guess, but for the couple of times I had been to Sarnia and Michigan to see Mother's relatives, this would be my longest journey. We got the chores done in a big hurry, washed up, changed our clothes, and got into the car. Wilson had written his mother and she wrote back saying she would be expecting us for dinner, about 12 noon. Maw was dressed nice, had on a big hat. Jock had on a white shirt

Willie Kell

and his best pants and shined shoes, and us boys were dressed up in our best, though I'm not quite sure what our best was at that time.

Jock drove the car and Maw sat up front with him. Wilson and Son and I sat in the back. It was a beautiful Sunday in July. Of course, with that old car you *needed* good weather. There was a canvas-type top that came down at the back with a see-through little window so you could watch what was coming behind, but no side curtains. If it rained, you got wet—real wet.

What a wonderful trip it was—in through town, way up the big, long, winding hill on the far outskirts and on down that long road. When we finally got there and drove in the laneway, everybody came out to see us. Jock was quite interested in this cousin, couldn't wait to see her, as Wilson had been telling him about her for weeks. It was one good way to get home; if it hadn't been for that cousin, I don't think we would have ever gone on that trip. Wilson had a younger brother about my age, and I was looking forward to meeting him—it would be somebody to play with for the day.

We were all so excited when we drove in the lane, I will never forget that day. Wilson was out of the car first, then Maw, then Son. Jock and I were the last to get out. I guess Jock was kind of sitting there looking at this good-looking cousin about half his age, with his big hand stretched across to the back door. He had that faraway look on his well-weathered face and that twinkle of anticipation shining in his baby-blue eyes. Jock had a big nose, as some of the Kells do, and when he got excited, his nose kind of twitched like a bunny rabbit's. While Jock was sitting there with his hand stretched out and his big awkward fingers hung down in the doorway looking at the pretty cousin, his nose twitching feverishly, I jumped out and slammed the door on his finger. *Ouch.* Took the whole tip of his finger off, blood

Willie

squirting all over the place. His nose stopped twitching and that beautiful twinkle he had in his eyes just a moment before was gone, and as he stared at me the look turned to some kind of inner rage. Well, Maw got him out of the car and everybody was making a fuss over him and looking at me like I was some kind of devil child from hell. I couldn't say I was sorry, I couldn't say anything. I was scared and ashamed all at the same time. Well, they took him into the house and put a huge bandage on that finger, a big white cloth kind of bandage. He could hardly handle his knife and fork at the dinner table. I sat across from him and every time I sheepishly looked up at him I got a look of hate. However, the dinner was delicious, I got to play with Wilson's brother, Wilson and Son went swimming back in a pond on the farm, but Jock didn't get the girl, and I think he always blamed me.

We spent most of that Sunday afternoon with those nice people and then started home. We had a long trip ahead of us, and when we got home there were chores to do, all those cows to milk and the pigs to feed. They let me off on the side-road so I could bring the cows home to milk. It had been a good trip; but for my slamming the door on Jock's finger and the big calamity that it caused, things went real well. He wore the bandage on his finger for over a week. It was hard to milk the cows with it on, and I was often reminded of this terrible deed that I had done.

During the summer, in the late afternoons, old Tom and me would go get the cows up out of the pasture and bring them home for milking. We walked back through the stony lane and along the paths that those cows had worn into the ground going back and forth. Old Tom was a good cattle dog; he would go chase them and bite their heels if they didn't move. Sometimes those cows

Willie Kell

would be away back near the highway. We had to cross over the creek on a log, and I often stopped and caught a frog. I would carry it around getting the cows, then drop it back in the creek on the way home. Sometimes there were snakes warming themselves in the late afternoon sun; black snakes, milk snakes. They say that those milk snakes milked the cows. There were several different colours and kinds of snakes back among those stones, and sometimes they would stand up and hiss at you if you came too close.

By the time Son and I went out to the farm to live, Dad had a real nice driving horse, a standardbred called "Delco Light," named after a lighting system that was used by some wealthy farmers where hydro wasn't yet available. Delco had been a pretty good racehorse, but was bothered by sore, brittle front feet. Dad took great care of the horse and the two of them were buddies. Sometimes in the summer Dad would drive me back to get the cows from the pasture. When he did drive me back, he would bring along a cake of Maw's Sunlight soap and a towel. It was time for the old man to take a bath! The horse had to take it real slow and wander around to miss all the stones in the pasture. Sometimes the old buggy would just about upset when Dad and the horse were trying to wiggle that buggy around those stones. Old Tom would walk along behind. When we got to the crick, Dad would drive the horse right into the water. It was good for his sore old feet and it tightened up the loose spokes in the buggy wheels at the same time, I liked it, too. It was fun riding along, bouncing over the jagged pieces of stone that lie on the creek bed. We must have scared the heck out of those frogs and fish as we came splashing along.

The creek, (everybody called it "the crick") started in the Long Swamp and ran on a winding westerly journey through the stony pastureland, ending near

Willie

Shallow Lake. It ran across the width of the farm, and was between just a few inches in depth to about a foot at the deepest part. That part of the farm back around the creek was all flat stone (ledgerock), melted like lava in some other time and flattened into different thickness in the aeons. This ledgerock was covered with a coat of soil a foot or two in depth, most places. The grass on top of that rock would soon burn off and be brown and dry in the hot summer.

The bed, or floor of the creek was like a cement floor—smooth and often slippery. In most places it was covered with pieces of broken ledgerock. But there were one or two spots that were clear of this debris—this was a great place to take a bath, shaded by a nice grove of cedar trees. Dad would tie the horse to a tree, take off his clothes, and sit down in the half-warm water. The old man would splash the water over himself and I'd roll up my pants, get into the creek and splash him some more. Then I got the big cake of soap and commenced to bathe this giant of a man. I would rub this cake of soap over his back, shoulders and huge neck and rub it in his hair. He always had short hair, so the hair was never a problem. The minnows would swim up and nibble at him as he sat in this big bathtub that seemed to have been made for him. It was my job to wash him where he couldn't get at, he washed the front and private places. Old Tom often would get in the water and walk around, then shake himself and go have a sleep on the creek bank. Once Dad was well soaped, I would splash water on him, lots of water; it was kind of fun. I'd get my clothes wet, but they would be pretty well dried out by the time I rounded up the cows and got back to the house. Anytime I have seen them washing the elephants at a circus, I am reminded of bathing Dad back at the creek.

Willie Kell

I used to like that old creek; it was kind of like a friend to me, with its millions of minnows, frogs, and snakes. Once, when I went to cross it on the log, there was a huge black snake waiting on the other end of the log. Didn't seem like he was planning to move out of my way, so I quietly backed up, took my shoes off, and politely walked around that snake through the creek.

In the summertime, after supper, when the hay was in for the day and the chores were all done, Son and I and the hired men would go to the crick for our bath. It was about a half a mile through the pasture. It always felt good to get the sweat and the hayseeds washed off after the day's work. We bathed in the creek with the green bullfrogs.

We did our bathing out near the road in a deeper part of the crick. Often, it was twilight by the time we got there, and the whippoorwills would be calling. Sometimes it was almost dark.

One night, Wilson Graham, Son, and me were back there, having our bath while the moon was coming up over the trees. When we finished playing around in the water and were drying ourselves, we saw this car coming slowly along the sideroad. It stopped, pulled off the road, and parked by some cedar trees near the bridge. Wilson said we should sneak around and investigate the situation. He was the leader, Son and I followed. We had to be real quiet. We got under the fence at the road, keeping down out of sight. As we crossed the bridge we went single-file, crunched over. Wilson seemed to know what he was doing, guess he had done this before. Once or twice one of us stepped on a dead twig and it cracked like a rifle shot. When we got to the cedar trees, we crawled on our stomachs—Wilson, then Son and I, one behind the other. I stayed real close to Son, right up behind him, it was so scary. Then, wouldn't you know, Son farted—it was a loud one, and although I was

Willie

scared, it seemed so funny, I started to laugh. Wilson put his big dirty hand over my mouth. We were getting pretty close to that car and couldn't make a sound. The only noises were the calling of a night bird now and then and the faint sound of a splash at the crick once in while.

When we got close to the car, we could see the back door was open, and by the dim light glimmering inside the car we could see two people. A man and a woman on the back seat—the man was on top of the woman, and it seemed to me that they must have been feeling the heat, 'cause they had most of their clothes off. They were talking very quietly in a kind of grunt and groan. After a while they more or less quit the grunting and groaning and sat up and kissed and talked some more in low voices. Then they got out of the car and stretched a blanket on the ground, and when they were doing this we could see that the man had no pants on and the woman was naked but for some kind of a brassiere. Well, they laid down on that blanket, the summer moon shining down on them, and darned if that man don't get on top of the woman again, and then the grunting and groaning started all over again, too. We were under the cedar trees, hardly breathing, 'cause they were right there in front of us. They bounced around on that blanket for quite a little while, making these weird, grunty sounds. Then at last they laid still for a spell. Stood up, kissed some more, then finally they got dressed, picked up the blanket, got in the front seat of the car, brushed and combed their hair, kissed some more, then started the car and drove off into the night, out towards the main road

After that interesting night down at the creek, we went for a bath as much as we could, every night that it was warm, hoping to find that man and woman there again, but I can't remember them ever coming back to their loving place on that winding old sideroad.

Willie Kell

Maw began talking of Aunt Lizzie and Uncle Bill and their kids coming from Toronto, and of course bringing our little sister Elizabeth. We hadn't seen her since early spring and I missed her so much, but soon she was coming to see us—I could hardly wait. I kept asking Maw when they would be here. When the big day finally arrived, a Sunday, I kept watching for their car. When the chores were finished, I walked out to the road and waited. At last Uncle Bill's Pontiac came over the hill and drove in the lane. I ran after the car as it slowly drove up to the back woodshed door. When they started getting out, I stood there and was so shy I could hardly talk to Elizabeth when I saw her. Everybody was shaking hands, hugging and kissing. We hadn't seen many of our relatives lately; Daddy hadn't been there, I don't remember the girls getting out to see us very much, Marian might have dropped in a time or two. Maw had friends that came out to visit from town quite a lot and she would make them tea and sit and talk to them.

Dad didn't say much when the Barbers came. Half the time he was mad at Lizzie for something. The Barbers unloaded the car, and they had brought me a scooter that Bud had got too big for. Then they put their things in the house, washed up, and it was soon time to sit down to a nice Sunday dinner that Maw had ready for us. Maw got a bunch of big, fancy clean towels out for the Barbers to dry on; they couldn't dry on our flimsy old towel. I remember them talking about the Dionne Quintuplets; they were just a few months old at the time, in that summer of 1934. Other big news—Jim Braddock had knocked out Max Baer to become the world's heavyweight champion, and the FBI had gunned down John Dillinger on a Chicago street. He was public enemy number one!!

Willie

After dinner, Uncle Bill got his barber stuff out and we went outside in the shade by the woodshed door and got a haircut. Dad, Jock, Son, me, and the hired man—everybody got a brush cut but the hired man. We all needed a haircut badly, hadn't had one in a while—we were waiting for Uncle Bill to come.

The Barbers were different than us; they were big-city folks, they talked city talk and dressed in city clothes. Uncle Bill was a handsome man, Aunt Lizzie was an attractive lady, Bud looked like his father and Isabelle was a beautiful fine-featured, fair-haired girl. She went back with me to the pasture to fetch the cows one day and told me a lot of interesting city things. I could hardly take my eyes off of her. She was 14, Bud was a couple of years older, and I would be 8 on the third of August, just a week or two from then. I gradually got to know my sister again and it was wonderful to be with her, we had a great time together. Having no other kids around to play with, and hardly any toys, I learned to invent toys out of things I found around the farm.

I used an old chicken shelter for my barn; it was just big enough that I could crawl part way into it. I rigged up string and little pieces of wire so it was a model of the way we put the hay in the big barn. There were old bones that were shaped like horses' feet that I used for horses. Sometimes I would bring a frog up from the creek and put him into a little pen that I built in my chicken coop barn and I'd pretend it was a pig. I kept this play barn out behind the house in the shade and spent some time there in the afternoons, if I didn't have things to do. Other times I would pretend that I was a horse, and learned to snort and whinny like one.

Well, that week when the Barbers and Elizabeth were at the farm, the time went by far too quickly, and soon it was time to say good-bye. Oh, I hated to see my

Willie Kell

little sister go away again, but I didn't cry; I stood and watched until they were out of sight. Sometimes when I was alone I would pretend that she was still there and I would talk to her. I talked to myself quite a lot and developed a wonderful imagination. I learned that if I didn't like things the way they were, all I had to do was imagine something I did like—it worked wonders for me.

The summer went along quite well. We had the hired men for company, had our trip to Wilson Graham's mother's place, (when I nearly took Jock's finger off). There was the intriguing night at the creek with the grunting man and woman, and then the Barbers coming and bringing Elizabeth and the scooter. I sure got a lot of mileage out of that scooter, played with it for a couple of years. Although we worked hard at times, Maw fed us good meals—not fancy but good food and lots to eat—often reminding us how fortunate we were.

When September came, I started to school in that little red schoolhouse, out on the main road. It was about a mile and a half, but I mostly went across the fields and saved some time. Maw gave me a lunch in a brown paper bag, and I used to sing as I walked along. For most of the time I was the only kid going to school from back on that side-road. Being a little fellow, slightly built, and coming from town, maybe a bit different from the farm boys, some of the kids picked on me for a while and tried to make my life more miserable. I never was a fighter and always hated violence of any kind. They would gang up on me at recess and noon hour and my first year at the school was not a very good one. But as time went on I kind of won them over. I became good friends with a bigger farm boy about a year older than me, and after that those kids didn't bother me. That boy, Jimmy Howie, and I were good

Willie

buddies and school became more fun. It was while I went to that little school that I started writing poetry, and some of it was pretty good. The teacher used to put it up on the wall. I did real well in literature, spelling, memory work and music. The rest of my subjects I found rather boring, but I got through them. They never knew at the farm how things were going at school, cause we hardly talked about it. They didn't know that I wrote poetry; I just didn't tell them. While I walked along that old side-road, I would put my poetry together or would be singing at the top of my voice—there was nobody to hear me. If it was the time of year when the cows were on pasture, I used to bring the cows with me on my way home. Those cows knew the old dog wasn't there and they didn't get in a very big hurry, so I had to holler and yell at them, or bark like I was a dog. Sometimes I would find some wildflowers; I'd pick them and take a bouquet to Maw.

One day early in the fall, when I was bringing the cows up the lane, coming from school, I saw Daddy's car parked by the house. I hurried those cows along, chased them into the barnyard, and ran fast as I could to see my Daddy. When I got to the car, he was just getting in to drive away. Mary was in the car. He said "I have to go now, Willie, I'll see you again," and then he drove away. My Lord, I hardly got a chance to say hello and he was gone.

I found out after that when Daddy and Mary came to the door, Maw wouldn't let Mary come in. Daddy came into the kitchen, and Dad got up and grabbed him by the throat and threw him up against the kitchen wall. He held him there like he was going to kill him. Daddy couldn't breathe with this giant of a man's hand around his neck, so he hauled off and hit Dad in the eye and the old man let go. When the scuffle was over, Daddy left

Willie Kell

and went to the car—that's when I came along. Dad wore a black eye for a week or so.

When the winter came, if Dad was at the farm, he often drove me to school with the horse and a little sleigh he had fixed up from an old cutter. Many a stormy, cold day, when school got out, there would be Dad and that horse waiting for me to drive me home; often the horse and Dad would be covered white with snow. Sometimes he would be in town, or over at the ranch; I missed him when he would go away for a week or so. He was a friend of mine. I could tell him things, kid talk, and he seemed to understand. He understood what life was like growing up without a mother, 'cause he had lost his mother when he was a little boy. Sometimes I would sit on his big fat knee and he would put his strong arm around me and it made me feel good and secure. He always wore a blue cotton shirt and overalls with a bib. He had a big gold pocket watch with a gold chain on it; that gold chain looked big and strong enough to tie a cow up with. He had the same nice pocketknife as long as I can remember. He would get a big cucumber out of the garden, peel it with that knife, put a bunch of salt on it, and eat the whole thing, along with a couple of tomatoes. He didn't have a tooth in his mouth, but he could chew anything, it seemed. Dad always walked straight and strong, sometimes with a long stick or staff in his hand and often in his bare feet. If he stepped on thistles or stones, it didn't bother him. I always thought of him as an oversized Moses.

Well, time went along out on the farm. Fall and winter came and went, and by the spring Jock was able to do more work. He started to get into purebred Yorkshire pigs—bought some registered ones and started breeding them and then started showing his pigs at the fairs and winning prizes.

Willie

Summer holidays came and school was out—I passed again. We got back to haying, hoeing, and all the other summer work. We had different hired men this year; they were nice guys, but we would never forget Wilson Graham and the good times he brought to us.

One day when Son and Jock came from town they brought our brother Jim! He had taken the train from Sarnia; Grandma Crichton bought his ticket and sent him home. There was no home for him but out at Maw's farm. I was so happy to see him—now half of us kids were together. By this time Sweet and Len Wilson were married, and soon Toots and George got married. Dad had bought our little house in town from the city. He bought it for a few dollars, the amount of taxes owed on it. Sweet and Len rented it from Dad for $5.00 a month, and Dad often stayed with them.

Jim was never cut out to be a farmer, and he and Jock didn't hit it off from the start. But he learned to do the work, milk the cows, feed the pigs, help in the fields, and help Maw in the house. If we couldn't work in the fields, after a rain, we would go picking wild strawberries or raspberries. Jim was the best berry picker on the planet. We picked berries all over the neighbourhood, and Maw made jam out of them. Jock liked that wild strawberry jam, but I can't remember him picking any berries.

We felt pretty lucky being out at the farm, it was kind of an orphan's home. They had raised the Anglin kids, Son and I had been there for a year, now Jim was with us. Maw treated us pretty good, and we were fortunate to have a place to live. A roof over our heads and three meals a day was a lot more than some people were getting in those times. But Maw never seemed to give us love, never a hug; mainly it was, "Hurry, boys, get the work done." I guess she was getting tired of

Willie Kell

raising kids by the time we came on the scene. When the meals were finished, she would say, "Come on, Willie, pick up the dishes and things from the table, put the milk and butter in the cellar where it's cool. Hustle around, don't sit there all day." I will always be grateful to her for this good training and this discipline. On Sundays, in the nice weather, she would walk with us out to Sunday school in the little red schoolhouse. Maw was a lady, and she taught us a lot about life.

Jock was okay with me, but never having children of his own, he seemed to have a strange way of dealing with kids. Maybe he resented having to take care of his nieces and nephews. He seemed to put Jim and me through some kind of a third degree over the littlest things. Again, Son was lucky; they needed him on the farm and catered to him more. He was able to do more work than Jim or me. Although, for the most part, I always thought we pretty well paid for our board and the few clothes and other things we got with the work we did.

Jock liked some special foods, cookies and things; we didn't get to eat this special stuff. One time I found some chocolate-covered marshmallow cookies in the cupboard, and they looked so good I ate a couple of them. The next day I ate another one or two. I couldn't resist the temptation—I had never tasted anything quite so good before. After a few days, these cookies were disappearing. Maw and Jock, like the three bears, noticed that "someone's been eating my cookies." I was hauled up before the high court, and I said that I saw Jim eating the cookies. They brought Jim in for his trial, and he proved he was innocent, so it fell back on me. I admitted my guilt, got a big lecture on stealing and lying, and was set free. I never remember getting a licking from anyone. Not Daddy, Mother, or anybody at the farm, just a couple of teachers that gave me a strapping a few times. I guess I deserved it.

Willie

Another thing I got in trouble for was neglecting my chores. I had to help feed the calves their skim milk, turn the veal calves on the cows to suck, and gather the frisky beggars up and put them in the pen when they were finished. Then I had to gather the eggs—they were all over the barn, upstairs and down. Fetch the cows in the late afternoon to be milked, herd them in the mornings on the road in the summer, and water the bull. They always had a bull tied up in the barn, summer and winter. This lazy bovine Romeo had nothing better to do than eat, drink, sleep, and keep all the heifers and cows on the farm sexually satisfied. This ungrateful critter had to be fed and watered a couple of times a day, and it was my job to do. I would go to the watering trough, fetch all the water I could carry (little more than a half of a pail), bring it back, lift it over the manger, and the bull would drink it down in a couple of slurps. Then it was back to the trough for more, until he was full. It generally took several trips to fill the brute. Well, sometimes I didn't get around to watering this bull; maybe a day or more would go by and he would start to get pretty thirsty. At a time like this, Jock would happen by with a pail in his hand, and this fool bull would do his best to come through that manger after that pail, with his tongue reached out like a saucy kid.

That's when I would hear my name called in a loud, sarcastic way, and though he never did hit me, I sometimes thought he might, so I treaded very carefully. Well, I would come running, I knew what was coming. Jock would be standing in front of that thirsty critter with the empty pail and that bull's long, pointed tongue trying to reach into that darn pail. "Did you water the bull, Willie?" Mostly I would lie and say yes, sometimes I would tell the truth and say no. Either way, there was hell to pay, but I had it coming. I should have watered that always-empty glutton and then none of this would

Willie Kell

be happening. If I said that I *had* watered the bull, Jock would say, "Go get him a little more, see if he'll drink it." I would go get the pail, walk out to the trough, about a half a city block, fetch the water back, and that thirsty fool would suck that pail dry in a second and a half, then try to go through the bottom of the pail with his tongue. Well, several trips later, maybe a dozen, and the bull would finally be filled up, but the lecture and the chewing would go on. "How would you like to be tied up with no water?" he would ask. He would go on making me feel like the most inhumane, meanest kid that ever drank a dipper of water. I would hate myself for being so careless, and always thought, never again will I forget that thirsty brute. But sure enough, every once in a while it happened, and the bullshit would hit the harrows again.

Sometimes Dad and me would sit in the front room and listen to the records on the old Baby Grand Phonograph. It had a crank on the side that you turned after every couple of songs. That wound up the spring that made the turntable go around. Aunt Lizzie gave the phonograph and records to Maw when they got their first radio. They had a lot of good tunes on those old 78s. Vernon Dalhart, a light opera singer who couldn't sell opera songs, made a big name for himself singing songs that I guess today would be referred to as folk and country songs. However, in the late 1920s and early 30s, when Vernon Dalhart was recording, terms like country and folk hadn't been invented. He sang great classics that never should be forgotten, and is in the Country Music Hall of Fame. Those songs—"The Letter Edged in Black," "Little Marian Parker," "Wreck of the Old 97," "Old Number 9"—and dozens more were being played on those old wind-up music boxes all over North America. Carson Robinson, a famous songwriter and

Willie

recording artist of that time, discovered the talent of Vernon Dalhart and urged him to try recording these songs. Years later I met and visited with Carson Robinson's granddaughter.

Then there was Jimmy Rogers' great songs: "Waiting for a Train," "Daddy and Home," "Frankie and Johnny." We would laugh at "Uncle Josh" and his silly stories, and cry when Dalhart sang "Lighting Express." I knew every word of those songs and would sing along with the records. When company came they would ask me to sing, and I'd feel so shy I thought I'd be sick, but I would bashfully sing my best. It was my very first taste of show business; I guess, in a shy kind of way, I liked it.

Son often went to town with Jock. Sometimes I would get to go, but not very many times in a year. They still gathered the buttermilk, stale bread, and garbage for the pigs and calves, only now they brought it home with the Model T Ford. The flies still followed behind, but now they couldn't keep up as well as they did with the slow old team of horses.

By the time the mid-thirties came along I was old enough to pay more attention to the news in the papers and what they talked about at the farm and at school. I knew that we had a prime minister by the name of R.B. Bennett. He's the one that pardoned the famous bandit Red Ryan. Yes, this army deserter had robbed banks and pay rolls and had escaped out of prison. He had a bad record from Toronto to Texas and was doing life in prison, but because he was such a crafty conman, everybody believed he had changed. He wrote the Prime Minister to please come and talk to him in Kingston prison. Now, here we were in this terrible depression, good honest people could barely feed their children. The

Prime Minister couldn't help them, but he found time to go talk to this low-life criminal, there in the Kingston pen. Well, I guess that low-life criminal said the right things, 'cause he was pardoned by the Prime Minister. It wasn't long after, May 1936, that Red Ryan shot and killed a policeman in a hold-up and was shot and killed himself by that policeman's partner. Politicians back then did the same unbelievably stupid things, which they continue doing today.

Our next prime minister was McKenzie King, elected in 1935, and he was the head of our country for the next 21 years. He is the man who used to ask his dead dog how to run the country. This was revealed in his own diary after that prime minister died. He would go to the grave of the little dog and talk to him, ask the mutt what he should do. It wouldn't have been so bad while the dog lived, but when he had passed away, let the poor dog rest in peace. This man King never was married. He also had great conversations with his dead father and mother, and liked to talk to the long-dead former prime minister Wilfred Laurier.

While these strange things were happening here, over in Germany this madman Adolph Hitler was planning to rule the world. He was building a huge army, navy, and airforce while the rest of the world sat and watched. Under Hitler's orders, hundreds of thousands of innocent people—Jews, gypsies, and anyone else they wanted to get rid of—were being murdered. As a young boy going to school, I knew that this terrible man and his gang of murderers had to be stopped, but the people in charge who should have been doing something about it turned their heads and pretended they didn't see.

The U.S.A. was busy trying to work out of the Depression. Franklin D. Roosevelt was re-elected president in 1936. That same year, King George of

Willie

England died and his oldest son, Edward (Prince of Wales), became king, but he was never crowned. He abdicated the throne of England to marry the woman he loved, an American divorcee named Wallis Simpson. Edward's younger brother, a shy, stammering man, became King George the Sixth. He was King of England and the Commonwealth, against his wishes.

Both President Roosevelt and Neville Chamberlain, the Prime Minister of Great Britain, wrote Hitler and asked him to please reconsider his terrible war-like ways. I guess he didn't get their letter!! Meanwhile, our man King said he believed Hitler could be trusted! Hitler had a plan, and those other so-called world leaders should have had one, too. It would have saved millions of innocent men, women, and children from the horrendous death, suffering, and desolation of the Second World War.

It was also in the mid-thirties that we had a terrible tragedy closer to home. Young Danny Dodge of Rochester, Michigan, 21-year-old heir of the famous Dodge automobile family fortunes, was killed while on his honeymoon on Manitoulin Island, Ontario. Seems the young man took along a male friend on his honeymoon, and somehow they were fooling around with dynamite (real dynamite), and young Dodge got badly injured, though not killed outright, as might have been expected. But while his poor, grieving bride and their friend were transporting the injured man in a little boat to get help, he somehow fell out of the boat and drowned in the icy waters of Georgian Bay! Things didn't turn out all that bad for the poor, grieving—now quite wealthy—widow, for soon she and this friend became lovers and were married. A happy ending to another wise, tragic story, although perhaps not so happy for Danny and the Dodge family.

Willie Kell

In 1936, the big news in the U.S.A. was that Bruno Hauptmann was convicted of kidnapping and murdering the Charles Lindbergh child. Hauptmann died in the electric chair for this crime.

With Dad spending most of his time in town at Sweet's place, Daddy showed up at the farm the odd time. It wasn't that he was afraid of the old man; he just didn't want to make any trouble. I remember one time I came from school and the boys told me Daddy had been there and just left not long before I got home. He was on his way to Manitoulin Island with Pop Eager, and couldn't wait to see me cause they had to catch the ferry at Tobermory. I was sorry I missed him. I asked the boys to tell me exactly where he had stood, so I could stand in that very same place, in his footprints. I loved him and missed him so much; I guess, in his own way, he loved me, too.

During the winter of 1937, Jock bought a nice 1928 Model A Ford. They were a lot different than a Model T. There was a gearshift on the floor and a clutch to deal with. A neighbour taught him to drive it. That winter there wasn't as much snow on the side-road. Most years, the roads were closed all winter for cars, the only traffic was horses. The mailman drove a horse and cutter and delivered the mail in all kinds of weather, six days a week. There was a winter road that cut across the farm, so everyone drove the team and sleigh or horse and cutter on this shortcut, that went between the barn and house. It was rare to see a car or truck from before Christmas until on in March.

Willie

Book Six: When Maw Died

The worst of the depression seemed to be over by 1937, but it was a long way from prosperity. Times were still hard, people couldn't find a job. Late in the winter, Maw took the flu and couldn't seem to get rid of it. The doctor got out to see her, but in those times, before antibiotics were discovered, folks had to rely on aspirins, mustard plasters, honey, and soda. She finally had to be in bed most of the time, in Aunt Birdie's room off the parlour. That old house was cold; there were no storm windows, no insulation to keep out the winter winds. They had never bothered to fix the place up; the Lord knows they could afford it. They had a barn full of livestock and money in the bank. Back then a new house wouldn't cost $1000.00.

Now that Maw was so sick, Jock did most of the cooking. Jim helped, and I had to make my own lunches for school, but I was big enough for that. When I got home from school, I would go and see Maw. Sometimes she would be sleeping; when she was awake, she talked to me. Seemed like she wasn't busy now and had more time. After supper, I used to go into her room and talk to her there at the side of her bed. She often would ask me to sing a hymn for her, and I would. It was in that Sunday school in the little red schoolhouse, when Maw used to walk out there with us boys, that I learned those old hymns. Now I could sing them to her when she was sick. I would reach out and touch her long, skinny fingers or put my hand on her forehead. I thought, any day she would start to feel better.

I guess Maw had been praying for some kind of miracle, and one day, sure enough, a miracle came walking in the door. It was Marian, Birdie's girl. Maw had raised her. She came with her little boy, Arthur, he was just 2 years old. Someone brought them in a car; it was early February and the roads were open. Things were not going well with Marian, and she needed to come home to Maw. But this time Maw needed her, and she was so glad to see her Marian come walking into the bedroom on that cold, February day. Marian couldn't tell Maw that her husband was confined in a mental hospital, that she didn't have any money, that things were going so bad for her. She had to smile through all of this pain, 'cause she could see that Maw didn't need any more problems than she already had.

It was wonderful to have Marian there to cook the meals and look after Maw, though she seemed to be getting weaker every day. Dad hadn't been at the farm for a while; he'd spent most of the winter in town.

One day, late in March, Daddy and Jimmy Sharpe came in a real nice Model A Ford—it was Jimmy's car. They stayed overnight, and it was great to see Daddy again. I hadn't seen him for so long, I just couldn't get close enough to him. By now he had a new family. He and Mary had two little girls of their own and were living in a log house over near Stayner and Wasaga Beach, about 60 miles away, which to me was about half way around the world. The next morning I didn't go to school. Daddy said that I could stay home 'cause he was there. It was wonderful to be with him. I loved him so, even if he had gone and deserted us.

After lunch, Daddy and Jimmy Sharpe left to go back to his other family, in that log house so far away. I

Willie

remember saying good-bye, then they drove away in the Model A Ford.

It was about five o'clock that day; the three of us boys were in the barn starting the evening chores, and Marian came running into the barn crying loudly, "Maw is dying, Maw is dying!"

Dear God, what sorrow we felt. Four of her grandchildren that she had raised rushed into the house, and there she was, lying in the same bed that Aunt Birdie had died in those years before. By the time we got to her, she was drawing her last breaths of life. This Maw that had been our mother and our grandmother, our teacher and our friend, was gone from our lives. Her lifeless body lay still in the bed, her white hair on the pillow. We kneeled there beside her bed and Marian asked Jim to pray and he did and we cried.

For Marian and us three boys, it was the second time we had lost a mother. Yes, for me, a 10-year old boy, I had been orphaned again. This time I was old enough to realise that there would be some big changes in our lives without our Maw. But none of us could have ever imagined the turmoil that losing her would bring. Jock stood by the bottom of her bed and looked as though the world had ended. She was the best friend he would ever have.

Marian's little boy woke up from an afternoon nap and was feeling poorly—little fellow was coming down with a cold. I held him and was putting his shoes on when the doctor came to pronounce Maw dead. He felt for a heartbeat, but there was none, so he covered her face, said some kind words, and left. The same undertaker that had buried Mother a few years before came to get Maw's lifeless body. He put her into some kind of a basket, backed the hearse up to the door, and carried Maw away.

Willie Kell

The next day he brought her back in a grey casket and set it up in the front room. Someone had let Dad, Daddy, Aunt Lizzie, and our sisters know. Dad came out with Maw in the hearse, Uncle Bill and Aunt Lizzie came from Toronto. Daddy had left the phone number of a neighbour; guess he knew that Maw was dying. Like us at the farm, he didn't have a phone or electricity in the log house.

When Daddy walked into the kitchen at the farm, he went over to Dad, who was sitting in the chair by the window where he always sat. Daddy reached out and shook hands with him, and the two were friends again. I wondered why it had taken Maw's dying to bring them together. There was a very uneasy feeling between Dad and Jock; they hardly spoke. Dad didn't go to bed while Maw lay there in her coffin. He kept the two wood stoves burning and sat by her coffin all night long; I think that he loved her dearly.

There were a quite a few people that came to see Maw in her casket as she lay there in the front room, before the funeral. Then, the day of the funeral, the yard at the farm was full of cars and they were parked all along the road. A preacher from a church in town was there to say some kind words. Aunt Lizzie cried and made such a fuss; she was very dramatic, but I'm sure she was sad for losing her mother. The little house was full of people, and a lot of folks I had never seen before were crying over Maw. I remember Con Gray and his wife being there and driving in with a fancy car. He was one of their old friends from the days on the road. But by this time he had become very successful running a big travelling carnival and midway. There was the Spearins—they ran a dairy, but years before had been on the road with Daddy. Yes, it seemed the Kells had lots of friends and were well respected. They owed no

Willie

one and nobody ever went from their door hungry, but now, worn out from hard work and raising three families, the matriarch, the very soul of our family, was dead at 68 years of age. On this day, folks were there to pay their respects. When the funeral was over, they took her in the hearse to the mausoleum at the cemetery. Her body would lay there until sometime in May. Then the frost would be out of the ground, they could dig her grave, and she would be permanently laid to rest beside Aunt Birdie.

After Maw's funeral, Dad went back to town to live. He never saw Jock or the farm again. He lived with Sweet and Len; by now they had a little boy. Aunt Lizzie went back to Toronto, Daddy went home to Mary and his new little family in the log house. Jock, my brothers, me, and Marian and her little boy were left on that sad old farm.

Maw had been a tower of strength from the very beginning. She was the one who knelt down by her bedside every night and talked to God, believing that He would take care of us. I remember this nightly prayer, down on her knees beside her bed when I was a small boy. I used to sleep in a little cot in the same room as Maw and Dad when I first went to the farm. She believed that there was someone, bigger than all of us, who watched from above.

If things didn't suit Dad, he got in that old buggy and drove away with his horse. Jock was somehow like a child who hadn't quite grown up; if things didn't sit well with him, he might start to pout. Daddy mostly cared about himself; I don't think he really wanted to hurt anybody, but if he did, even his own children, well, that was too bad—as long as he got what he wanted. Maw was the one who cared, Maw was the one who looked out for us, but now she was gone. Our tower of strength

Willie Kell

had crumbled, and the chaos that came upon us was testimony to that.

Marian's little boy had to go into the hospital soon after Maw's funeral. He came down with pneumonia. Marian stayed in town and spent day and night at the hospital for almost 2 months. That child came very close to dying. It just seemed like one thing after another for poor Marian—life tried to be cruel to this beautiful girl. Marian stayed at Sweet's place, our little white house, when she wasn't at the hospital with her child. When the little fellow did get well enough, Marian took him and went to the city of Hamilton to live. She got a job there and raised the boy. Later they moved to St. Thomas, Ontario, where she bought a little house of her own.

Meanwhile, back on the farm, things went from bad to awful. Jock and Jim took turns at cooking, and sometimes I would have to do it. Oh, why hadn't we learned some of Maw's good recipes? The place started to get awful dirty; sometimes we swept up the dirt off the kitchen floor and once in a long time we washed the floor, but mostly things just stayed dirty. Jim and Jock didn't get along too well. If Jim cooked something, Jock would make fun of it. Sunday mornings, when the chores were finished, Jim would walk out to the main road, hitch a ride to town, and go to church. He spent the day with the girls or with church friends and came back at night. He liked to be with church people and play the piano; the only thing we had to play at the farm was the old gramophone. Later, Son got a guitar. It wasn't very long until Jim moved into town and boarded at Sweet's place.

In the morning, I'd get up, do some work around the house, have my breakfast—mostly oatmeal porridge—make my school lunch, and head off for school. Often

Willie

I'd be late. Looking back, I guess there were times I wasn't as clean as I would have been if Maw had been there with that soapy washrag.

Daddy and Mary were still living in that log house. We hadn't seen them or heard from them since Maw's funeral, until one day when the local paper came and the front page headlines screamed out in big black letters across the top of the page:

CAR THEFT RINGLEADER CAPTURED IN FARMHOUSE

Sure enough, Jimmy Sharpe had been hiding out at Daddy's log house down that lonesome side-road. Yes, that log house hidden out of the way was an ideal place to hole up. That's what Jimmy Sharpe had been doing—hiding out from the law, a fugitive from justice. Daddy knew all about his crime, but Jimmy was like a wayward brother. He needed help, and Daddy didn't want to let him down at a time like that. Daddy always told him to quit the crazy stuff and go straight, but he never did, and now he was going to have to pay for breaking the law.

He was in big trouble this time. It seems that, for the past couple of years, Jimmy and about four other fellows were involved in what at that time was Canada's biggest car-theft ring.

The way it worked—or was *supposed* to work—was that they would buy a car that had been totalled in a wreck. It would be a popular make and model, almost new. Nothing over a year old would do. Then some of the gang would steal an identical car, same make, model, colour as the wreck. Suppose the wreck was a 1936 black Dodge sedan. They would find the identical car

Willie Kell

and steal it from somewhere off the street, in a parking lot, maybe from somebody's driveway. Then they would take all the identification from the wreck and transfer it to the stolen car and all serial numbers and licenses from the stolen car went to the wreck. Then they would sell the stolen car with the new identification. It worked quite well for a while. One of the gang was a metropolitan Toronto policeman—yes, one of Toronto's finest. It wouldn't be very difficult for him to steal a car. Nobody would suspect wrongdoing if a police officer got into a car and drove off with it. Jimmy was a car salesman, and they peddled these stolen cars all over Ontario. I guess everybody had a specific job to do.

One time they sold one of these stolen cars to a fellow in a smaller town who had been pricing a similar car at a local dealer. That dealer became suspicious and contacted the law. Their little game was starting to come unravelled. The police cracked the ring and every one of them was arrested but Jimmy; he was hiding out with Daddy and Mary in the log house.

He drove Daddy around, selling medicine or going anywhere else they wanted to go in that nice Model A Ford. He promised to give the car to Daddy when he was through with it. Well, he was through with it now; he wouldn't need a car where he was going. Daddy took Jimmy everywhere with him, or I guess Jimmy took Daddy. They used to play cards with the neighbours, and Jimmy fit right in with them. Jimmy had a fine wife and a beautiful daughter back in Toronto; they had to struggle while he was away.

One late afternoon, Mary, Daddy, the little girls, and Jimmy had been out to the little nearby town shopping for some groceries. When they got home, Mary was putting the groceries away, Jimmy was reading the paper—I guess to see if his name was in it—and Daddy was splitting some kindling wood to light the fire to cook

Willie

supper. He saw two men in a late-model car drive by slowly, and thought it looked like the law. He went in and told Jimmy and Mary about his suspicions and Jimmy went upstairs. Those strangers didn't go far before they turned around and came back and drove in the driveway. Daddy was still getting the wood when the two big fellows got out of the car and identified themselves as police officers. They asked if Jimmy Sharpe was there, and Daddy said he didn't know him. I suppose, right then, he was wishing that he really *didn't* know him. They said they would like to go in and check for themselves, which they did, with Daddy following close behind. They walked in, spoke to Mary and the little girls, and then walked to the bottom of the stairs. One of them said, in an authoritative voice, "JIMMY, WE KNOW YOU ARE UP THERE, JUST COME DOWN WITH YOUR HANDS OVER YOUR HEAD, WE DON'T WANT TO HAVE TO COME AND GET YOU." With those few kind words, Jimmy came down, hands over his head like they told him. He knew that his little game of hide and seek was over. Daddy asked if Jimmy couldn't have supper before they took him away. They said, "No, they'll feed him supper where he's going."

Daddy never did get that nice car. Turns out that Jimmy was so broke he had to sell the car and even pawn his watch before his trial came up. Guess Jimmy Sharpe's crimes didn't pay after all. Fortunately for Daddy, he was not implicated; his name never came up, not even in the newspapers. Jimmy Sharpe was sentenced to 3 years in Kingston Penitentiary; the Toronto cop in the gang got about the same.

It was about that time Daddy's heart started bothering him again. The doctor said he shouldn't drive the car for a while. Mary never had learned to drive. He

Willie Kell

got a young man to drive him around for one dollar a day. By this time he had sold the old Model T and had a 1928 Chevrolet sedan. The young man that drove him around was quite mechanical and liked to drive. His name was Adrian Craddock. The Craddock family lived up the road a few miles; they were very talented in music, but like most other people of that time had to struggle to make a living. The family had worked with medicine shows around the country, but now they were living in an old run-down, rented house and trying to find work. But what wonderful stories they had to share about their life on the road. Daddy had great times when he and Mary would visit with these people. They would get out their guitars and sing and play.

Along about October that same year Mary wrote to Son at the farm and said that Daddy would like us boys to come and see him. I guess, with his heart bothering him, he wanted to see us, and I suppose he had thought about things he might have done, or perhaps should not have done. Son got in touch with Jim, asked him if he would like to go with us, and he said that he would. So arrangements were made and soon the day came for us to go. We left the farm in good time on a Sunday morning, right after the chores were done, in the 1928 Model A Ford. Son had been doing most of the driving by now, which was going to town and back and other little trips. Now we were heading out on a long trip—60 miles—to see our father, and we were excited.

Son had the instructions on how to get there and Jim was the navigator. I was content to sit in the back seat and enjoy the trip, and even went to sleep for a little while. It was late morning when we arrived at the log house, and it was great to see Daddy. We got to meet our half sisters for the first time—they were beautiful little girls. The oldest one was Marybelle, named after Mary

Willie

and Maw. The other little girl was quite blond, eleven months younger, and her name was Gwendolyn. The little girls had nicknames, too: they called Marybelle "Bubs" and Gwendolyn "Ben." They had Daddy's blue eyes. I guess at that time Bubs would have been almost 3 and Ben almost 2. We had a wonderful day there with Daddy, Mary, and the little sisters. They took us to visit the Craddock family and they did some singing and playing for us. When we got back to the log house, Mary cooked a real nice dinner, and a good meal was a treat for Son and I. When late afternoon came, we started on our long journey home with happy memories of a great time with our father, Mary, and our little sisters. Mary couldn't have treated us better, and Daddy was his usual charming self.

When we got back to the farm, Jock was quite inquisitive about how everything went. We told him of our wonderful day, what a great cook Mary was, that wouldn't it be nice if Daddy, Mary, and the girls would come and live with us and Mary could do the cooking.

This talk of Daddy and Mary and the girls coming to stay with us seemed to be catching on, and it wasn't very long until the arrangements were made for them to come. They would come for a while, and if we got along, their stay would be extended.

It was early winter when they moved in. I could hardly wait to be living with my father again after all this time away from him. It was interesting to think we would be happy to have Mary come live with us, after the unhappiness she seemed to bring to our family just a few years before. But that was then, this was a different time, we were desperate—we needed a good cook in the house. The touch of a woman in the home, we had missed that since Maw was gone. Mary could never take Maw's place, but we would have our father with us, too. And it would be nice to have those little sisters around

Willie Kell

Mary had canned a lot of fruit and pickles that past summer and fall and they were just sitting in the cellar at the log house. Son drove Mary over to Stayner to get them. She brought jars of pickles and fruit and we ate that good stuff like we might never eat again. It was like a good rain after a long dry spell.

Things went along real well, as I remember. It was great to get to know Daddy again. He helped with the chores, split wood for the fire, fixed some things that nobody else knew how to fix. The little girls were fun to have around, and for a time I was about as happy as I had been for quite a while. When Christmas came, we had a tree, the first one I ever remembered. I even got a Christmas present from Mary, a pair of lined leather mitts, and we enjoyed a really great Christmas dinner. Mary was a fine cook. It was she who saw to it that we did have the tree and the nice Christmas dinner, and those mitts were the first Christmas present I ever remember getting in my life. Yes, it was Mary who made our Christmas.

It was more than a year now since our sister Elizabeth had gone to live with Toots and George. They lived in a small apartment in town, and once in a while I would get to go spend overnight with them. This was wonderful, to be with my sisters, even if just for those few precious hours. It was great too to be in a place with electricity and an inside bathroom and a radio! As time went on, Toots and George adopted Elizabeth. They had a baby, but it died at birth. So Elizabeth was raised an only child.

As winter became spring, there began some more changes. My best friend, Jimmy Howie, took very sick and died. I was asked to be a pallbearer, but at the time of his funeral I was sick with a cold. Daddy said I

Willie

shouldn't go. I was disappointed that I couldn't say a last good-bye to my best buddy. Life at the farm was changing too. There seemed to be more disagreements between Mary and Jock. He became suspicious that she was stealing the cream and giving it to her brother to make butter. Mary alleged that Jock wanted her to go to bed with him. These petty things, and the fact that both Mary and Jock were difficult to get along with, ended with Daddy, Mary, and the little girls having to move out, at Jock's request. By now all the canned fruit and pickles were eaten, the nice Christmas was history, and the dream of being together as a family was now just a memory. Once again back to bachelor life.

Well, this bachelor life didn't last very long, because Jock went and found us a young housekeeper, kind of a wild one. Maybe she found Jock, but it wasn't long before there were hot times at the old farm. There would be parties, booze, women, and all kinds of interesting happenings. This pretty good-looking gal would twirl around and show off her frilly panties. I had never seen anything like that before, but even at 12 years of age, I found it quite exciting.

One winter's day, who should come along but our old hired man, Wilson Graham. He was dressed up like some kind of millionaire. Jock had been under the weather for a while and was in bed. I can remember old Wilson being kind of taken with this wild, whore-like housekeeper that first night he was there. After the chores were done, he got Son's guitar out and was singing "I'm Thinking Tonight of My Blue Eyes." It was the first time I had ever heard that great song, written by A.P. Carter and made popular by the famous Carter family. I thought it was wonderful, even if Wilson wasn't that good of a singer or player. I can remember the wild house-keeper dancing around, showing off her frilly underwear. Wilson stayed around for about a week, I

Willie Kell

guess until he became bored, then he moved on. That's the way he was.

Sometimes when we had company, which seemed to happen a quite a lot of times, I had to sleep with this wild gal. I can remember waking up on more than one occasion to find her big, bare leg lying across mine, and it would arouse my boyhood manliness. Guess a young fellow could easily have lost his virginity, or whatever it is that young fellows lose.

However, like Maw used to say, all good things have to end sometime. By this time, Son was married. He had found a nice girlfriend over at Shallow Lake. They went together for a while and got married. It probably wouldn't last long. Her name was Irene and she was good-looking, with dark brown eyes. She and Son lived in the back part of the farmhouse, Jock and the wild housekeeper and me lived in the front part. And when Son told Daddy about some of the wild happenings at the farm, and me sleeping with this horny housekeeper once in a while, it meant another change of scenery for me. Daddy came and got me and took me to stay with Dad in town. That was in early spring; I would be out of school until September.

By this time, Sweet and Len had their second child and had moved out and were renting a place of their own. Now I was back living at our old house, back to my first childhood memories. Maybe these past few years had all been some crazy dream after all.

Book Seven: My Life With Daddy and Mary

By this time Dad also had a housekeeper; he called her Mammy. She was a little skinny old girl, legs like broomsticks and a squeaky voice. Poor old girl didn't have a place to go, so Dad took her in. She cooked the meals on Mother's old stove and kept house. There were just two beds—Dad slept in one and Mammy in the other. Well, I couldn't very well sleep with Dad, there wouldn't be much room; he weighed about two hundred and seventy five pounds by this time. So I slept with Mammy—there was lots of room in her bed. You know, getting out of bed with that wild gal at the farm and then having to sleep with this skinny old lady ... even at 12 years old, it seemed like I was moving backwards in life. To me, this was progress in reverse.

Dad had a horse and old democrat wagon with wooden wheels that was his only means of transportation. I used to go with him around town. We would do the shopping, then go to the butcher's to visit his friends and get some meat. Then we would shop from the garbage cans behind the restaurants, get those fish skeletons with the heads. Dad would cut the heads off and find nice, tender fish in those cheeks. They weren't all that bad when they were fried in grease, and along with some garbage-can vegetables cooked up, we made out pretty good. Sometimes we would have some cake or muffins that had been thrown out by the bakery. No, Dad hadn't lost his touch for gathering up garbage.

We still had great talks riding around in that old democrat, and I liked being with that old man. He was

Willie Kell

the world's original hippie, not your ordinary grand-pappy.

One day when we were out driving around with the horse and wagon, we saw some signs posted that I found very interesting.

"COLE BROTHERS" THREE RING CIRCUS—WITH CLYDE BEATTY THE WORLD FAMOUS WILD ANNIMAL TRAINER—ALONG WITH COWBOY MOVIE STAR
KEN MAYNARD—COMING TO TOWN!"

I brought this to Dad's attention, and he agreed that we would go to see the big circus unloading at the railway station. I could hardly wait for the day when one of the biggest circuses in North America would be coming to town and Dad and me would drive old Jenny down there to the station and watch this great event.

Finally the big day came, and we were up bright and early. Mammy got us our breakfast of thick slices of stale bread spread with butter, washed down by black tea. Then we hitched up old Jenny and headed for the station to see the circus train come in. It was a huge train, painted in every colour. We could see the elephants, horses, lions, tigers, camels, ponies, and dogs through the open, cage-like boxcars as they pulled into the station. Then the men—must have been a hundred or more of them working to unload this gigantic circus train filled with people, animals, and paraphernalia brought to town for the sole purpose of thrilling and entertaining the local folk. It was without a doubt one of the most spectacular events of my entire life. Not only as a boy of twelve—it still remains one of my all-time favourite days. I didn't remember my first circus, I was just ten days old.

Willie

Well, when they finally had the train unloaded, they lined up the elephants, horses, and riders, wagons with big cages filled with tigers, lions, and leopards pulled by beautiful teams of horses and ponies. There were beautiful dancing girls, clowns, acrobats turning cartwheels, all dressed in colourful costumes. When the band lined up and started to play, they began the big parade up 2nd Avenue—it looked like a mile long, maybe more. Dad and me followed along behind with Jenny and the old democrat. The streets were lined with people. They said it was the biggest circus to ever come to town.

Well, we followed the circus parade as it wound along the streets, across the Potawatami River bridge, and over on 14th street to Harrison's Field. Then the task of building this wonderful fairy-tale circus city began. Tents were unrolled, including the big top itself. It was huge, like a canvas-covered football field, when it was finally put up. Elephants grunted and roared as they pulled and pushed, teams of horses groaned and pulled. Then the roust-a-bouts, 4 or 5 of them around a steel post with big hammers, started swinging in time, driving those posts into the ground.

There were dozens of tents. I asked Dad if I could try and get a job helping, cause they needed help carrying water and doing odd jobs. Well, I got a job. My pay would be a ticket to the feature show in the big top. I couldn't believe my fortune. I worked hard, doing all kinds of chores, my eyes wide open to see every sight and hear every sound of that exciting day. When the work was finished, the boss gave me a ticket to the big matinee show. What a spectacular extravaganza: Clyde Beatty, the world's greatest wild animal trainer, in that cage with those roaring tigers and lions. They would growl and roar, bite at him and paw at him. He would crack his whip, and sometimes shoot his gun, BANG!! You could see men lying on the outside of the cage with rifles, ready to shoot one of those big cats if he really did attack Clyde Beatty. Then came Ken Maynard, the famous Hollywood cowboy- star, with his beautiful horse and gold-plated western saddle. There were trapeze artists walking a tightrope high above the centre ring, and beautiful girls with very little clothes on being thrown back and forth from one swinging trapeze to another by muscular men hanging upside down. There were the clowns in their colourful clothes, the trick riders on beautiful white horses, prancing around the ring. There were trick horses, ponies and dogs doing amazing things, while the big band played music and the ring announcer introduced the different acts as they performed. I loved every moment of that wonderful circus. When the show was over after the night performance, just as quickly and with precision-like efficiency, the whole circus-city was loaded onto that big train and headed out of town. I could not think of anything else for days and weeks.

After I had spent a couple of months or so with Dad and Mammy, I went to live with Daddy, Mary, the little sisters, and a Dalmatian dog named Spot. By this time they were living about 40 miles south, near Hanover, in a little brick cottage. The landlady was an old maid and was still living there in one room—she was kind of weird. I had looked forward to moving in with Daddy again; if I remembered right, Mary was a much better cook than Mammy, and it would be fun having a bigger family around. I turned 13 years old on August 3 that year and had already seen quite a lot of life.

When I went out selling medicine with Daddy, I would wait in the car—sometimes it seemed forever— until he came out of those houses. Daddy was trying to talk those nice people into buying some of this great

Willie

wonder medicine. Whenever he sold some, he would come to the door and, in his smooth way, would say, "Bring in 10 bottles," or "Bring in 2 bottles, son." Then I would get the medicine, take it into the house, and he would introduce me to the people. What a smooth, intelligent man he was. Dressed in his best clothes, shoes shined so you could see yourself in them—although he only had the one pair—and a tie that was tied just so. He would wear a nice straw hat in the summer, and as soon as he got to that door, off came the hat and the smile came on his handsome face. "How do you do, lady?" he would say. "You have probably heard of this medicine, that has helped so many people in this area with rheumatism, arthritic, and similar complaints." While he talked, he would hold up the bottle of Ton-A-Lax in his left hand and give a rub over it with his right hand, like a magician going to do a magic trick. That's exactly what he was doing—performing magic, with words. At that time, a lot of good men were glad to work all week, 6 days, to earn 10 or 12 dollars. Daddy would often make 20 or 30 dollars in a short day, driving around doing what he liked to do. But when that case of medicine was sold, he would have to spend a day or two getting another batch ready. Then he would take some time for doing other things—sitting and reading, or talking. Most of the money would be gone by the time he went out to get some more. His needs were few; he never thought of being rich, he didn't dream of a new car, a new home, a cottage at the lake, or those things that ambitious men crave. He was content, it seems, with an old rented house without electricity, bathroom, or telephone and some old car to drive that he got somewhere on a good deal. Maybe he was just as well to be this way.

    Life with Daddy and Mary was different than being on the farm. He taught me about life. He was a

Willie Kell

gentleman, and had a good sense of humour. We had good talks on the road, and I got to know him, especially when Mary wasn't around. He liked the harness races, and sometimes we would stop some place and buy the morning paper to see about horses that were racing—how fast they went, what breed they were, who drove them. He knew all about them, though it hadn't anything to do with gambling on them. He was just interested in the horses. Yes, being out on the road with Daddy, opening farm gates, taking the medicine in the houses when he sold some, and just spending time with my father was kind of nice for a change.

When September came, it was time for school, a new school—another one-room building about a mile and a half away. I got to know some new friends there and was getting along pretty good, though I was a little behind the other kids and confused with the schoolwork. I seemed to have lost something that I would have to somehow find. However, I started to catch up and things were going along pretty good.

Then it was time for another change of schools. This time we moved into a smaller house, about 8 miles away. Now we lived on the other side of town a few miles, in this smaller two-room house. There was a little eat-in kitchen and living room combined, and a bedroom where Daddy, Mary, and the girls slept. There was a small stairway up from the kitchen to an unfinished upstairs—there wasn't much between that place and the outside. That upstairs was my bedroom; my furniture was an old iron bed with Daddy's tent on it for a mattress. I had never seen that tent, although I had heard a quite a bit about it, and now I was sleeping in it. Or I should say I was sleeping on it, and it was kind of hard and bumpy. At the farm we slept on Maw's old

Willie

lumpy feather ticks, and they were much better than that tent to sleep on.

That upstairs was cold in the winter. I could easily count the nails protruding through the shingles, 'cause they were often white with frost. In the summer it was like a baker's oven. There was no electricity or telephone, but a little two-hole toilet out back. The place had a small barn and there was 40 acres of swamp, sinkholes, and a couple of cleared fields. Daddy liked it cause he could get his wood out of that swamp, keep a horse or two, and Mary could get a couple of cows to milk, and the rent was only $40.00 a year.

The school was about two and a half miles away at Campbell's Corner, which was a mile and a quarter from Hanover. It was a nice one-room school. We had a very strict, bossy teacher, and I soon learned a few things about school. I began to take it a little more serious. I had to, or that teacher would be liable to make life very uncomfortable, and even cause permanent damage to a boy's careless attitude. I soon learned to like her and respect what she was trying to do. By now, kids didn't pick on me anymore and I soon became quite popular. I was a good singer, good at the Christmas concert, and was beginning to like school a little more.

However, things were not as great at home. By this time Mary was beginning to show her old self again—temper tantrums, treating me kind of awful at times. I think she was jealous that Daddy spent some of his time with me. She seemed to begrudge me the little bit I ate. She made me terrible lunches for school. No one ever went in my bedroom, except to put more junk up in that miserable place. Of course, she didn't have to wash my sheets—I didn't have any, just a couple of blankets. My clothes were getting worn out, shoes were nearly off my feet. Daddy was okay with me, but he couldn't treat me

Willie Kell

too good or Mary was jealous. I began to feel unwanted and alone; it was worse than the farm ever was. Of course, Daddy and Mary would have some rather loud fights at times; she was an impossible person. Daddy told me, when we were alone, how she had behaved at times in the past, how she came into a hotel where he was having a beer with friends and she threw the beer on the floor. How she had kicked the windshield out of the car one time right at the main intersection of the city of Barrie. Yes, she could be an interesting woman.

When the fall and winter came, I had to help Daddy cut wood with a crosscut saw, and then we piled it in the woodshed. Daddy would buy a horse once in a while, something to sell again and make a dollar on. It was my job to ride these horses home sometimes at night, often several miles. No saddle, just bareback and a rope for reins, with a bit strapped to the halter. I soon got to be a pretty good rider. It doesn't take long to learn if you get one of these half broncos that have never been ridden before. You either ride the horse or the horse will ride you. After you get bucked off a few times, you learn that the ground is quite hard. Soon I would jump on those horses—no saddle or bridle, just a rope in my hand—and ride them all over the place. One time we had a western horse, and I had been riding him a quite a lot. But this day Daddy was in some kind of bad mood. He was fixing the rope that was my reins—it was about 20 feet long. Well, he hauled off and hit the horse, 'cause he wanted to show who was boss or something, I'm on this bronco's back, this rope is now between the horse's legs, and the fool horse takes off, bucking like something in a wild west show. The rope caught around Daddy's foot and it pulled him over. I rode that maverick and he didn't buck me off; I brought him to a stop by reaching up to his halter. Turned him around, rode him back to

Willie

the old man, who was just getting up off the ground. Daddy had a half grin on his face by now, as if to say, "You did good, kid, to stay on him; sorry for acting dumb." Of course, he didn't come out and *say* it.

One day he bought a little brown standardbred mare about 7 miles from home. I rode her back and we used her in the cutter, she could go pretty good. Daddy gave $12.00 for her. By this time, Son and Irene had a little girl and Irene was quite pregnant again. But they came to visit us in that little house; it was a big event to have them come. It was the second day of December, but the roads were still open for cars. However, it started to snow and blow overnight, and the roads became blocked. The next morning, I guess Irene thought it would be a good time to have a baby, so she started having labour pains, and Son had to hitch that old brown mare and go fetch the doctor; in those days you could do things like that. Well, Son brought the good doctor to the little house and the baby was born, a healthy boy, in that little house surrounded by huge snow drifts. Another Arnold—yes, they named him after his father, his grandfather, and his great-grandfather. When the doctor was finished—and with Mary's good help, it didn't take long—Son hitched up the old brown mare and drove him back to town. The fee was $15.00, and that included a lot of nice clothes for the baby— dress, bonnet, booties, and more. The Women's Institute had left these clothes at the doctor's office for an emergency. This was definitely an emergency.

Son went home on the train after a couple of days and came back in two weeks, loaded up his wife, the little girl, and the newborn baby in the car. The storm was gone, but the roads were only partly open. A kind-hearted neighbour hitched Son's car behind a team and sleigh and pulled the car with Son, Irene, the little girl,

Willie Kell

and the new baby to the highway, more than 2 miles. Mary had taken good care of them while they were there. She always had been nice to Son and Irene.

That little house was sure crowded, with three adults, three children and the baby living in those two rooms. I was lucky; the upstairs was so bad, I didn't have to share it. My older sisters and their husbands and families came a few times while we lived at that place, but never overnight. The only other person that stayed overnight was old Alex McDonald, Daddy's hobo friend. He slept on a couch in the kitchen one cold, stormy winter night. Even that old hobo didn't have to sleep in my frosty room.

We got through that winter; I helped cut wood for the fire, did the few chores. Mary milked the 2 cows they had by this time. After school I rode that old brown mare; I just got on her back and guided her with the lead rope. Sundays, I would ride her several miles, often just letting her walk along. I'd be singing, talking to myself, dreaming I was somewhere else. Sometimes I was a cowboy and I helped drive the neighbours' cattle.

When school was out in June, I had passed into grade 8—just one more year left and I'd be through public school. I wasn't even thinking of high school. During the summer, I picked wild raspberries with Mary, and she made jam with them. And I picked some on my own and sold them, enough to buy a new engineer's cap for 25 cents and I had a dollar left over. I hid it away in my room, for a stormy time.

When school started in September, we had a new teacher. She was real nice, just 18 years old, and I loved her from the first day. Bubs started to school that year; it was a long walk for her, but there were always other kids to walk with. Christmas came and went; I really

Willie

don't remember much happening, except the big Christmas concert at school. I had several parts; I sang, helped other kids with their parts, and when the night of the concert came, I seemed to be in everything. Even in my worn-out clothes, folks liked me, I got lots of applause, and I was the star of the evening.

Well, that cold, snowy winter crawled along. Mary would get Bubs up for school, fix her a nice breakfast, and pack a lunch for her. Most of the time I would still be sleeping, 'cause she didn't call me. I was always a sound sleeper. But finally I would wake up and run out to the barn, feed the horse and cows. Then pump some water, carry a few pails to water them. Run to the house, wash, grab some breakfast, pick up the brown paper bag containing my not-so-good lunch, and take off for school. And although I ran most of the way, I was late every morning. I just hated going into that school, every kid turning around to look at me. The teacher didn't punish me for being late, and I never told anyone why I was always late.

In spite of the problems at home, I excelled in school, was on top of all the subjects, and got along great with everybody. When it was time to go home after school, I got to walk with the other kids. In the mornings I was by myself, being late all the time. When I got home from school, I would get the horse out and ride around, do the work that had to be done, and start to dream of a time before long when I could get away from this unhappy life I was living.

When late spring came we moved again; Daddy rented another place about 12 miles down the road. But because I was in my last year of public school, he thought it best for me to continue at the same school until the end of the term. I was happy about that, 'cause I didn't want to change schools.

Willie Kell

I stayed with neighbours. They were old people who had never had children, and they liked me. I felt quite at home with them. I used to help him sometimes drive the team of horses. Being there with those old folks was much better than living with Mary. I stayed with them about six weeks, until school was out for the year. I always felt welcome at the table, and Mrs. Gilespie made me nice lunches. I continued school and passed with honours, second highest marks in that part of the county. I sang at the big music festival in Owen Sound, at a huge church. The teacher took me in her car; it was at night. I had a terrible attack of stage fright—could hardly get the words out of my mouth. It was awful, standing on that large stage by myself, with those worn-out clothes on, and the judges listening and watching so closely. I only sang a few lines; it was so embarrassing. However, the kind judges gave me a 72 out of 100. I felt bad that I had done so miserably and let the teacher down.

I kept thinking of a time when I would leave that unhappy life behind. One time, when Sweet and Len were visiting, they told me that I could get a job at the factory where Len worked, and that's what I intended to do. When school was over, I went to live with Daddy and Mary again in the new place; it was a much bigger house, and they had a barn and ten acres of land, but still no electricity or phone. I told Daddy that I planned to leave home when school was out. But he had a field of turnips planted and I stayed and hoed the weeds out of them before I left.

Daddy knew how it was with Mary and me, that I wouldn't stay in the same house with her any longer than I had to. He knew that Mary would be happy to see me go. Then it would just be the four of them again. Though he told me he didn't like to see me leave, I thought it would be better if I did. Maybe I was the cause of some of Mary's bad moods and the reason for some of the fights between them. I remember one time when we left her, Daddy and I, we packed our few things and took off up to Son's farm in the old 28 Chev. We were only there a day or two when Mary came with a taxi. After a little fight and a big making-up, we all got in the old Chev and went back home. Lord, I was disappointed.

Willie Kell

Book Eight: Out On My Own—At 14

It was Saturday, July 12th, 1941 when I left my happy home. The Orangemen were celebrating the 12th of July in Durham. Daddy, Mary, and the girls were going to the parade, so I got a ride that far with them. I hung around for a while, watched the parade, and then I headed out of town. I had packed all of my belongings into a little cardboard carton that I found on the road. I had rigged a little leather handle on it, for easier carrying. There wasn't much in that little cardboard box—some things from school, and a pair of socks; I still had the dollar that I had earned picking berries the summer before, and three stamps worth 9 cents. My clothes were the same ragged pair of jeans that I had sewed up a few times with string, they were split down the side of the legs at the seam. My shoes were pretty well worn out, and I had that engineer's cap on my head.

I had a 30-mile trip ahead of me. I walked through town, up the hill, and started out north on the highway. I stuck my thumb out and waited for someone to give me a lift. It seemed to me that Daddy was a little ashamed to see his youngest boy leaving home like that at just 14. Maybe he was getting used to being ashamed by this time.

I soon got a ride that took me right through to my destination, and arrived at Sweet's place in time for a nice supper. I felt good about getting away from Mary, though I didn't argue or have words with her. After supper, I unpacked my "suitcase," but when I tried to

Willie

find my stamps, they were not there. However I wrote Daddy, Mary, and the girls to say that I had arrived safely, and borrowed a three-cent stamp from Sweet to mail it.

On Monday morning, I got up early, when Len got up, and we had our breakfast and went to his factory. He introduced me to a foreman in the shipping department, and in about five minutes I had a job. Packing and shipping furniture, mostly wooden chairs; the pay was 19 cents an hour. We worked eight-hour days, five and a half days a week, and payday was every second Friday. I used to take home about $ 16.00 every two weeks. I paid Sweet $5.00 a week board, so after I paid the two week's board, I still had $6.00 left over. Of course that had to last me for two whole weeks. But I had enough to buy cigarettes—they were 10 cents for a package of ten. Everybody smoked cigarettes: Daddy, Son, Irene, Len, Toots, and George. Sweet didn't smoke, nor did Mary. Yes, now that I was on my own, earning a living, I would have to smoke.

Meanwhile, while I was so concerned with my own little world, the war was raging in Europe. The Nazis were bombing the hell out of England, had taken several countries in Europe, and were herding Jews and Gypsies by the hundreds of thousands into gas chambers— killing them, men, women, and children, and then taking out their gold teeth and cutting off their hair to be recycled (though the word hadn't been invented yet). Our Prime Minister, MacKenzie King, had been to visit Hitler and came back here saying that Hitler was someone to be trusted. Hitler gave him a portrait of himself, and King seemed to admire this murdering madman. As the war raged on, our soldiers were being killed or taken prisoner in huge numbers. The news was

Willie Kell

bad; many thought we would lose that crazy war. But thank God, by this time they had got rid of that silly old man with the umbrella—Neville Chamberlain, Britain's Prime Minister—and a great and wonderful statesman named WINSTON CHURCHILL became Prime Minister of England. He had been telling anyone who would listen that Hitler had to be stopped. Too bad he was not running things a few years earlier. Churchill said, "WE SHALL NEVER SURRENDER."

France fell apart like a wet piece of paper, quickly surrendered, and over a third of the population joined the Nazis. Meantime, our young men were being called up for military service. Unless you lived in Quebec! Yes—they were exempt from military service. Several of the great hockey players from Quebec didn't go to war for Canada. Can anyone believe that our young men were being slaughtered over on the battlefields of Europe, thousands gave their lives to rescue France, while the Frenchmen in Canada didn't have to go and fight? Some did. But I have read that our former Prime Minister, Pierre Trudeau, like many Quebecers, didn't believe in the war. In fact, he protested it emphatically. Was he a Nazi-lover? I don't know; he let Nazis come to Canada when he was Prime Minister!!

Wages and prices were frozen. Although there were lots of jobs, the wages were quite low. But things were still cheap to buy. If you could get what you wanted at all, most things were going towards the war effort. There were soldiers, airmen, and sailors everywhere; it was a very interesting time to be living. The country and the allies stood together against the tyrants who were out to destroy our way of life.

In my little world, things were going well. I was learning to be a city boy, meeting all kinds of interesting people. After about three months in the shipping

Willie

department, I applied for the job of office boy. I got the job, and had my own desk right there with all the big shots. I could hardly believe that I was rubbing elbows with the president, vice president, general manager, purchasing agent, and the president's secretary! Had I really come this far in such a short time? Of course, I still took home the same pay, about $16.00 every two weeks. I walked around out in the factory, talked to the foremen and the girls, and wore a white shirt and tie. Everyone knew my name: it was, "Hello, Willie." This was great—a far cry from being in that little house back in the sticks, having to deal with Mary. In the afternoons we would have tea and cookies, which I served. Yes, I thought that at last I had made it in the world of high rollers. I had my own bicycle—bought it second hand for $5.00. I think it was about the second week that I was riding it, going to work one day, when a car pulled across the street in front of me and I ran into it, flew over the hood of the car onto the pavement. I had a few scratches and scrapes, nothing serious. The police came and blamed me for running into the car. I was just a kid off the farm didn't know my way around yet. The bicycle had a bent front wheel that I soon got fixed.

It was while I was at the factory that I met a young fellow there about my age. We seemed to get along and hung around together. After being at the factory for about ten months, I was starting to get bored with the routine. Seems my friend was feeling the same way, so we decided to quit and take off for Toronto. Find a job in the big city, see the sights, find out how others lived. My friend had an aunt living there, and we could stay at her place. She lived at the corner of Jarvis and Gerard Streets, in the red-light district. We didn't know about red-light districts. My friend was a pretty good-looking fellow. However, he had two thumbs on each hand,

Willie Kell

which made him look a little awkward with a knife and fork. I suppose those thumbs hampered him in several activities. Anyway, we started out on our trip; we each had about ten dollars in our pockets, and we didn't take very much luggage with us. We walked out of town and stood at the outskirts with our thumbs out—me with just one and my buddy with his two—and we soon got a lift and were on our way to the big city, to make our mark in the world!

It was a quiet Sunday morning in June, and there didn't seem to be many cars on the road. However, it wasn't very long until someone stopped and gave us a ride. We were both about the same size, not very big, guess we didn't look like much of a threat to anybody. Now we were on our way down the highway that would lead us to a better life. We would get a job in Toronto, make big money, meet some nice girls, and maybe live happily ever after, for a while.

It was just a few hours till we were riding on a streetcar in the big city that would take us to our new home. When we arrived, my buddy's aunt seemed polite; she had been expecting us. It was a big, older brick house with a veranda across the front. We could see a lot of interesting happenings from that veranda on those warm June evenings. There was a hotel across the street on the opposite corner; Aunty told us that the famous bank robber and underworld character, Mickey McDonald, lived there from time to time.

The next morning we got up, Aunty fixed us some breakfast, and we were soon on the streetcars, that would take us to find a job. We went to the factories out along the lakeshore. We walked and rode miles on the buses and streetcars. When the day was over and it was time to go back to Aunty's house for some supper, we didn't have a job. The next morning we followed the

Willie

same plan as the day before, but this time we went to different places. We did this every day. We rode buses, streetcars, and walked the streets of that big city for the whole week, and we didn't find anyone who would give us a job. That $20.00 we had between us was running mighty low. Before we left home, Son drove in from the farm to ask me if I needed a little money and gave me $5.00. That, with the $5.00 I already had, left me with $10.00. We gave Aunty a little for board.

It was a wonderful experience for both of us, and we got along well together. We would sit on the big veranda and watch the goings-on around that hotel at night. We might see Mickey McDonald come blazing along, shooting everybody in sight, or we might just see him. Well, I don't know if we saw him or not, 'cause I wouldn't have known him if I had. But we did see a quite a few real pretty girls. They used to go in and out of that hotel, or just stand in front. They had short dresses and lots of rouge and lipstick on. Sometimes my buddy and I would walk along the opposite side of the street to get a closer look at them. They seemed so friendly; folks would drive by in a car and these girls would wave at them and smile. Sometimes these friendly girls would hitch a ride in cars. I would have liked to get even closer to them, get to know them, but Aunty told us we couldn't talk to them, or go near them. So we just watched from across the street.

Things were not going as well as we thought they would. We were kind of disappointed. No job, or not even a prospect of a job. Our money was gone. So after about a week, Aunty packed us some lunch in a paper bag, we said good-bye, and told her thanks for having us. Then we rode the streetcars and buses to the edge of the city, got off, and started up the long highway home. We stuck out our thumbs, his two and my one, and soon we were riding in a truck, heading back where we came from. I reckon that we were a little bit wiser. We had met a few nice people; Aunty treated us real good, although she didn't cry when we left. We didn't get to see Mickey McDonald, and I've often wished we had got a little closer to those good-looking, friendly girls. Those pretty girls were a big improvement on what was happening in my life just a year before—hoeing Daddy's turnips on that little ole farm back in the country.

When we got back to Owen Sound, my buddy and I went our separate ways. I didn't see much of him after that, but I often think of him. I went back to my sister's house to live. She said she had worried about me being in the big city, just 15 years old and not long off the farm. Well, I knew Sweet was happy to have me back in town, but I also knew that I would have to pay my board, so that meant get out and find a job. I was hoping that it wouldn't be as difficult as it had been in the city.

Book Nine: The Innkeepers

It was one of the first days in July, and I was walking past the Seldon House, a hotel on the main corner of 10th St and 2nd Avenue, downtown. There was a sign in the window: PORTER WANTED—APPLY WITHIN. I had often been by the place, always thought it looked kind of fancy. Of course, almost anything looked fancy to me in those times. It was close to noon when I went in to apply for the job.

The lobby seemed big. Terrazzo floors, nice furniture, stone fireplace in the corner, and an open stairway leading to the second floor. The chairs in the lobby were mostly red leather, and there was a cloth-covered chesterfield suite trimmed with maple wood surrounding a large pillar in the middle of the rotunda. Shining ashtrays on stands were placed here and there by the chairs. The place was so clean! The main dining room, just off the lobby, would soon be open for the noon meal, and there were a quite a few people milling around, waiting. I walked up to the man at the desk and told him I was interested in the job. He was a fine-looking man of about 33, a little on the stout side, and he wore glasses tinted in green. He was well-spoken, had a wonderful voice, and introduced himself as Jack Alles, the proprietor's son. I was quite impressed with the man and the place and perhaps a little frightened. If I did get the job, could I survive in this atmosphere? He told me they paid $40.00 a month plus meals and tips. He asked me to come back a bit later after the noon-hour rush and meet his father.

Willie Kell

When I went back an hour or so later, there was hardly anyone around. I met Jack's father—he called him Pop. His father was even a bit bigger than Jack, had a great personality, and seemed to like me. He offered me the job; I could start the next day. Jack explained that the job was actually several jobs in one, and the hours were long. You mopped the lobby floor every day, vacuumed the mats, kept the glass doors and windows clean, and polished the brass handles on the doors. Keep the ashtrays clean and polished. Sweep the sidewalk out front, mop the big kitchen floor every afternoon, and take out the garbage. Help set up tables in the dining room for special events. Set up the sample rooms for the travellers and keep them clean. Take the travellers' bags to the rooms. That's where I made the tips—a dime or a quarter. I had to watch the doors, run out and get their bags, and help them in. Some would come on the train; the taxis would pick them up at the station and bring them to the hotel. It was hustle, hustle, smile, help all the time when we were busy. The first day was kind of confusing, trying to find my way around that big hotel. Take the travellers bags to the rooms, open the door, turn on the light, run down stairs and bring up the next one as fast as I could. There were three floors and no elevator; you sure got a lot of exercise. You also had to be sharp and smart; I soon learned to be both. All that early training from Maw was paying off.

What a strange new world I was experiencing. It was noon hour, just my second day on the job, and people were coming for lunch. The lobby was half full, everybody talking, laughing, going here, going there. I was watching the front door, opening it, and smiling at the people as they came in. The switchboard was buzzing, it seemed like a madhouse. I was taking bags

Willie

up, running back down for more, and trying to please everybody.

There was this big fellow in his early forties; he came in for lunch with a couple of ladies. Fine people, well dressed, passing through, stopping at the best place in town for lunch. The big, handsome fellow came over to me and asked if I could show him where the washroom was. "Just follow me," I told him cheerfully. Then I headed up the big, winding stairway to the washroom on the second floor. I walked along the hallway ahead of the man, making some small conversation as we went along. When we came to the washroom, I reached in and turned on the light, then pointed my outstretched hand to the inside and stood there, smiling. Maybe he was going to give me a tip.

"Step inside, son," he said in a very mannerly voice. Then he unzipped his fly, took out a giant-sized penis, and commenced to masturbate, while at the same time trying to persuade me to do likewise. He took my hand and put it on this monstrous thing and with his other hand unzipped my pants and reached in with his slimy fingers. I was completely dumfounded by all of this. Was this part of my job? Jack told me I was supposed to be nice to the customers. What should I do? I had never encountered a dude like this one before.

Well about then, I came to my senses and thought, "If this is what they expect of me, they better get another boy." I zipped up my fly, turned, and walked out while he continued on with his strange sexual behaviour alone. I went downstairs, washed my hands 2 or 3 times with soap and hot water, and went on with my work. I didn't say anything to anyone about my experience. The big fellow came down the stairs after a while, smiled at me, smiled at the ladies he was with, and then they went in and ate dinner. When they finished their meal, they paid their bill and left in a nice car, still smiling. Was this just another day in the life of a bellhop in a small-town hotel? Lord, I thought, what must go on in that hotel in Toronto, across from Aunty's house!

The Seldon House hotel was owned by a family. There was Pop, Mama, Jack, his vivacious blond wife, Naomi, Chuck, and his lovely wife Helen. Chuck and Helen had a child, a little girl. Later they had another girl, and Jack and Naomi adopted a baby girl. The boys, both in their early thirties at the time, worked as desk clerks. One on the morning shift, from 8 AM until 8PM, the other on the evening shift, 8 PM until 8AM. They alternated every week. The place was open 24 hours a day, seven days a week, 365 days a year. I worked from 8AM until 8PM six days a week. But you never got out of there on time. It was always, "Could you do this for me? Would you run here or there? Could you help with this before you go?" Naomi and Helen were hostesses in the dining room and waited on tables when it was busy. The girls always worked the shift with their husbands, though not as long hours. The one on the evening shift could go home when the dining room closed and everything was cleaned up.

The commercial travellers would come through the week. Some would stay all week and work the surrounding towns. We had the same ones all the time, and new ones would keep coming along. We were filled up all through the week with the travellers, who mostly ate at the hotel. In the summer we were filled up with tourists on the weekends. People would stop over, waiting for the cruise boats that went back and forth to Manitoulin Island. We had a lot of American tourists who came from all over the U.S.A. The tourists were good tippers.

Willie

It wasn't very long until I was answering the switchboard; I could talk just like Jack and Chuck. Everything came natural for me, and I liked being around all of these interesting people. A little more than a year before that I had never talked on a phone in my life! I could check people in and out, handle the cash register, and work the desk at mealtime. Take the money from the dining room customers, ask if they enjoyed their meal, and talk to them. All of this came easily for me; guess I was like Daddy.

These innkeepers taught me to dress, how to walk, what to say, what not to say. It wasn't long and I was like one of the family. They bought me clothes and took me around with them. I even started eating with the family at their table, just inside the dining room. Some of the other staff became jealous of this curly-headed kid from the country. But I earned my special privileges, by hard work and a desire to exhibit my ability. Yes, I was learning all about the hotel business. I soon learned that you could meet a lot of pretty girls, lonely girls. I met quite a few, had some very interesting encounters on the job. My vocabulary was becoming enriched; I kept learning new words. I learned to type the menus; I was quick at making change and calculating the customers' bills. This was before electronic calculators were invented—it all had to be done manually.

We had a French Canadian chef, Danny, a well-travelled but excellent chef. Danny was married to the cutest little Chinese girl I ever saw, and they lived at the hotel. That poor fellow got T.B. and died, and after that it was one chef, then another; they kept coming and going. Sometimes Jack did the cooking, then I had to do his job *and* my own. Sometimes the dishwasher woman wouldn't show up. Then I had to clean the plates off, put the big stacks of dishes in the dishwasher, and dry them.

Willie Kell

When the winter came, I had to sweep and shovel the sidewalks and look after the furnace. Fill the hopper with coal—we had a stoker. If you let that hopper run empty, the gassy smoke seeped back into it from the furnace and you could smell it all over the hotel. There would be times you could hardly find the furnace for smoke in the basement. That's when Pop would yell some of his favourite profanities. It kind of reminded me of the times when, back on the farm, I'd forget to water that bull.

As time went on, I stayed at the hotel all the time—that was part of the deal. Mostly in the guest-rooms; I just chose one that was empty. If we were full, I had a room in the basement of Pop and Mama's apartment. It was nice down there, but I couldn't sneak any girls in.

After a couple of years, Chuck got his call to join the service; he went into the airforce. I had to take his place, only I worked all nights and Jack worked all days. This had disadvantages, but there were some bright spots as well. I had to mop the lobby floor and clean the place up. That didn't take long. So, after about 1 AM, I would get a little rest. Sometimes I slept so soundly that customers would come to the locked front door and I wouldn't hear them. Other times, girls would come by and we would talk, and sometimes these girls would be staying at the hotel. I would invite them to come keep me company. We would sit in the quiet darkness, with just a small light at the desk and the light that filtered in from the street ... yes, I was getting my education. That hotel was my high school, learning about life on the job. Once or twice poor Danny's Chinese wife stopped by in the stillness of the night. She was determined to teach me a lot of things, and although I enjoyed the company, I never got involved with her.

Willie

During these times, I would visit Sweet and Len. He got his call and went in the infantry. Once in a while I would get out to the farm. Toots and George and Elizabeth had moved to Whitby, east of Toronto, and I visited them with Sweet a time or two. I often walked up the hill and visited with Dad and Mammy; sometimes I would take them ice cream or some other little treat. Their place was interesting. They had a big box stove in the front room and still had Mother's old wood cook stove in the kitchen. They did have a radio to listen to the news, but there was hardly a curtain left on the windows; it was pretty basic. They still used the old back house, with a couple of new boards added to it. But they were always happy to see me; Dad and I had great talks. He still hated Jock and they never saw each other after Maw died. Daddy and Aunt Lizzie went to see him once in a while, when they got to town.

Willie Kell

Book Ten: Learning About Girls and Other Things

The summer of my seventeenth birthday, a cousin, Betty, came to visit me from Michigan; she arrived on the evening train. As usual, I was working. Sweet met her at the station with a taxi; she planned to stay a week at Sweet's place, and I could hardly wait to see her. They stopped in at the hotel on their way from the station, and my heart was beating the jitterbug rag.

We had been writing to one another for almost a year and falling in love through the mail, although she had a boyfriend and was engaged. Our letters started out innocent enough, but soon gained momentum, like a freight train going down a steep hill. We hadn't seen each other since I was about three years old, and I had but a faint recollection of her. She was Aunt Alice's daughter—Alice was Mother's sister. By the time she came to visit, our letters were filled with love. It was "my dearest darling Willie," and "my dearest darling Betty." When she walked into that hotel lobby and I saw her for the first time that I could remember, she was just as beautiful as her picture said she was. Oh, I loved her so much. We kissed and held each other. I could hardly believe she was there in my arms.

When she got settled in at Sweet's place, she called me. And for the next week she was either at the hotel or I was at Sweet's house. Before the week was over, she wrote to her mother and told her she was going to stay another week. She wrote her boyfriend and told him the engagement was off, that she loved me. Aunt Alice wrote her back, telling her to come home in the next day or two, or they would come and get her. Sweet also got after us to stop the foolishness; after all, we were cousins, she said.

Betty went home, but she cried when she got on the train. As the train pulled out, it seemed to be taking my heart with it. We spent a wonderful nine days together and said we would always love one another. There was no sex between us—we didn't pursue that angle. I loved that girl with the sweet American accent, the cute nose, and the pretty blue eyes. She was 13 months older than me, but I guess, for all the things in life I had seen, thirteen months didn't really matter. She liked when I would sing her love songs, said I should come to America and sing for a living. It was all so exciting.

She wrote when she got home, said how she missed me. I wrote her and told her how I loved her. We continued to write, but somehow along the way we began to drift apart. She went back with her boyfriend, who had been her sweetheart through high school. He went into the army, and soon they were married. During that time her letters cooled, and the "dearest darling" stuff became "Dear Willie," and we only wrote to each other occasionally. After a time, her husband was shipped off to Saipan to fight in that old Asian war.

At the hotel things continued about the same: people kept checking in and checking out. Eating in the dining room and buying cigars and cigarettes. One day in the fall, it was late afternoon, a fellow checked in to a room on the first floor. It was a Friday, we weren't busy, and Jack gave him his room. When the tourist season was over in the fall, we were not busy on weekends, and were glad for any stragglers that came along, although we allowed no riffraff.

Willie Kell

After a little while, there was a big commotion in his room, like he was trying to tear the walls down. We didn't use keys in any of the rooms. The doors were locked from the inside with a little night bolt. We couldn't get the guy to answer us and we couldn't get in the room. So we got a stepladder and looked in through the half- open transom above the door.

Here was this fellow, not a stitch of clothes on him, bouncing around on his hands and knees like a Shetland pony. He would get on the bed and then jump off. We thought sure he was going to kill himself. Chairs were knocked over, and he was snorting like a rhinoceros. He paid no attention to Jack hollering at him and threatening him. Jack finally called the police, and after a while we pried the door open and got into the room. We even called the Mounties in.

We discovered that this fellow was a medical doctor, but also a drunk and a dope fiend. He had been mixing booze and barbiturates and got himself on one enormous high. The combination of the two caused him to act like a dangerous lunatic. After a while he settled down and went to sleep. The next day he was back to being a real nice man. But as the afternoon came, he started to act a bit strange again. Jack told him he would have to check out. Just about that time, an innocent fellow came along driving north, luckily in the same direction the "Doc" was headed. Jack arranged with the fellow to take the good doctor with him. He was starting to get pretty funny by the time we said our good-byes and saw him off. We wished that innocent and very naive fellow good luck as he drove away. He needed it.

I continued my education there at the hotel, learning and growing as the days and weeks came and went. My teeth had been neglected and needed some repair; I was always a big baby when it came to dentists and doctors.

Willie

Pop paid for getting my teeth fixed, and Jack came with me to the dentist.

I would sometimes go on the road with the travellers to the nearby towns. All the local businessmen came to the hotel. The Rotary Club, Kiwanis Club, Kinsmen Club, and just about every other organisation held their dinners there and met once a week. I was able to meet so many interesting people, and it was my job to talk with them and play the part of an evening host. It meant that I got to learn a lot about people and about life.

It was in the mid-1940s that there was a federal by-election, between a local conservative and a famous general. General McNaughton was a big liberal and knew all the important politicians in Ottawa. Several came to stay at the hotel, including William Mullock, the former Post-Master General of Canada. One day Mr. Mullock told me he was expecting a call from the Prime Minister, and that he would be in his room. It wasn't busy in the afternoon when the switchboard lit up and started to buzz. I answered, and a secretary asked to speak to William Mullock—it was long distance. I had it all figured out that I was going to talk to this famous Prime Minister; he was nice to Hitler, why wouldn't he be nice to me? I asked if it was the Prime Minister, and the secretary said it was. I told her that Mr. Mullock was expecting the call and asked her to put Mr. King on the phone.

The Prime Minister said, "Hello, is that you Bill?" I said, "No, Sir, this is Willie. Mr. Mullock is expecting your call; he is in his room and I will call him. He was just here in the lobby a little while ago." The Prime Minister and I made a bit of small talk about the weather and things, and I finally said, "Here he is now,

Willie Kell

coming to the phone." He said, "Thank you, Willie." "You are welcome, Mr. Prime Minister," I proudly said. Then I switched him over to the Post Master General.

It was kind of exciting talking to the Prime Minister. But not nearly as exciting as the time I went to sleep one night in one of the rooms smoking a cigarette. It fell out of my fingers and onto the rug and started to burn. Burnt a big hole in the rug. Jack could smell the smoke downstairs and came pounding into my room, woke me up, got some water, put the fire out, and opened the windows. Woke everybody up—they were all standing in the hall in their nightclothes. That was a bad scene—I could have burned the hotel down and everybody in it, including myself. It taught me never to smoke in bed. Pop gave me such hell the next morning, I thought my hotel days were over—but they weren't.

Then there was the exciting time Jack caught me in bed with a pretty girl from Toronto. She was trying to seduce me. I was lucky Jack came along to rescue me just in time—I told him so. Then there was the time Jack's wife caught him in bed with a sexy young chambermaid. It just seemed like one thing after another.

There were always pretty girls around; they either stayed there or worked there. But of all the girls I met at that hotel, the one that really caught my eye the most was a sweet, innocent-looking girl who delivered telegrams. She had long blond hair, big blue eyes, and rather fat legs. I used to tease her when she came in. I had to sign for the telegrams and I would always talk to her. I found out her name was Irene. She was a couple of years younger than I, but there was something about her

Willie

innocence and beauty that got to me. I loved that sweet gal.

My brother Jim, by this time, had moved out of town and we didn't see him much. Daddy and Mary didn't get up that way very often, but once in a while I saw them. Son and Irene and I went to their place sometimes. But one time Daddy came up to the farm and I hitched a ride out to see him. He was telling me that he had got a little mare called Topsy. She was a little part Indian pony, part standardbred, a pretty, dark bay with a little white blaze on her face, and she had the heaves. He would sell her to me for $30.00 and deliver her. I bought her and bought a nice wire-wheel buggy from Son. I really had a wonderful time driving this horse and buggy around town. Up and down the main street, up to the park, take my girlfriends for rides—it was better than some of the things I was doing. It kind of kept me out of mischief.

Before I bought that horse, I used to drink and hang around with a fellow who ran a taxi. We went to bootleggers, got booze, and did lots of foolish things. Now I spent more time with the horse, and the family at the hotel encouraged me. That taxi fellow had a nice girlfriend. She lived next door to Sweet's house, and I knew her, but she was a couple of years younger than I and I wasn't interested, though I liked her, she was very wholesome-looking. She used to babysit Sweet's children sometimes.

One night I went to Sweet's place; they were away, but I didn't know they were away until I got there. This nice neighbour girl was babysitting the kids. Well, I was sitting on the chesterfield beside this sweet girl, reading the funny papers, not paying much attention to her. The kids were in bed. She keeps getting closer to me, reading the funnies too. She must have had a short skirt on, because she put her leg over mine as we sat there. And her dress is up and her fat thigh is right under my eyes. I felt so shy, and yet I liked this warm feeling I was getting from that innocent neighbour girl. I didn't touch her, I didn't say anything, just went on reading the funnies. It was a quiet street; I saw a car drive slowly by, but I was too busy trying to be a gentleman to pay much attention. Finally I got up, said good-bye to that sweet, innocent girl, and walked downtown.

When I went into the taxi stand, my friend was very quiet with me, and then accused me of fooling around with his girlfriend. I couldn't tell him what really happened. I suppose what I did tell him, he really didn't believe, and we were never as friendly after that. I guess he drove by, maybe he stopped and looked in the window. The blind was up and the curtains were back. I wasn't hiding anything, didn't have anything *to* hide except that girl's leg. I sometimes look back on that night and wonder what that nice girl had on her mind.

I was eighteen now, and would soon be getting my call to join the armed services. Pop had told me I wouldn't have to go—he had friends in high places. They would have my job at the hotel declared an essential service. However, when the letter came asking me to report to the army depot in Toronto, I told Pop that I was going to go and serve my country. It was like the war had broken out in the lobby of the hotel. "You can't run off and leave us after all we have done for you!" Well, I figured I had done just as much for that hotel as they had ever done for me. At the time I got the call, I was working seven days a week, running my butt off and not getting very much for it. I wanted a change.

I was grateful for what I had learned, and for what they had done for me, but I had earned every thing I ever got and then some. I had a couple of weeks until I had to report to the army. In the meantime, I kept on working at the hotel as usual, but preparing to leave, getting things in order. I sold my horse and buggy to a couple of bachelor brothers out on a farm. When the time came, I was ready to go. I had everything looked after. I even had a little money—not very much, but enough until I got my first army pay.

Willie Kell

Book Eleven: I'm In the Army Now

I reported to the army recruiting headquarters at the CNE grounds in Toronto. I passed my medical, got my inoculations, was issued uniforms, shirts, socks, boots, coats, and a .303 rifle to kill the enemy with. I lived in the horse palace, in a box stall on the second floor. It wasn't that bad; I think there were four men to a stall, in bunk beds. The first morning, at 6AM, some crazy guy played reveille on his bugle, and it seemed like he was blowing that ugly horn right in my ear. Some of us recruits had been out drinking beer and celebrating the night before and had a pretty heavy hangover happening—hearing that silly bugle wasn't music to *my* ears.

We hung around the CNE grounds in Toronto for a couple of weeks until we had had all our needles, got our clothes, and that heavy old gun. There were some official papers to sign, and we made out wills in case some German killed us, and we did a bit of *left-right, left-right*, while some over-zealous corporals and sergeants yelled out commands to us like we were deaf, or soon would be. Then we shipped out to Brantford for our basic training. Basic training is where they march you, run you, build up your muscles, and break down your spirit. They teach you discipline, they tell you that you might break your mother's heart but you can't break ours. Everywhere you go it seems you have to carry that heavy old rifle with you. Out on the parade ground, on route marches, everywhere but to the toilet. The bugle

Willie

blows at 6AM—it's out of bed and ready for roll call outside the barracks in five minutes. This I hardly remember, 'cause I was never awake for it. Though I was there with the rest of them, having worked nights at the hotel for the past year or so made getting up at 6AM seemed like cruel and unusual punishment.

I soon had some good buddies: Johnny was Italian, Fred was a native Indian, and Herman was a Jew. There were several more I hung around with. We would go to town and meet girls, if we had some money. If not, we stayed at the barracks. The fellows would ask me to sing wherever we went. Those times I used to imitate Bing Crosby, Perry Como, Al Jolson, The Ink Spots, Mills Brothers, and even George Formby, the Englishman.

It was about the time we were finishing our basic training that the Germans surrendered and the war in Europe was over. The allies had defeated those terrible Nazis. Adolph Hitler supposedly shot himself and his girlfriend, Eva Braun, on April 30th. The armistice was signed one week and one day later—May 8th, 1945. At our army camp, they asked for volunteers to go and fight the "Japs" in the Pacific. There was a bunch of us outside when this announcement was made, and those of us who were volunteering ran to the office to sign up. I was always a pretty good runner, especially for a short distance, the fastest in our platoon. I got there ahead of everyone and was the first to sign up.

When basic training was over, after about six weeks, we shipped out for Camp Borden, Ontario, for our advanced training. Camp Borden was one of the biggest army training camps in North America. It seemed that it wasn't near any place, but it was in the Barrie vicinity. I guess it was not long after we got there, President

Willie Kell

Roosevelt died and Harry Truman became President of the United States.

Advanced training is tough—twenty-mile route marches with full pack and that ever-present heavy old 303 rifle on your shoulder. Then there are the obstacle courses, designed by some over-patriotic shell-shocked sergeant-major. They were so much fun—that is, if you get fun out of crawling under barbed wire fences on your belly, running through ditches half full of muck, climbing up ropes hand over hand across rivers (I couldn't swim). Then we had to learn how to shoot heavy artillery and bazooka guns; we fired live ammunition, and I almost got killed accidentally by my Indian buddy Fred. Those of us who had signed up for the Pacific got special training. There was bayonet practice, gas attack drills, and we also had a few tear-filled encounters with crying gas. We were hungry at the end of the day when it was time to head for the mess hall. The meals weren't bad, especially when you were starving, and we always were.

The letter-writing between Betty and I had continued, and again the letters became more frequent between us. The words "Dearest Darling" had crept back into the lines somehow as well. When my advanced training was over, I would be taking a fourteen-day furlough, so we arranged that I would spend two weeks at Aunt Alice and Uncle Herb's place at Pontiac, Michigan. Yes, Betty's mom and dad would be happy to have Florence's youngest son spend a little time at their house. They hadn't seen much of us Kell kids since Mother died; it would be a good time to get reacquainted.

Willie

It was a beautiful Sunday in July when I got there. I had ridden the trains and buses and arrived in the early afternoon. Betty had a nice car, and met me at the depot. It was great seeing her again. When we got to Aunt Alice's house, everybody made a big fuss over me. My other cousins, Laura and Florence—named after Mother—were there with their mother and father. And we all went to a friend's place at the lake. This friend was a doctor, and had a beautiful cottage and a big boat. We had a great time that afternoon. But the best part was just being with my Betty.

Aunt Alice and Uncle Herb lived in a big white house out on Elizabeth Lake Road. It sat back on a beautiful park-like property. There was a tall flagpole in the middle of the front lawn where Old Glory proudly waved in the summer breeze. It seemed everybody was so easy-going and full of fun. Uncle Herb was slowing down some, but still kept busy. He had built a quite a few homes in and around Pontiac. When he got home at noon for lunch, Aunt Alice always had a nice dinner ready. He would open up a bottle of beer and have it with his lunch, and he would always offer me one. I mostly refused his offer, but made up for it at night when the girls took me to clubs. They took me every place they could think of. I met all of my long-lost relatives. They took me to see Grandma Crichton in Sarnia; I hadn't seen her since Mother died 13 years before. Grandpa wasn't living anymore, and it was the last time I saw Grandma.

Betty had a little apartment in town, and we went there a few times to get some things she needed. Once we lay across her big bed kissing, and we spent some precious passionate moments together. But the strength of our determination to avoid going any further kept it from happening. Betty stayed at Aunt Alice's while I was there, and we were always together. She worked

Willie Kell

part-time as a cashier at a big grocery store managed by her father-in-law. I went to work with her and helped around the store. Betty and I and her sisters went to night clubs, where there were entertainers, singers, dancers, magicians, jugglers, and comedians. I guess it was obvious to the girls that Betty and I were more than just cousins. But not much was ever said, and we both did our best to hide the fact that we were so in love.

We were always the last ones to go to bed. We would sit on Aunt Alice's chesterfield in the living room, holding hands and whispering love words, stopping to kiss often. Then we would walk together up the big, winding stairway to my bedroom. Betty would come in and we'd spend some more precious time quietly saying good night.

Well, the good-times were coming to an end; all too soon the day came when we had to part. I had to go back to that silly old army at Camp Borden, Ontario and leave my precious Betty.

It was on Sunday around noon when I said good-bye to Aunt Alice and Uncle Herb and told them thanks for having me. Betty and her sisters drove me to Detroit. That way we could spend a little more time together. We went to Belle Isle, an interesting place, and spent the afternoon. Walking around, seeing the sights, and just being together. Then it was time to catch my bus and say good-bye. Betty cried when I got on the bus, and blew me a kiss when we pulled away. As the bus manoeuvred its way along the quiet, late-Sunday-afternoon streets of Detroit and across the Ambassador Bridge at the border into Canada, I pushed back my seat and reflected on the most exciting two weeks I had ever lived. It was a lonesome old ride on that bus heading back to the army.

When I finally got back to Camp Borden, after riding what seemed like endless miles on trains and

Willie

buses, things hadn't changed very much. It was good to see my buddies again. We all told stories about what had happened on our first furlough. I think my stories were the most exciting, and I didn't tell everything.

It was around this time that we heard on the news about America successfully testing some kind of weird bomb that, when dropped on something, had devastating effects. It was just three days after my nineteenth birthday—August 6th, 1945—that the United States dropped one of those weird new bombs on Hiroshima, Japan. It killed about one hundred thousand people and devastated the city and surrounding area. But those stubborn Japs wouldn't give up. It took another bomb, this time on Nagasaki, to convince them to lay down their guns and sign an unconditional surrender.

It was a terrible thing to have to kill those people like that. But President Harry Truman felt that he had no alternative. The war had dragged on long enough; too many innocent people had been killed and tortured. Japan surrendered on August 14th, just 5 days after the second atomic bomb was dropped. It was estimated that some 45 million people lost their lives in that crazy war, and too many millions more maimed, crippled, and left homeless. It is so sad to think that this war never should have been—Hitler and his gang could have been stopped before they ever got started!

After the war ended, I lost interest in the army and all that silly *left-right, left-right* stuff. We had to stay on and soldier, but now we didn't take it as seriously. There was more time now for fun. But no girls for me: I had my love, my Betty. We wrote every few days. I'm sure she loved her husband, too, and she wrote to him as much as she did me. It was really a crazy situation, as I look back on it.

Willie Kell

Early in the fall we were shipped back to Brantford, and some of my buddies were discharged, depending on their age. I spent about a month there and then was shipped to Niagara-On-The-Lake. What a nice part of the country, just a few miles from the famous Niagara Falls. But it seems nobody told them at that army camp that the war was over. They kept right on soldiering like before.

Our commander was a Scottish-Canadian colonel who had won the Victoria Cross in World War I for wiping out a German machine gun nest by killing every last one of them with a club. Sometimes I thought that old colonel was going to kill me too. I had sold some of my clothes and equipment in Brantford; didn't think I'd be needing them anymore, though it's against the army law to sell it. The first time we went on parade, supposed to be in full battle dress, I didn't have half my clothes and packs with me. The old colonel came to me in inspection, stood in front of me, looked me up and down, and said, "Well, ain't you a fine-looking pickle." I could tell right then we were not going to have a good relationship, and we didn't. I told him someone stole it from me, and I had to buy new stuff from the quartermaster stores. Well, that old colonel had us doing 20-mile route marches and the whole thing, just like when the Germans and Japs were mad at us.

I had new friends and buddies now; all my other friends were either discharged or had moved somewhere else. The only thing good about the army now was when the mail came and I got a letter from my sweetheart Betty. One day she wrote and said she was going to Hollywood, she and her girl friend. We had talked about going to Hollywood sometime. She always wanted me to pursue my music, but Hollywood seemed a bit much ... though I really liked the sound of it.

Willie

It seems there was an advertisement in the paper, that someone was driving to Hollywood in a Cadillac and wanted somebody to help with the driving. Betty answered and made a deal to go. I got letters and cards from New Mexico, Arizona, and finally Hollywood, California. They had arrived, found a room, and were finding a job. The letters kept coming, and this magic love affair was becoming more magical and somewhat bizarre all the time.

But again, as Maw always said, good things have to end sometime. One day it ended—awfully sudden and quite dramatically. I got a letter from my sweetheart in Hollywood, saying that her husband was very sick with a tropical disease and was being sent home. To her credit, she said she had to be by his side when he needed her. He was being shipped into San Francisco, and she would be there to meet and take care of him. This must have made him feel much better, 'cause about a month before, she had written and told him of her love for me.

Well, my heart was broken, but I wasn't a bit angry, because I felt Betty was doing the right thing. I started to feel sorry for that poor fellow and what I had helped to put him through. But it didn't do much to ease the pain of my broken heart. Our dream had ended, that magic love affair was over. I went AWOL, goofed around, drank too much, and acted like some silly kid who had played a game of sidewalk marbles and lost.

One night a buddy and I hitched a ride to Buffalo and started bar-crawling. As the night went on, we found our way into an interesting place with music and quite a big black lady singer. My friend told the lady that I could sing, and she invited me on stage. Well, I got up there and sang something, I don't remember what, but I remember that lady saying, "Sing it again, son." That room was going around like painted ponies on a carousel. We had a good night, but we didn't get back to

Willie Kell

the army camp until noon the next day. The colonel wasn't happy about it, and I got hell again.

When you were brought up on charges, a sergeant would take you before the colonel. Then he would read out the charges. The colonel would ask what you had to say for yourself, then pass sentence. Usually it would mean you were confined to barracks for a length of time, perhaps a week or 10 days, and have several days' pay deducted. With wages of $1.40 a day to begin with, sometimes it would leave a person awfully short of cash.

Sometimes a few of my buddies and me would walk into town a couple of miles up the road and hang around the hotel, drinking beer. The people got to know us, and they would often ask me to sing a few songs, I would imitate Jolson and Crosby or someone else, and they would buy us beer. This often came in handy, especially if the old colonel had taken some of my pay away. I didn't go out with girls, though; I was still carrying a torch for my Betty.

One winter night, I think it was near the end of January, a friend of mine—a bit of a wild guy—and I were at the hotel in the little town, having a bunch of beer. My buddy got talking to a lady a bit older than himself. I don't mean that she was some high-class lady; she was a drunk who hung around trying to pick up lonesome soldiers. My buddy wanted to take her to a room, kind of fool around. Well, me being somewhat of an expert in the hotel business, I said, "Follow me." We went upstairs, tried some doors, and soon came to one that was unlocked. We went in, turned on the light, and made ourselves at home. I could see that this room was occupied; there was nobody in there, but there were things hanging on the hall tree and stuff on the dresser. We locked the door with the bolt, just like the Seldon House locks.

Willie

One of my other friends had loaned me his Scottish hat; it was a plaid tam, with a couple of ribbons hanging down the back—a real nice hat. "Don't lose it, Willie," he said as we left the barracks that night. Well, I hung the thing on the hall tree and watched as this wild-animal buddy of mine helped that over-sized gal undress. Just when she got all of her clothes off, there was a loud knock on the door. It was the hotel owner and the waiter pounding on the door. "Let me in, let me in," they shouted, in loud, angry voices! They had heavy accents, sounded Greek. My buddy jumped up, went over to the window, opened it, and jumped out, leaving me holding the bag!

I have always been afraid of heights—there was no way I was going to jump. We were up on the second floor; a guy could get killed. So, being a better talker than a jumper, I opened the door and tried to explain. The naked woman was standing behind me, screaming at these two Greeks at the door: "You are disturbing my husband and me!" These two fellows were talking a mile a minute, and the naked woman was screaming at them. I just tried to calm everyone down. I couldn't help wonder if my wild friend was lying in the snow down below that window with a fractured skull, or maybe just a broken leg. I kept getting closer to the door, still talking as nice as I knew how, and wondering how did I get into this mess in the first place. When they started talking about police and things like that, I left very quickly; after all it wasn't *my* party. Maybe those two Greeks knew what to do with that naked woman; I sure didn't.

I ran out of that room and down those stairs two at a time, I had over three years' practice running up and down the stairs at the Seldon House. When I hit the front door, I was in high gear; I just pushed it open and kept on going. I was a decent runner in those days, but when I left that hotel and started running down that sidewalk, I was probably running close to a world's record! I slowed down when I got to the corner, thinking that I would circle around behind the hotel and help that poor buddy who may have a broken leg, lying beneath the hotel window. But there in the snow were fresh footprints about four feet apart, heading for the army camp. My wild friend wasn't lying behind that hotel with a broken leg. NO, he had two good legs and was using them to run as fast as he could to get away from that naked woman and the two Greeks.

When I got back to camp, he was there—so was my friend who had loaned me his good Scottish hat. When he asked about the hat, I told him it was hanging in that hotel room uptown. The next morning, he and I sneaked away from camp, into town, to get his hat. The front door to the hotel was unlocked, so we went quietly up the stairs and opened the door to the room. The room was in darkness and the blinds were drawn. I crept quietly over and took the hat off the hall tree and we left, without closing the door. I could hear what I thought were two people in that bed, snoring. I think one of them was the naked woman of the night before!! My friend was happy to get his hat back and I was happy that the late-night caper with the naked woman and the two Greeks was over and had ended peacefully, without anyone getting hurt.

I went up home for Christmas for a few days and dropped into the Seldon hotel. They were so nice to me, treated me like some kind of prodigal son. Pop said, when I got out of the army to come back; they would be glad to have me. It was a far cry from the way they had treated me when I went into the army, almost a year before. It seems they tried to find someone to take my place and it hadn't worked out. Pop suggested that I

Willie

could get a leave from the army if I had a job to go to. They offered to pay me $85.00 a month plus room, board, and whatever tips I might get.

As time went on, we made arrangements for this leave. I thought it would be better to be back at the hotel than doing those silly route marches. I was getting bored with army life and was ready to give it up. One day in March, after having spent about a year in the army, my papers came through. We had just got in from a 20-mile route march; I had had my pack on my back and that heavy old gun on my shoulder all day. Now I could get back to living a better life at the hotel. Anything would be better than that old colonel and his gang screaming *left-right, left-right*!

Book Twelve: Love, Marriage, and Irene

When I got back to the hotel, everyone was so nice to me; the travellers and the staff all welcomed me home. Jimmy Yemon, the big Chinese chef, and his beautiful, sexy, blonde wife, Irene, were still there—what a nice fellow and a wonderful chef. He and Irene had come there from Toronto before I went into the army. They lived at the hotel in a room on the third floor. Jimmy always said, "I fix you something weely nice, something number one." His wife worked in the dining room; she was very nice, but a bit of a whore! Jimmy was crazy about her and bought her beautiful clothes and jewellery, but she cheated every chance she got. That big guy was over six feet tall and was very handsome, with a great personality.

Most of the staff that had been there were still there when I came back. But there were a few new ones. One of the new ones was that sweet blonde girl with the big blue eyes and the fat legs, who used to deliver the telegrams. Her name was Irene Grenfell. She had just started at the hotel a few weeks before I got back from the army. She had worked about a month as a chambermaid, then she began waiting on tables in the dining room. That innocent, sweet girl was just as beautiful as ever, only now she was sixteen, would be seventeen in a few weeks, and looked eighteen.

One thing I knew for sure, I wanted that girl. I used to talk to her and tease her. But I was shy, and I didn't want to scare her off. She seemed to like me, but she was shy too, and would blush when I talked to her. I wanted

Willie

to ask her to go out with me to the show, but I was afraid she would turn me down. But when I found out that she went out with a married man a few years older than me, in town doing construction work at the hotel, I wondered if she was as innocent as I first thought she was. I was kind of jealous about her going out with this married man. Finally I asked her to go to the show with me, and she said she would. When I walked her home after the show and said good night to her at the door, she said, "Aren't you going to kiss me?" I couldn't believe what I was hearing—that sweet, innocent girl asking me to kiss her! Well, sure, I was going to kiss her—and I did!

I used to have Saturdays off, so the next Saturday night we went to the show again. It was a long walk out to her house on the other side of town, but it was great being with her. Yes, I kissed her good night again. Sometimes, in the hotel, I would meet her in the hallway going into the kitchen and steal a little kiss. She was so pretty in her white uniform. She was quiet, but had a beautiful smile. We were going to go to the show the next Saturday, and I could hardly wait—I was falling for this girl, head over heels!

She used to go swimming in the afternoons, up at the old mill dam, she and the other Irene (the chef's wife). They met two fellows from Michigan while they were swimming on Friday afternoon. These fellows asked them to go out with them that night, and they did. They went driving and whatever else they were doing, and the chef's wife didn't get home until after 1 AM. I was working—or at least I was there, half asleep, I guess—when she came in. She was in a bad way; she had taken off her wedding and engagement rings and couldn't find them. She was crying and had been drinking.

Jimmy was going wild. He had been down to tell me, "Irene not come home yet, I kill her!" He had ripped her

Willie Kell

good dresses up and thrown her shoes in the garbage—she had at least a dozen pairs of shoes. He was furious! That was before he knew she had lost her rings! There wasn't anyone else on the third floor that night, so the yelling and screaming didn't wake very many people up. After a while, things settled down and they went to bed. She always said she had a way of making that Chinaman forget her faults.

I had a room just down the hall from them, and when I was off duty in the morning, I went to my room to have a little sleep. Jimmy was in the kitchen; his wife came in to my bedroom and told me that he had thrown all her good shoes out and ripped up her clothes. She was still crying about her rings. Then she told me that she and my sweet, innocent Irene had gone out with these two fellows. I was hurt; I wanted that gal for my own.

This thing went on with Jimmy and Irene several times. Once when she got him mad, he threw a long-handled sharp meat fork at her across the kitchen. It just missed her, and stuck in the door!

Well, it was Saturday again. I had a date with my Irene (the innocent one) to take her to the show. We held hands in the show, and after the movie was over, we took a walk up to the old mill dam, where she and the other Irene went swimming and had met the guys from Michigan the day before. My Irene told me that the other Irene got in the back seat with the fellow the night before and they seemed to be doing some great love-making. Of course, my Irene was disgusted with all of this; she would never do anything like that. If ever there was a virgin, it was that girl.

She told me about her boyfriend; he was a sailor in the navy. He was about six years older than her, but stayed at her place when he was on leave. He bought her

Willie

nice gifts and wanted to marry her. It just so happened that he was at her house that very weekend. She wanted to give him up. Her mother and father thought this sailor was a wonderful fellow, and that Irene should stick with him. As we talked, leaning over the little bridge, she reached down with her slender fingers and scratched her leg, above her knee. I looked, and in the dim light I could see her thigh. When I mentioned it to her, she casually showed me a little more of it. Then she gave me that shy, schoolgirl smile. What was happening to my sweet, innocent girl?

We sat on the wooden deck, leaned back, and kissed. She was on her back, one leg out straight and the other leg bent at the knee. Her skirt had slid up, revealing her fat thigh to the very top; our kisses became more passionate. It seemed that if we kept this up, that innocent girl wasn't going to be a virgin much longer.

It was a warm night in June, and the dim light from the street lamps shone across the little river. In the shadows, I could see her full lips, her laughing, big blue eyes, her round face, and long blonde hair. She didn't wear makeup, just a little lipstick. She had just turned 17 a few weeks before, on the 4th of May. If I didn't have any better reason for getting out of that silly army than being with that beautiful girl that night, she alone would have been reason enough.

We decided to go back to the hotel. We walked along the main street; it was getting way past midnight. When we got to the hotel, the door was locked. Young Perry, the boy who took my place Saturday nights, was on duty. I knocked on the door while Irene stood at the side, out of sight. Perry came to the door to let me in. I told him I would lock up. He hardly saw me, he was so sleepy; he didn't see Irene I held her hand tightly as we tiptoed through the lobby and up the big stairs to my room on the third floor. There wasn't a sound from

155

Willie Kell

Jimmy and the other Irene; guess they were tired after the wild time they'd had the night before. Irene and I slept warm in each other's arms the rest of the night.

The next morning she called her mother and said she had stayed overnight with a girlfriend. Well, I was no girl, but I sure was proud to be her friend. She had to work in the dining room that morning. She washed up, put her white uniform on, kissed me, and went to work. I thought I must have been in heaven—what a beautiful, sweet, perhaps not-so-innocent girl.

It was Sunday, the hotel was not busy, and Irene got off work early in the afternoon. She walked home, had a fight with her boyfriend, and broke up with him. Her parents sided with the boyfriend, and thought she had been unfair to him. However, their romance was over.

From then on, Irene and I were together every precious minute that we could be. We were buddies, friends, and lovers. The fact that we both worked at the hotel gave us the wonderful opportunity to be in each other's arms often. When she came to work in the morning, I was there, working the desk. We ate together as much as we could. In the afternoons, when she was off work between the noon meal and the evening meal, we were mostly together. In the evening, when she got off work, we were together, and I walked her home most of the time. I had free passes to the theatre across the street, and we went to every new movie that played there.

It was around the time that Irene and I started going together that I bought a grey saddle horse. Her name was Mickey; she was very intelligent and had a quiet disposition. I started teaching Mickey some tricks, and I bought a new western saddle for her. I didn't have quite enough cash to pay for it, and Irene loaned me some. We spent a quite a lot of time together, Irene, Mickey, and

Willie

me. I didn't miss Betty anymore; I guess my fickle heart found love anew.

It wasn't long after Irene and I started going together that I met her parents. They lived out on the northwest part of town, in a small frame house covered with cedar shingles. They had an eat-in kitchen with a wood cookstove, a living room, and one bedroom upstairs, with a tiny room off of it where Irene slept. They had electricity, but no bathroom, just an outhouse out back. They had bought the little place for $150.00 in the Depression. Irene's mother paid for it a dollar or two at a time, by doing housework.

Irene's parents had migrated to Canada from England in the fall of 1928; Irene was born the following spring, May 4th, 1929. They had nothing when they came to Canada, and it was a struggle for them. The Depression started the following year. Her father, Bill Grenfell, was a labourer, and took jobs where he could find them. Half the time he was out of work, and the poor fellow would get himself into difficult situations, trying some scheme to better himself. Her mother, Belle, was a kind-hearted patient woman; she had to be, to live with old Bill.

They had two children. Fourteen years after Irene was born, they had a boy. He had brown eyes and almost black hair. David was just three when I started going with Irene, but already he was showing signs of being quite clever, although he was spoiled by his mother.

Bill became very deaf and wore a hearing aid; he was a strange man. He was fair-haired with blue eyes. Belle was dark with brown eyes, good-looking, a very charming happy nature and a wonderful laugh, but she could show a temper if you crossed her.

Willie Kell

The little home was quite comfortable, for those times. Bill had fixed it up; he was kind of a jack-knife carpenter. I went there for dinner a few times. They were okay with me, but still liked that sailor that Irene had gone with from the time she was 14—he had been over 20 at the time.

The summer went along just great. I had found the love of my life in that sweet, blue-eyed girl. We had wonderful times together; we used to walk up to the fairgrounds and play with the horse in the afternoons. In the evening we often visited Sweet and Len and their kids. Sometimes we baby-sat for them, other times we would get out to see Son and Irene at the farm. Jock was there, and I would spend time talking to him. By now I kind of liked Jock; it was different from when I was a kid.

On August 3rd that year I turned 20, and Irene and I talked about getting married. Why not; we loved each other, were together all of the time. I couldn't see how we could ever part. Seemed like God had made us for one another.

In September, I bought her a diamond engagement ring. I should say *we* bought her a ring. When we went into the store to get the ring, the one she chose cost $10.00 more than I had at the time, so she paid the extra ten bucks. I really don't remember if I paid her back or not. However, she had her ring, and she loved it. We walked out to her place to show her mother, who didn't seem all that happy about it. Looking back now, I can't say that I blame her. After all, Irene was just 17 at the time ... though it hadn't seemed to matter when she'd talked of marrying that sailor. I tried to treat those people the best I knew how, but they just didn't like me. Even young David seemed to hate me. That sailor always bought them things, and sucked up to Mom (by

Willie

now I called her Mom). He used to flatter her by telling her she had nice legs.

But Irene and I were going to be married, and set the date: October 26, 1946. Irene was a good saver; she had a couple of hundred dollars and a nice cedar chest full of things. I had the horse and saddle. I sold Mickey and the saddle to Billy Bishop's brother-in-law, a local lawyer, for $150.00. So, all together, I had about $200.00. In spite of not liking me and preferring the sailor, her parents consented to the marriage. Because she was under 18 years old, her father had to sign a paper giving her permission. As time went on, her mother went along with all the plans and preparations for our wedding.

We were married at the minister's house. They belonged to The Reorganised Church of Jesus Christ of Latter Day Saints (Mormons). It was a beautiful Saturday afternoon, and Sweet and Len stood up with us. Irene had no white veil, but we each had a new suit for the occasion. Her dad and mom were there, and Daddy and Mary. It was the first time Daddy had been to the wedding of one of his children. Irene's mother cried all through the ceremony. There were just a few people there, but we had a nice reception at her parent's place after the wedding, and a quite a few of their friends from the church came.

About 5 o'clock, Sweet and Len drove us to the station and we took the train to Toronto. We had reservations at the old Ford Hotel. We arrived at the hotel about 9 PM and soon were in bed after our busy wedding day. I think I was the happiest person in the whole world. I was married to the most beautiful girl I'd ever known. But our honeymoon didn't last more than a day or two, 'cause we had to be back to work on Monday.

Willie Kell

We had rented an apartment for $25.00 a month. It was the attic of a big house, about three blocks from the hotel. The family at the hotel wasn't very happy about us getting married, but they gave us some used furniture, a bed with box spring and mattress, a little table to eat off, some chairs, and a couple of lamps. We bought a used pullout couch and a new china cabinet to put our dishes in. Irene already had her cedar chest full of things and we got some nice wedding presents, dishes and things. We were so happy in our little home, even though we shared the bathroom with the people on the floor below.

We continued working at the hotel for the winter, but made plans for me to start selling Ton-A-Lax in the spring. I was only earning about $21.00 a week at the hotel, and we thought we could always go back to something like that—why not have some adventure? We bought a car, a 1931 Chevrolet Coach, for $265.00; it was sixteen years old. We took a trip or two down to Daddy's place during the winter. I could drive a little and got my license, and taught Irene to drive. It wasn't long before she was a good driver. Sometimes we would go out to the farm; that old side road was often kept ploughed open by that time.

We went to visit Daddy and Mary in March, about 50 miles away. They had a Dalmatian dog, and she had a litter of nice, spotted pups, and Mary gave us one. That's the way Mary was—she giveth and she taketh away; anyway, we were thankful to get the dog, and Irene loved it.

It was about the middle of April when we gave up the apartment and put the furniture in storage, sold some things. I remember that I mistakenly sold one or two of our wedding presents, and Irene wasn't happy about that. I don't blame her; I should have known better. By that time, Irene wasn't working; she'd had a

Willie

disagreement with one of the Alles boys and quit. So, when the time came, I quit my job and we drove to Daddy's place for a case of medicine. Daddy had said we could have it at cost, but when we went to pay for it, Mary said that we would have to pay 25 cents a bottle for it. I had no problem with that. It was priced at $1.25 a bottle, or if you sold 5 or 10 bottles to a person, it was $1.00 a bottle. There was lots of profit in it if you could sell it, and I thought I could.

We got it in cases of 72 bottles. A case cost $18.00. You could buy gas for the car for around 30 cents a gallon. If we stayed in a hotel in the little towns, it would be about $1.50 a night. Meals were about 75 cents.

Willie Kell

Book Thirteen: Being a Medicine Man, Like Daddy

So we loaded up a case of medicine in the old Chevrolet and headed out for the Stayner area—Irene, me, and the spotted pup. We'd be going to Daddy's old stomping grounds. Daddy and Toots had made an arrangement, when she first took Elizabeth, that her address would be on the labels and any letters that came for Ton-A-Lax, Toots would get the money for it. She used to keep a few bottles at her place and sometimes would deliver it to people; that way, if they wrote asking for five bottles, she would go and try to sell them ten. $10.00 was lot of money in those times. The rent for their two-storey house at the time was only $8.00 a month. However, this arrangement stopped when they adopted Elizabeth.

When Toots moved to Whitby, Sweet and Len moved into their house and started renting it. That was just a month or so after I started boarding with them.

One day, just about the time we were moving from our apartment and getting ready to start selling medicine, a letter came to Sweet's place from near Stayner. It was from a lady wanting 10 bottles of Ton-A-Lax; she had the old address. Sweet brought me the letter and said I might as well go sell it to her when I was going that way. Why not—that $7.50 profit on the stuff would about buy our gas and pay the first week's rent in the hotel, although the letter rightfully belonged to Daddy and I should have given it to him; I later apologised for that.

Willie

We drove over roads neither one of us had ever seen before on our way to Stayner from Daddy's place. We got to the town in late afternoon and booked into the nice old hotel on the main street. The lobby was full of antique furnishings; the light fixtures were ancient, and everything about the place was beautiful. We had a room on the second floor, with a bathroom just down the hall. After we had checked in and washed up, we went out to sell some medicine. We found the lady who had ordered the 10 bottles of medicine, delivered it to her, got our money, and they invited us to stay for a nice supper. We sold another $25.00 worth of medicine that afternoon and evening to the neighbours, had the lovely supper, and went back to our hotel. We had a wonderful time our first day on the road: we had sold $35.00 worth of medicine, more money than the two of us could earn in a week working at the Seldon House.

We got up the next morning and had a good breakfast in the dining room. It was less than a week before that I had been working in a hotel, and now we were staying at one. We were high rollers for sure. I was 20 years old and Irene was 17.

In a few days the medicine was sold and we were on our way back to Daddy's place for more. We were two happy kids; it didn't seem to worry us that we had no home and very little money. And but for the few sticks of furniture that were in storage, the old car, and the spotted pup, about all we had was each other. At the time, it seemed enough.

Someone had told Irene's mother that my father had left his wife and kids and run off with another woman. Whoever told her that just had part of it right. Her mother told her that I would keep her knocked-up and bare-footed and when she had a bunch of kids I'd run off and leave her. "He is just like his dad," she would

Willie Kell

say. Well, I guess I *was* a lot like my dad. If I could ever be as smart as he was and as talented, I'd be happy. He had a hard time to pay his bills sometimes, when he was younger, but he always told me to keep my credit good and to be honest. Always do what you say you're going to do. Keep your word and don't back out of a deal, and keep your eyes open. Those are some of the things he told me. I tried to remember them.

We would stay at Daddy's place for a day or two. The girls were growing up by this time, and they seemed happy to see us. Sometimes we had to help label and wrap the bottles, but we never knew how to make the stuff. I knew what was in it, but I didn't know the exact quantity of some of the ingredients, and didn't bother to find out. Mary tried to keep it a secret, and we didn't really care. We got the stuff, paid for it, and went selling it. We stayed at Stayner as long as we could keep selling Ton-A-Lax.

As time went on and a month or so passed by, it seemed that everybody in that part of the country had bought all of the Ton-A-Lax they were planning to buy for the time being. Yes, we even sold our spotted dog to a wealthy farmer; he got a wonderful home. By this time he had grown up, and it became a problem taking him around in hotels. Yes, we had to move on; it was time to find greener pastures.

We tried other areas a few miles away, around the hilly places of Horning's Mills, Mansfield, and Honeywood. It was a beautiful part of the country, but there didn't seem to be as much money around. We stayed in a private house with an old lady for a couple of weeks, and although we didn't sell as much medicine as we did the first while, around Stayner, we enjoyed the scenery and earned enough to pay our way. One day when we were travelling around in that part of the country, we sold a few bottles of medicine to some nice

Willie

folks, and they asked Irene and I to have dinner with them. It was noon hour, and we were getting hungry. It was back in those hills, and these people were not wealthy farmers; they were poor, but fine people. I guess it's hard to grow crops on the side of a hill. We sat down with them in the big, plain kitchen with their kids and a hired man. All the doors in the house were wide open—they had no screen doors. They had a lot of hens running around the farm, and these hens walked in the house, messed on the floor, cackled around, and none of these folks paid a bit of attention to them. You had to be careful where you walked in that house, 'cause you might step on an egg or something. Irene put a spoonful of what she thought was sugar in her tea. It turned out they had no saltshaker; that "sugar" was salt. After that, she always made sure it was sugar in the bowl before she put it in her tea or coffee.

Those times, we used to go to the harness races around the small towns. We got to know all the owners and drivers, and would bet $2.00 on a race. The betting system was different at those little one-day tracks. They set up a book system: they wrote you a ticket, and if the odds on the horse were 5/2, that was written on the ticket, along with the horse's number. They had different coloured tickets, for win, place, and show. They had a little place about eight feet square, put together with a few boards and a bit of a tarpaulin over the top. There was a small platform out front where the booker stood, taking your bets. It was a good day when we got to the races. Often Daddy and Mary would be there, and sometimes Son and Irene. Son bought a horse and trained him and raced him around at these small tracks; he was a trotter named Scott Express, and Son drove him. We tried to be at every place that horse raced. He

Willie Kell

didn't win many races, but sometimes would be second or third.

Daddy was a walking encyclopedia on the sport of harness racing. He knew the breed of every horse in the country, it seemed. Harness horses are standardbreds, an offshoot of the thoroughbred, through Messenger, a thoroughbred stud imported to the United States in the early 1800s from England. This great sire, and his sons—down through a horse called Hambeltonian 10 and bred to American mares known for having speed at the trotting gate—produced what became known as the standardbred. They are said to be perhaps the most noble of the equine species. These are the horses that brought the family doctor to a sick child in the night, through rain and snow. These are the horses that brought the mail, often pulled the stagecoach across the dusty roads and through the winter storms. They worked alongside the draft horses in the fields, pulling a plough. It was these very same horses, the standardbreds, that raced at the trotting and pacing gate and started to earn big money and become famous. Back in the mid 1800s, Stephen Foster wrote the popular song, "Camptown Races," and it soon became known all over the world. The song was about harness horses, racing at what was then Camptown, New Jersey. The song tells about "a blind horse sticking in a big mud hole." Yes, he was blind, but he was one of the best pacers of his time. His name was "Sleepy Tom."

Through the years some of the best trainers and drivers in the world were Canadians. Men like Ben White, Ralph Baldwin, Vic Fleming, and many more of that era. There was Nat Ray, who won the very first Hambletonian Stake, for three-year-old trotters, with a horse called Guy McKinney, back in 1926 at Goshen, New York, the birthplace of Hambletonian 10. Later, there were many more Canadians who were the best in

Willie

the game: Clint Hogins, Johnny Chapman, Morie McDonald, and little Joe O'Brien. Today the sport is dominated by talented Canadian trainers and drivers, headed by John Campbell, the biggest money-winning driver of all time, who was raised on a farm near Ailsa Craig, Ontario; I knew his father and grandfather. Clint Galbraith was raised near Tara, Ontario, just a few miles from Maw's Keppel farm, where I went to school as a young boy. We knew his family well, and I remember him before he ever drove a racehorse. He went on to train, drive, and be a part-owner of the famous world-champion pacer, Niatros, winner of over two million dollars.

Daddy never owned a racehorse; at least, he never actually raced any. But, with his great memory and intelligence, he became quite an authority on the sport. However, the way he was with his lack of ambition and being content with life, he never used this knowledge for financial gain. He often told me stories of horses and drivers, and I became interested in the sport and in horses generally. Daddy told me of the time he had traded a horse for Billy Bishop; that was before he became a great racehorse. It was in 1918, the time of the flue epidemic. Daddy took sick with the flu just about that time, and the deal fell through. The horse later became a local hero, like his namesake, the World War I pilot.

Irene and I were having the time of our lives, although we weren't making much money. We drove that old Chevy car all over—selling medicine, going to the races, staying at hotels, at Daddy's place out at the farm, and at Irene's parents' house. We didn't stay at her parent's house very often, 'cause Irene's old boyfriend, who was out of the navy by this time, was there quite a lot. When we were in town, we would

Willie Kell

always go and see Dad and Mammy. Dad was always glad to see us. For the last couple of years, we had made sure that there was a pint of milk on his doorstep every morning. Daddy and I took turns paying for it to be delivered from the dairy. His old radio had quit working, so I gave him ours. They liked to hear the news.

We were struggling, trying to sell Ton-A-Lax in an Irish community. We had hung around the area for a couple of days, went to the races in the local town, and the next day went to try and sell this great wonder medicine. When late afternoon came and we hadn't sold one single bottle, we started to get a little anxious. I'm not saying that we panicked, 'cause we didn't. We spent the last $2.00 we had on some gas and headed south down a gravel road. I knew that somewhere a few miles down that road there was a sect of people called Mennonites. I had been through there the year before, when Son and his wife and I went to New Hamburg to the Canadian Pacing Derby. I saw these people driving their horse and buggies along. They wore black clothes, and the women had bonnets on their heads. I didn't know if they believed in taking herbal medicine or if they talked to strangers or what. But I knew we had to try something if we were going to eat supper and have a hotel room to stay in that night.

We started to drive slowly when we came to some farms with no signs of electricity. Then we saw a man who was fixing a fence at the side of the road. Irene was driving; we stopped, said hello. The man walked over to the car; he was on the driver's side. I showed him the bottle of Ton-A-Lax and explained some things about it, and that we sold 10 bottles for $10.00. The man said, "I'll take it."

"You mean the ten bottles?" I asked, trying not to seem surprised. He said he wanted the 10 bottles. He

Willie

lived just down the road a short way, so he stood on the running board and we drove to his house to deliver the medicine and get the money.

Well, I hadn't been at the business very long, but long enough to know that you can carry that medicine into a house and think you have a sale and the woman can be the boss and throw a monkey wrench into the deal. So when that fellow jumped off the running board of that old car, I grabbed up that medicine as fast as I could and was right on his backside when he got to the door. I was prepared for a bossy, hard-to-convince woman; I would just have to sell her on the stuff. We needed that money—it was after 5 o'clock in the late afternoon, and we were getting hungry.

The man opened the door, held it for me, and said to the woman, "Get my wallet." The woman didn't even look, she just went and got the man's wallet and handed it to him. When he gave me that $10.00 bill, I could have kissed them both.

His name was Manasah Martin; I asked him who lived across the road and he said Alvin Martin. How lucky could I be, must be his brother. "No, he was no relation," the man said. "You will find a lot of Martins around here," and I sure enough did!

We drove across the road and just about as quickly sold that fellow $10.00 worth. We sold all of the medicine we had with us and ended up with $33.00 and a real nice supper. Our first venture into the Mennonite country of Wellington and Waterloo counties selling Ton-A-Lax proved a profitable and worthwhile event in the history of our life on the road.

We stayed in a little hotel that night and the next day went to get more medicine at Daddy's place, and told him of our good fortune finding these wonderful Mennonite people. We headed back down that way as fast as we could and sold medicine all over that country

Willie Kell

to those great people; they seemed to trust me. They were good farmers, prosperous, hard-working honest people with big families. Often grandpa and grandma lived in part of the house, so you might sell the young people some Ton-A-Lax and then go to the other side of the house and sell the old folks some. They all had so many relatives, they would sometimes send you to them, and often the relatives would buy from you too.

Because the medicine was so new in the area, we had nobody to recommend it, or no letters asking for more. It wasn't very long before the many cards and letters came.

Book Fourteen: The Derby

When the second Wednesday in August came, Irene and I were staying at the local hotel in New Hamburg, ready for the famous Canadian Pacing Derby. I had been there the year before for my first time. I saw Harold Wellwood drive the world's champion, Blue Again. He won the derby and broke the track record twice that day, pacing a mile in 2.04 1/2. Blue Again had established a world's record for a mile and a quarter out in California earlier that year while defeating the best pacers around. Another good horse, The Count B—a roan gelding driven by Cliff Chapman—had won the prestigious derby the two previous years, but couldn't catch the mighty Blue Again in 1946. These two great racehorses were going to be racing in the derby, along with other fine horses from Canada and the U.S.A., and Irene and I would be there early to watch them warm up. Irene had never been around horses or been on a farm growing up, but with me having the trick horse, then going to the races and seeing Son's horse, she was starting to like them.

We were both looking forward to the Derby; it was an exciting time for us. The secretary for the Derby was a local insurance agent named Earl Katzenmier; everybody called him Katzy. He had lived in New York for a time and was a terrific salesman. He sold that Derby and made it into the greatest one-day harness event in North America. There was the Derby, McCall Derby Day Pacing Stake, Junior Derby Trial, and the prestigious F.S. Scott Memorial Trot, partly sponsored by the Scott-Mchale Shoe Co. There would be some 8000 people there from all over. There was mutual wagering and the old bookie system as well. The infield would be filled with cars. The grandstand and the sloping grounds between the barns and the grandstand were filled with people from all walks of life. They mingled, wagered, and watched the races, in an atmosphere seldom matched anywhere else. The big maple trees swayed ever so gently in the warm summer breeze, bringing comfort to those on the grassy slope. There was a big fountain in the middle of this shaded area, where the water trickled down over the rocks in a refreshing friendly sound. Inside the arena that stood just behind the trees, the local ladies served up wonderful home-cooked meals, with a big assortment of pies.

Irene and I had been in town a day or two, selling medicine around the countryside. We were over to the fairgrounds, seeing some of the horses working out and watching as they shipped in and unloaded. That year The Count B, driven as usual by the legendary Cliff Chapman, won the derby for the third time, defeating the famous Blue Again and several other high-class pacers. We had a wonderful day at the races, then in another day or two sold out our Ton-A-Lax around the area and moved on to farther fields.

Irene and I kept moving around, peddling our medicine, having a pretty good time, but not saving any money. Just living and learning, and we sure had a lot to learn. It was about this time that we took up fishing. We got a couple of fishing rods and a bit of tackle and used to get up at the crack of dawn and go try to catch a fish in a nearby stream. If we were at Daddy's place, we would clean the fish, Mary cooked them, and everybody enjoyed the catch of the day. If we were up at Son and Irene's, she would cook the fish.

Willie

So, between selling Ton-A-Lax, driving around the country roads, going to the races, fishing, and making love, we seemed to put the time in. One evening in the fall, we pulled into the Queen's Hotel in Hanover to get a room for the night. The fellow that checked us in had been a traveller at the Seldon House and knew us both. He got into the hotel business by marring the owner, a good-looking widow. He wanted Irene to come and work in the dining room there. She would get paid, have a room and meals, and when I came into town I could stay there free on the weekends. The weather was starting to get cold and Irene liked the idea. She would have a warm place, and she didn't mind the work. By now she might have been getting tired of doing nothing but driving the car around.

She seemed to like the work at the hotel and the bit of money that it brought her, and I kept selling the medicine. Finding someone to buy that home-cooked conglomeration of medicinal ingredients was, at times, difficult, but I always managed to put gas in the old car and keep going. I missed having my sweetheart with me, but I felt good about her being there, doing what she liked doing.

One time when I came back to the hotel, Irene told me she was pregnant. I was going to be a daddy. Well, I hadn't planned on starting to raise a family just yet, but things would work out somehow.

It was getting into December, not so long before Christmas, when I got back to the hotel one Friday evening and found Irene concerned that she was going to have a miscarriage. She quit her job at the hotel and we went to Owen Sound, so that she could go to her own doctor. We stayed with her parents; by this time we were back on friendly terms with them, although Irene's old boyfriend still came around once in a while. Her doctor soon admitted her to the hospital, but he couldn't save our baby.

We went on staying there at her mother's place. Irene needed some time to rest up and get over the trauma of losing her first child. We spent Christmas with her family. Irene had spent some of her hard-earned wages to buy me a nice gold ring for Christmas. After Christmas, I kept selling medicine among the Mennonite people around Wellington and Waterloo counties. By now we were getting some good feedback from our customers, people were being helped with the Ton-A-Lax, letters were starting to come in, and word of mouth was positive.

I had sold ten bottles to a man near Elmira in the summer. He had been diagnosed as having arthritis, walked with a limp for some years. His name was Henry Martin. He was a prominent farmer who had a herd of Holstein dairy cattle. He and his wife also attended the big Waterloo market on Saturdays and sold poultry, summer sausage, eggs, and just about anything else that farmers sell at a market. He was well known and respected all over the area, especially among the Mennonites. This man was improving every day. His arthritis was better than it had been in years. He quit taking anything the doctor had given him and drank Ton-A-Lax, out of the bottle, three times a day. He had written for more, saying in the letter how the medicine was helping him.

Early in the New Year, I made arrangements with this fellow and his wife to stay at their place when I came down every week with a load of medicine. They had four children, two still going to public school. I paid them $1.00 a day for room and board. The meals were great. The breakfast table was laden each morning with sausage, potatoes, eggs, bread, and homemade coffeecake, washed down with good coffee. Supper was

Willie

like something you would get at a famous German restaurant, including a wonderful dessert. My room had a double bed with a big, thick feather tick for a mattress with homemade quilts on it. The room was cold, but with all of these covers, I was comfortable.

Every week when I would arrive, usually in the afternoon, Henry would have some new customers for me. All I had to do was go and deliver it to them. Sometimes half my week's medicine was gone the first day. Of course I had to go out selling the rest, finding new customers and reselling to those who had bought it earlier. It was a very cold winter; 20 below zero was common that year. There were huge piles of snow all over the place. A couple of times I borrowed a horse and cutter and delivered medicine on roads that weren't open for cars. It was a wonderful experience for me, living with this Mennonite family. Of course, these were the more modern ones. They had electricity, telephone, cars, and tractors, though the women wore the bonnets and the old-fashioned dresses.

Mennonites are of German descent, mostly. Some are Russian and German. But they speak German; the children speak German until they go to school, then they learn English. The little boys are dressed in plain, dark clothes and the little girls in the homemade dresses and their hair done up in braids. Their dresses are long and they wear cotton stockings and black shoes.

My routine that winter was kiss Irene good-bye on Monday morning, drive 50 miles to Daddy's place to pick up the case of Ton-A-Lax, then drive another 50 miles to Elmira. I would spend most of the week there and then drive back to Irene at her mother's place about Friday. We didn't pay board at her mother's place, but we bought groceries and paid our way, treating them the best we knew how. They didn't have a car, so when I was in town we could take them places they wanted to go.

The winter went by and I met some real nice people, and learned quite a few things about the Mennonites and their way of life. I learned that there are several different sects of them. Some drive cars, trucks, and tractors and have electricity and telephones, even radios. Although the bishops don't encourage them to have radios, some hide them. Other sects drive horses, but will ride with neighbours in their cars. Some will not ride in a car, but will ride in a bus or train. Some have a buggy with a fancy arched axle, but most use a straight-axle buggy. Most wear an overhead rein check and breast collar on the buggy horses. But some only use collars and side checks on them. I soon got to know these different sects and could easily refer to names within certain sects, people that they knew, and relatives. This was valuable in doing business with them.

For the most part, I found them wonderful people to deal with, although there were always those who were unfriendly and didn't trust strangers. And while some of them would tell of relatives and friends that might be interested in our medicine, others wouldn't.

I had an interesting experience with one lady. She got five bottles of Ton-A-Lax ($5.00) from me in the fall, when she was apparently suffering from sciatica. When she bought the medicine, she was sitting by the kitchen stove with a blanket wrapped around her, keeping warm, hardly able to walk. Later on in the winter, I went to see her to find out how she was getting along, and she wasn't home. She was at a quilting at a neighbour's house. That sounded very good to me, so I drove over to the neighbour's place to see her. The man of the place was just coming in from the barn; he said his name was John Martin. I noticed a slight limp in his walk. I asked the man if this lady was there, and he said

Willie

she was, and about a dozen more Mennonite quilters. I was expecting a great testimony from this lady who was now running around to quiltings. The last time I saw her, she was sitting in that chair by the stove and could hardly move—what a great advertisement she would be! Those ladies would probably all want to buy some Ton-A-Lax; I was hoping I had enough to go around.

The man followed me into the house, where these ladies were sitting around a giant quilt there in the big kitchen. I recognised the lady and reminded her who I was and that I was so happy to see her getting around so well. As I proudly stood there, holding up a bottle of this great wonder medicine in my hand so everyone could see it, I asked her, "Do you think this medicine helped you?" Of course, I was expecting a positive answer. The women kept on working and, without looking up from her work, this lady said in an off-handed voice, "Oh, I probably would have got better anyway."

Everyone laughed and kept right on sewing that damn quilt I couldn't have *given* them a bottle of that stuff for nothing. I was very disappointed, but there was really nothing much I could say. When the man came outside with me, I started talking to him about his condition. He said he had been going to the doctor and taking some drugs for the problem. He explained that it bothered him in the heel, and with other things he said, I told the man that he had arthritis, and that he should start taking this medicine right away. He said that the doctor told him that it wasn't arthritis. Well, I couldn't persuade the man to take the medicine; that neighbour lady had made sure of that.

However, in spite of the little setbacks now and then, I was doing okay; it was a way of making a living. I liked it better than working at the hotel, and it had that silly army beat by a mile. Still, we seemed to spend all I could

Willie Kell

earn, which wasn't very much after I took my expenses out. But we managed to get through the winter of 47/48. Irene went with me to stay at my boarding place a few times and seemed to enjoy the change, although she was having a good rest at her mother's house for most of that winter. It was great to be with her even on weekends, I loved her so much.

When early April came, we got a furnished apartment on the outskirts of Hanover. Actually, it was two rooms in the upstairs of a house. But we were comfortable, and the people that owned the place seemed nice. They lived downstairs, but their bedroom was upstairs, beside ours. We paid $20.00 a month for the place. Soon Irene got a job working at the dry cleaners on Main Street; she seemed to like the work and a little extra money. Living there, we were closer to Daddy's place and it was not as far to drive to get the medicine.

One day Daddy got me a prospect to sell my old Chevy. I sold it for $400.00. That was a pretty good deal; I drove it all over the country, selling Ton-A-Lax, and had bought it the year before for $260.00. I bought a 1932 Chevy half-ton pickup for $125.00 from Henry Martin, the man I boarded with. I drove that old truck around for about a month, then traded it for a 1938 Chevy car. That car was in tough shape, but it was a lot newer. I fixed it up and drove it selling medicine, hoping to find a buyer for it.

Willie

Book Fifteen: God Bless Our Borrowed Tent

It wasn't very long and Irene got laid off at the cleaners; I really don't know why. Then, one time when I came home from the road, she told me that while the lady of the house had gone away overnight, and she was there all alone with the landlord in the house—her sleeping in one room and him in the room next—the son of a bitch had asked Irene to come and get in bed with him. Thank goodness she didn't! I didn't say anything, and we didn't tell the lady; why ruin their life, or mess her up? We soon gave up the apartment; we hadn't planned on staying there very long anyway. Daddy had kept telling us that we should save our money, and how he had lived in a tent on the road, why didn't we try that? So we borrowed his tent.

It was sometime past the middle of May when Irene and I headed out for the Stayner area. I had been selling Ton-A-Lax for over a year by this time. We were getting to be road people, getting to know the game. We had the 38 Chevy all shined up, the tent in the trunk, and a case of Ton-A-Lax on board. Daddy had given us instructions on how to set up the tent. I had slept on it for two years when I lived with Mary and him, but had never seen it when it was up. Now I was going to be sleeping in it with my beautiful Irene. Daddy told us how to make a bed out of cedar boughs, laying them on the ground; "They'll keep the dampness from going through your body," he told us. We had lots of blankets; it was going to be fun living in the tent.

Willie Kell

We went to the place where the old log house had been, where Daddy and Mary had lived, where their little girl Ben was born, where Jimmy Sharpe was arrested, down that lonesome side road. The old log house was gone; it had been moved away and made into a fancy cottage for someone at Wasaga Beach. The same man still owned the place, though. He lived on a farm down the road a half mile. He said he would be glad to have us camp there. There was a good well for water, and there'd be no charge, stay as long as we liked, he told us. He came over, showed us how to drop the pail down the well with a rope, give it a flip, and draw up a pail of water. We set up the tent just inside the gate at the road. It was a nice tent, 12 feet square, with a veranda out front, a cottage roof, and a pole in the center to hold the roof up. We bought a little basin and a mirror at the hardware store, hung them on that center pole so we could look at ourselves when we washed our faces. We put the cedar boughs on the floor and made our bed, and built a fireplace not far from the tent out of some old bricks and stones from the foundation of the house. There was the old backhouse still there, so we just about had all the comforts of home. There was even a nice patch of rhubarb growing along the cedar rail fence; Irene cooked some up for dessert. We made a nice supper over the fire and were hungry after the big day. I guess we just about had everything anyone could ever want.

We bought a lantern and hung it on a veranda pole after dark and had the campfire blazing away until bedtime. Then we lay down on those cedar boughs and blankets, cuddled warm in each other's arms, and slept until morning. To say that we were roughing it would be somewhat of an understatement, We found out that May is still pretty cold for living in a tent in that part of

Willie

Canada, but it seemed to us that we had the whole world, we had each other, we were happy.

The next morning, while looking around where the log house had been, we found an old bed-spring, just what we needed. It was a big improvement over the cedar boughs. And we found a grate out of an oven, to set the frying pan on, for cooking on the open fire. Our home was beginning to resemble the Taj Mahal more all the time.

After we washed the breakfast dishes, did our morning chores, and I shaved my few whiskers off, we were ready to start out on the road and sell some medicine. We would try a new territory; the familiar places had been picked clean. We found out that it was much more difficult to sell medicine around that area than it was among the Mennonite people. We would sell five bottles, two bottles, and even one at a time, unlike selling perhaps two dozen to one person among the Mennonites of Waterloo County. It was hard to find someone who would try ten bottles.

The first or second day in that part of the country we saw a nice little shorthaired terrier dog. Irene fell in love with this little chestnut-coloured dog with four white legs, so I traded three bottles of Ton-A-Lax for her. Her name was Trix. The first morning we had that dog, she ran away across the fields, and Irene was broken-hearted, but by calling her and waiting for a few hours, she finally came back. That little dog was part of our family for the next several years, until she got old and sick, and we had to have her put down.

When we finally sold the 72 bottles, we headed out for Daddy's place and got some more. We came around to see Irene's parents, stayed overnight with them. Her mother and young David decided to come with us and spend a week camping. A week for them seemed a long

Willie Kell

time, though, and they were happy to get out of the tent and get back home. I guess we spent about 6 weeks in that tent altogether, struggling along, trying to coax some money out of those folks in that area. The weather was gradually getting warmer and we had a wonderful time. We didn't earn very much money, but the living was easy, and it didn't cost much.

It was while we lived in the tent that Dad died, in June 1948. He was 84, would have been 85 on August 3rd. For a fellow who thought he wouldn't live long, he did pretty good. He was sitting outside on a Sunday afternoon, walked in the house, went upstairs, laid on the bed, and died. I knew I'd miss that old man; I had been close to him.

He always said he would leave the house and whatever he had to Mammy, and when she was through with it, she was to give it to me. After the funeral, Irene and I drove Mammy home, and there was the old stick Dad had cut from a limb that he used for a cane. It was leaning by the kitchen door where he had left it. I asked her if I could have it, and she said I could. Well, that old cane is something that I have kept and treasured, but it's all I ever got, or wanted. After he died, her folks came around like vultures, and we never did bother the old lady after that. I never was inclined to wait on a dead man's shoes.

After about six weeks in the tent, Mary decided that she wanted it back. Although they hadn't used it in over ten years, she wanted it now; she was going to put it up in the yard on the little farm and let the girls play in it. Irene and I would have to move out of our little home. Oh, well—we were getting kind of tired of it anyway. It was time for a change, and back to staying at hotels and with relatives. Taking a bath was much easier in a hotel—although it was kind of a nice job, washing

Willie

Irene's back as she stood naked beside the tent, her long, blonde hair hanging down on her shoulders.

We never lived in that tent again, and I don't know if anyone else ever did either. They had it up in the yard at their little farm for only a week or so and a couple of cows got in the thing and ripped a hole in it.

It was about this time that Daddy bought a beautiful, like-new '32 Pontiac from a farmer a few miles from his place. He bought it cheap and traded it the next day for a 1929 Model A Ford, and got a couple of hundred dollars more than he gave for the Pontiac. The man he had bought the Pontiac from was looking for a newer car. Daddy told me about the man, and I went to him and sold him my '38 Chevy for $700.00 cash. Just what I had been waiting for; I had put about $300.00 into that car. That $700.00 was more money than I ever had before.

I bought the Model A Ford coach from Daddy for $112.00. We picked up a case of medicine and headed down to the Amish country around a little place called Wellesley. There was a nice old hotel on the main street, the Queen's Hotel, and the owner's name was Joe. His sister Mary ran the dining room. The food was great; some good German cooking happened in that kitchen. Mary would make us a lovely lunch to take with us on the road for our noon meal. We had a real nice room, and the bathroom was just across the hall. It cost us $1.50 a night for the room and the dinner was about 75 cents. We covered a territory that reached all over the Amish country, up into Perth County. The county where old John Kell cleared the land and made a home, where his children and grandchildren were born. We sold medicine to the Amish people within 10 miles of John's old farm.

Willie Kell

The Amish are something like the Mennonites. They speak German; the men start growing a beard when they get married, and their hair hangs down over their ears, with bangs in front. They wear wide-brimmed black hats, like the Mennonites. Even the little boys wear these nice hats. Perhaps they're not quite as well-disciplined as the Mennonite people; it is quite common for them to drink and smoke, something that you would hardly see among the Mennonites. Most of the Amish I dealt with drove a horse and buggy and used horses to work the land. I found them honest, hard-working people. This Amish country soon became the second-best territory that we had for selling medicine.

It was getting close to my 22nd birthday, and perhaps even more important, it was getting close to Derby Day at New Hamburg. We were starting to get excited about the races. We kept working around the Amish country and over close to New Hamburg, struggling along. We generally spent about seven or eight hours a day on the road. Irene liked to drive, and she did most of it. By now we had traded the Model A Ford for another '31 Chevy two door. Things were going along pretty good. Or at least *I* thought they were.

One morning in the hotel there at Wellesley, we were just getting out of bed and Irene started crying. When I asked her what was wrong, she said she would like to have a house and settle down. She was tired of living like a gypsy. Well, now, I couldn't have my darling crying like that, so I said that we'd buy a house. Why, we must have had all of $300.00; we would start looking for a nice little place in the country. Why not right there in Perth County, where my great-grandfather John Kell lived, where Dad and Maw and Daddy and his siblings were born?

Willie

Our Tent

Irene and Me

Book Sixteen: This Old House

It was just a day or two later that we were selling medicine in the Amish district around Millbank and Poole. They were all gravel roads at that time. We drove down one of these roads and saw an old frame house on a corner lot in a little hamlet. The place was empty, and there was grass and weeds growing up around it. There were only three other houses and a couple of small barns in the neighbourhood. We inquired about the empty place and learned that the people that owned it lived in one of the houses there. When we knocked at the door, a grey-haired Amish lady answered. She told us we would have to talk to her husband, when he got home from work. She asked us to come back that evening.

After supper we came back to see the man. He was a little Amish man with a dark grey beard and wearing little round, thick glasses. His clothes were the traditional clothes of the old-order Amish sect: blue cotton shirt, a vest, and the black barn-door pants. They don't use buttons; they fasten their clothes with hooks and eyes. He said his name was Johnny Bellar, and his wife's name was Nancy. They had an adopted daughter about 11 years old; they called her Ruby.

He said they would sell the old place for $400.00. He told me that the house needed a lot of repairs. Although it was old, it had never been finished. It had been owned and lived in by an old maid by the name of Liza Forrest.

The man invited us to walk up and have a look at the old place. It was less than a city block up the road.

Willie

Nancy and the girl came along. The little house sat on 3/4 of an acre of land. There was no well; we would have to fetch our water from the neighbour's pump with a pail. Just like back at Maw's farm. We went in through the woodshed and opened a pine door into a large room. There were two smaller rooms, divided by wide pine boards covered with wallpaper. A door at the bottom of the stairs in the large room led to the second floor, where there were two rather small bedrooms and another room that had never been finished. The old house had a musty smell and there were cobwebs hanging in corners. There was a cellar under the house, but every pane of glass had fallen out of those cellar windows and the stone cellar wall had caved in by an outside door. Of course, there was no electricity, no, not even a back house, but Johnny and Nancy had a chemical toilet that Johnny had made. In spite of all the faults of this old place and the enormous amount of work there would be to fixing it up, there was still something intriguing about it that Irene and I both liked. We wanted it, it was a challenge, and the price was right!

We walked back to Johnny and Nancy's place, they made us some tea, and Nancy insisted we try a piece of homemade pie she had baked that day. I offered the man $350.00 for the place, he said he would take $375.00, and we made a deal. I gave him a $50.00 bill I happened to have in my pocket and told him we would pay the rest when we drew up the deed. There was no hurry he said. The taxes were $10.00 a year, and he would pay them when they came due in late fall.

Irene and I drove back to the little hotel down the road. We were so happy—we had bought our first house! I had just turned 22 a few days before and Irene was 19. It was no mansion, but we had the money to pay for it, so we wouldn't have a mortgage.

Willie Kell

The next day was Derby Day at New Hamburg. Irene and I got up, had breakfast at the hotel, and went to the races. We were more excited about buying the old house than about the races.

It was a beautiful day; the warm August sun beat down on the tall maple shade trees that stood on the grassy knoll between the grandstand and the horse barns. The sounds of the large crowd mingled with the pounding rhythm of the horses' hooves out on the racetrack, as the pacers and trotters warmed up for the day's events. The barking of the operators of the hot dog and hamburger stands, urging people to come and get one, seemed to make the place come alive with a special feeling that made you feel happy to be there.

The great roan gelding, The Count B, was there to try and win the Derby again, but he would have his work cut out for him, because there were several classy pacers in the field. The supporting card was also full of good horses. Irene and I had our dinner in the arena. The meals were always so good. We sat just across the table from the famous Johnny Chapman, who was to drive The Count B that day. He had been racing him at the tracks in New York and had brought him back for the Derby. The purse for the Derby was $5000.00, more than he'd race for in the U.S.A. Those times, before Prime Minister Trudeau, the Canadian dollar was a real dollar, at times more valuable than its American counterpart.

During the afternoon, while Irene and I were walking along on the shady knoll, we saw our old boss from the Seldon House, Pop Alles. He was looking into the crowd with his hand above his eyes as if he was searching for someone. He didn't see us until I put my hand on his shoulder and asked who he was looking for.

Willie

"YOU!" he said. "We drove a hundred miles, hoping to find you here at the races."

He said that he would like me to come back to the hotel for a couple of months and take Jack's place. Jack, his son, had come down with bad nerves and was ordered by the doctor to take some time off. I told him that I hadn't thought of working at a hotel, that we had just bought a house the day before. Pop said that he and Mama were with Wes Litt and his wife, at their car parked in the infield. He pointed to a light-coloured Cadillac and said he would be there until after the races. He told me to think it over and come and let him know. He would pay me $40.00 a week and my board. Irene could stay at the hotel weekends, after the tourist season. That was a pretty good deal.

Irene and I talked it over and decided that we would take a couple of months off the road and go back to the hotel. The road could use a rest.

The Derby was won again by The Count B for an unprecedented fourth time. What a wonderful horse! But he came to a sad and tragic end a year or two later. They were training him on the road and he was hit and killed by a car. He was buried in the infield at New Hamburg, and they put up a monument to his memory above his grave. Johnny Chapman became one of the best drivers in America, but he died a young man. That same day that The Count B won his fourth Derby, the prestigious F.S. Scott Memorial Trot was won by a famous trotter, bred, trained, and driven by The Honourable Earl Rowe, who would later become the Lieutenant Governor of Ontario.

After the races, Irene and I headed across the infield to Wes Litt's Cadillac, to see Pop. I remembered Wes Litt. He had been a friend of Pop and Mama Alles for years. One time when he had stayed at the Seldon House, I was working nights as usual and Wes had an

Willie Kell

early call. He had to be back at his hotel at Stratford in the morning. I got him up and made him breakfast before he left. We talked a little, and he told me that he wouldn't take me away from Pop, but if I ever needed a job, I could work for him anytime. I had often heard them talking of how successful he had been, with the hotel and his racehorses.

When we got to the car, they were waiting for us. They had drinks and food and they offered some to Irene and I. Wes remembered me and introduced me to his beautiful wife, Nora, and I introduced them to Irene. We told Pop and Mama that we would see them at the hotel in a couple of days, said our good-byes, and left for our hotel out at Wellesley.

When we got to the Seldon House a couple of days later, we found that most of the staff was still there, including Jimmy Yemon and his horny blonde wife. And although we had been away for a year and a half, I hadn't forgotten the routine. Irene and Trix, her little dog, stayed at her parent's house during the week. Irene had the car and could take her mother shopping, go visit her girlfriends, and she and I would sometimes drive out to the farm and visit Son and Irene. We used to go fishing and take our catch to Mom's or bring the fish back to the hotel and Jimmy would cook them. One day Irene caught a nice Northern Pike; Jimmy cooked it and we all had a good feed of fish.

As the summer changed to autumn and the October leaves turned red and brown, Irene and I were thinking about our home down the road a hundred miles or more in that little hamlet. It was just about the time of our second anniversary when we loaded the few things we had kept in storage on Son's small trailer and headed out for our new old house down in the Amish country of

Willie

Perth County, about 14 miles south from Old John Kell's homestead farm where Dad was born.

Johnny and Nancy Bellar said that we would be welcome to stay at their house for a few days while we cleaned the old place up. Nancy even came and helped us. They had ladders and things that we didn't have, and every kind of tool, wrench, and shovel that was ever invented. We were welcome to borrow anything they had.

I bought a nice second-hand cookstove. It had a reservoir and a warming closet and it burnt either coal or wood. We ordered some coal, we set up our bit of furniture and put a rug on the floor that we'd had in our first apartment. We had Irene's cedar chest by the front window, and set some ornaments on it to make the place look like home. We had our pullout couch, a little table, and a few chairs the folks at the hotel had given us when we got married. Then we bought a small table to set the washbasin on; there was a shelf underneath for the water pail. We still had the little mirror, the basin, and the coal-oil lantern we had used in the tent. There were two old-fashioned windows in that big room. We got some curtains and a couple of blinds to hang on them. In just a few days that little place was starting to look like home, and we were proud of it. Why, it was only a few months before that we were living in a borrowed tent.

I traded a few bottles of Ton-A-Lax for a real nice Aladdin coal oil lamp and it shone a wonderful light until we had the electricity installed. We lived in that one big room and slept on the pullout couch all that first winter; it was quite comfortable, with the warm fire burning.

There were always things to do in my spare time, and Irene was a great help. I bought glass and putty and put all the cellar windows in and hired a man to fix the cellar wall. It looked like new again. I paid him $20.00,

Willie Kell

he worked at it for 2 days, and I helped him. Johnny made a new cellar door and we put in cement steps going down from the outside. There was a door to the cellar from the inside as well, with steps going down.

We were happy in our little home. We paid Johnny the balance of the $375.00 and had a deed to the place. We had been married just a little more than two years.

Although I sold Ton-A-Lax close by in the Amish country around there, some would come by with a horse and buggy and get it from time to time. My best customers were still the Mennonite people in Waterloo and Wellington counties. The heart of the Mennonite country was less than 25 miles away, and I spent a lot of time up there. We were getting good results by this time, and a quite a few repeat orders. Of course, there were always new customers to find and new challenges to face.

People up there had been telling me to go and see John Martin, that he walked with a cane; then, go see John Martin, he walks with *two* canes. I told these people that I was to see him the winter before and that he didn't seem interested in our Ton-A-Lax; I told them about those ladies at that quilting, laughing about our Ton-A-Lax. Finally they said, "Go and see John Martin. He's in bed and has two neighbours come in each night to turn him in bed. He is in bad shape with arthritis."

It wasn't long after that we got a letter from his wife; John wasn't able to write. She asked us to bring some Ton-A-Lax to John. It was in December that I knocked on their door. Mrs. Martin came and showed me to the bedroom just off the big kitchen, where John lay helpless. They certainly remembered me, and it wasn't very difficult to sell them—I should say, deliver them—three dozen bottles of Ton-A-Lax. They had tried about everything else, doctors, chiropractors, and very expensive medicines, but he just kept on getting worse.

Willie

I found them to be wonderful people. Mrs. Martin stood at the foot of John's bed; you could see such love and caring in her eyes. I have always thought that she was about as close to a saint as anyone I have ever met. I told them I couldn't promise anything, but that I believed the medicine would help him. I said he might start noticing a little improvement in about a month. If he did, and kept on with it, taking large doses 3 or 4 times a day, with God's help, he could be walking by spring. They didn't believe he would walk by spring, perhaps ever walk again. Mrs. Martin shook her head when I mentioned it. I wished them well, said that I would ask God's blessing, and told them good-bye.

Irene and I spent that Christmas with her parents and David. We told them all about our little place. They mentioned that they would like a home in the country, sometime.

After Christmas, we kept busy. I had to drive 45 miles to Daddy's place to get the medicine, then go out and sell it all around those country roads. Then it seemed there was always something to do around that old house. If I didn't have money to spend on it, I would get a pencil and paper and draw pictures and plans of what I wanted to do to fix the place up, when I did get the money. Irene was learning to cook. Nancy kept giving her those good Amish recipes of hers. She spent a lot of time with Nancy when I was on the road. The Bellars had no electricity, telephone, or bathroom; the old-order Amish don't have those things. Johnny had sold his horse and buggy, so they had no transportation. If they wanted to go anyplace, we took them in the car. If they needed something from the store, we got it for them. Of course, they had relatives with cars and they took them places too. Sometimes they would take trips to Indiana to their relatives there.

Willie Kell

One evening when I got home off the road, our next-door neighbour came with a phone number for me to call. I recognised the number right away; it was the Seldon House in Owen Sound. I went to the neighbours to make the call, and it was Pop Alles. He said he would like me to come back to the hotel, and talked of giving me an interest in the business if I would. He suggested I think it over for a day or two and call him with my decision. The next evening I called him from town, told him I was happy with my life and wasn't interested in going back to the hotel.

Most of our neighbours seemed friendly. There was a couple that lived in the little hamlet, several years older than us, but we sometimes went to their place and played cards. That lady used to get a little jealous of Irene; she thought her husband was taking a shine to her. He used to stop and visit her on his way home from work. He was often there when I would get home off the road.

Sometimes we went with them to another neighbour's house, where they had homemade cider and wine. It only took Irene and I a couple of times to learn what a potent kick that stuff had. We used to visit Johnny and Nancy, and they visited us. We went back and forth for meals and played a game called Lost Heir. Although I never got a great kick out of playing cards and games, Irene did, and we often went to card-game gatherings in the neighbourhood.

We also went to a couple of dances with neighbours. One night at a dance, Irene found a partner and spent almost the whole evening with him. I was very disappointed with her, and when we got home, I told her so. She said she was just having fun, and because I wasn't much of a dancer, she needed to kick up her heels. I forgave her, as usual.

Willie

It was early the next spring when her parents sold their little home in Owen Sound for $1700.00. They wrote and asked me to try and find them something in the country, where Paw could keep a couple of pigs and some chickens. I knew of just such a property. It was just down the road from Daddy's place, not far from the village of Clifford. I went and got Paw and took him to the place. If he liked it, I'd make a deal for it. He wasn't good at dealing.

It was a good-sized frame house, with electricity. A little barn and hen-house, a good well and it sat on a nice, fenced, quarter acre of land, with a couple of shade trees along the front. It was on a country gravel road, but there were neighbours close by and the church and school was within a half mile. Young David would be starting into grade 1 that September.

Paw wanted the place, and I knew I could buy it cheap—the people were anxious to sell. I bought it, along with a nice brown and white cow and a good brood sow, the whole package for $675.00. They could have possession in 6 weeks. They had to move out of their other house right away, so they came, brought all their belongings, and moved in with us.

Irene and I cleaned up the bedrooms upstairs, put some wallpaper on and a bit of paint, so they would have a place to sleep. It felt nice to be able to return the favour. For how many times had Irene and I stayed at their place when we didn't have a home?

Irene's father did some fixing around our place during the six weeks they were there. They still had some money burning a hole in their pockets, about $750.00 more than they needed to pay for the little place. They wanted to buy my car. At the time, I had a 1929 Model A Ford roadster. Never being one to turn down a deal, I sold it to him for $150.00 and taught him to drive

Willie Kell

it while they lived with us. He got his license and was about as happy as I had ever remembered seeing him.

We helped them move into their new house, and they were settled in just in time to plant a garden in late May. Paw tried to get used to milking that cow, but he never did. It wasn't long until he sold her, but kept the sow and sold several litters from her.

It had been a busy time around our little house, with all the extra company. But we got along fine. I went on selling medicine and kept the groceries on the table. It felt good to be able to help Irene's folks. Maybe they would have what they wanted, with that place in the country and a car to drive. Maybe they would get to like me after all. Before they sold their place in Owen Sound, they had a falling-out with Irene's old sailor boyfriend, who was married by that time. He claimed they owed him money. It was around the same time he got into trouble, something to do with a young girl.

We would often see Irene's parents; they only lived about a half-mile from Daddy. So when I went up for a case of Ton-A-Lax, Irene would mostly go with me and stay at her mom's place while I went to Daddy's. Sometimes they would drive down to our place on a Sunday and have dinner with us, now that they had a car. Paw did some carpenter work for the neighbours, and he started selling Raleigh's products. But life was always a struggle for that man. He was becoming very deaf as time went on, and trying to make a living was never easy for him at the best of times.

My business was still pretty good, but it would slow down some in the late spring. After working in the Mennonite country all winter, by spring you started to run out of customers—they'd be all stocked up.

Remember John Martin, the fellow who couldn't turn himself in bed in December? Well, by early spring, he could walk out to the barn with a cane. By late

Willie

spring, he didn't use a cane at all, and never did again. He continued taking the medicine for years.

The last time I was at their place, it was a cold, wet day in the fall. John was in town with the team and wagon. Mrs. Martin bought a supply of Ton-A-Lax for her and John that day. Yes, she had started taking it too. Word spread all over that country about John Martin and the help he got from taking Ton-A-Lax. That sister-in-law of his did me a big favour that time at the infamous quilting. So many people bought our medicine because of John Martin.

During that summer, I saved enough money to have the electricity installed in our old house. It was great to just flick a switch and, like magic, a light would come on. We moved our kitchen to the other side of the house, ripped out a partition and made it into one bigger room. Then we had two rooms downstairs, a good-sized eat-in kitchen and a nice big living room. We put the cookstove in the kitchen and got a nice coal heater for the front room. We bought a second-hand washing machine, electric stove, refrigerator, and a little radio. By that time we had a 1934 Dodge car. So we were slowly progressing.

Irene and her mom kept saying it was time we started having a family. I didn't think there was a big hurry; I wanted to get that old house fixed up decent before we had children. Another thing that concerned me was that we were married so young, especially Irene. And there were times she acted a bit frivolous around men. I wanted to make sure that, once we had children, we would stay together and try and raise them right. I didn't want to bring kids into the world to have their mother and daddy split up and leave them orphans with nobody to love them, like I had been raised. However, about every time we saw Irene's mom, she asked us when we were going to have kids. She'd say: "You're going to wait until you're too old." Irene was only 20, and I was 23; we weren't "too old." It had only been three years before that her mom kept telling her that I would keep her pregnant, then run off and leave her with a bunch of hungry kids. She must have changed her mind about me, but if she did, she didn't come out and say it.

We kept on fixing the place. Johnny made Irene some nice kitchen cupboards. I had dug a ditch across from the neighbour's place and put the water in on tap. Then I bought a second-hand electric hot water heater, and more magic—hot water on tap!

It was a few weeks after New Year's, and one night we had been out to a neighbour's house. We went with the people down the road, the jealous-wife couple. We had some of that homemade cider, and when the neighbour drove us home, he walked to the door with us. I had been rather suspicious of what might be going on between him and Irene, so was watching for signs. While I was turning on the lights, Irene was kissing the neighbour at the door.

When I confronted her with it, after the fellow left, she denied it. When she finally admitted it, she said that she was frustrated. She wanted a baby. She said she was sorry, she would never do anything like that again. It was just a day or two after that, a Sunday afternoon, we made passionate love on the couch. She told me not to be careful. I wasn't; she got pregnant! Maybe that would be the answer to our problem.

During that winter, when I had saved a little money, Johnny would come up with his ruler and measure whatever it was we wanted to fix or build. He would tell me what material we needed, I would get the things, and we would have something else done in the old house.

Willie

As the spring and summer went on, the baby was growing inside Irene. She had a wonderful doctor, old Dr. Tye; he had a practise in Milverton, about four miles away. She went for her regular visits; the old doctor's fee was $1.00. When the baby started kicking and moving, I used to put my hand softly on her bare belly and feel the tiny feet and hands reaching and stretching. We were getting excited about having a child. Both the doctor and Irene thought it would be a girl, so we prepared for a girl. Irene got a clothesbasket and fixed it up for a little bed. She bought diapers, sweaters, and all the things that a baby needs. We expected her to be born about mid-September. We would name her Susan Elizabeth. Irene liked Susan, and I wanted her named after the sister I didn't have an opportunity to grow up with.

It was through that summer that Irene's father had been feeling poorly. He had a pretty good local doctor, if you caught him when he was sober. Strangely, he was that very same doctor that we had the wild episode with some years before at the Seldon House, the one who mixed dope and whiskey and went crazy.

They finally X-rayed the old man and found that he had TB. Yes, he was a sick man, and the doctor arranged that he would be sent to Freeport Sanatorium, near Kitchener, on Monday, September 18th, just one day after his birthday. I was to go and get him and take him to the TB hospital.

It would be tough on her mother, 'cause they sure didn't have much and it would be a while until she could get help from the county. We would offer to bring her and David to our place, at least until she could afford to make it on her own. David could go to school from our house, it was just a mile up the road.

Willie Kell

Book Seventeen: Billy Was Born

While we sat talking on that Sunday afternoon, September 17th, 1950, about taking her father to the hospital the next day, Irene began to have labour pains—she was going to have the baby. I called the doctor, and he said to take her to Stratford hospital, and he would be there soon.

That evening, a little after suppertime, our baby was born. IT WAS A BOY! He weighed 5 lbs., 14 ozs. What a beautiful baby, bald as a bald eagle. When I got to hold that little fellow in my arms, something happened to me inside. I could hardly believe that Irene and me could bring that beautiful creature into the world, and God would breathe life into his tiny body.

I stayed at the hospital as long as they would let me. Irene was breastfeeding him. What a magical, wonderful thing had happened. Irene and her mom were right all along; it was time to have a family. On the way home from the hospital, driving along that 12 miles, I sang and hollered and thanked God for giving us that child.

The next morning I got up and drove 50 miles to get that poor man and take him to the sanatorium. They were happy when I told them about the baby being born, especially that it was born on his birthday. It was somebody else's birthday too; yes, Hank Williams was 27 years old that same day. He was at the very top of his career at the time. He had made his debut at the Grand Ole Opry a little more than a year before that, on June 11th, 1949, singing not one of his own songs, but an old Tin Pan Alley tune called "Lovesick Blues."

Willie

We loaded up the things Paw would need at the sanatorium, got Mom, Paw, and young David in the car, and we started out on that sad old journey, about 75 miles. After he was admitted, we stayed around for a little while, then we went to Stratford Hospital to see Irene and the new baby. We found everyone fine; Mom was excited about her first grandchild and couldn't wait to hold him in her arms. Looking back, it could have been a little scary going right from a tuberculosis hospital where folks are dying with TB to be with a day-old baby, but at the time we didn't think of it that way. Mom and David stayed overnight at our place, then I drove them home the next day.

After about ten days, Irene and the baby came home from the hospital. By that time, we had decided to call him Billy. His second name would be Paul; mine is Peter. Our initials would be the same—W.P.—and our second name would be borrowed from a biblical apostle. Nancy Bellar came up to see them right away. She was like a mother to Irene. She helped her with the baby and anything else she could do

We talked with Mom about coming to live with us for a while, and she agreed that it was the only thing she could do. So, in a week or two, I went and got her and young David and their things. By now they only had one pig left, and it was about half grown. I loaded that stinky porker in the car on the floor by the back seat, and we headed home—Mom, young David, and the pig. We kept that pig in Bellar's barn, fed it until it was big enough to butcher, then we had it made into sausage, hams, spareribs, and anything else you could make out of a pig. We ate lots of pork that winter; I guess you could say we lived high on the hog.

On Sundays, I would take Mom to see the old man; it was about 60 miles there and back. We all had to have several check-ups to make sure we didn't have TB, but

Willie Kell

thank God, none of the rest of us got it. Irene liked having her mother to help with the baby, and now she had two helpers. Young David went to school. He was an excellent scholar, wherever he went to school.

It was around the time Billy was born that I got myself into a very bad situation. I began to play the pinball machines in the poolrooms when I went to Elmira. This habit kept growing until it became quite a problem for me. I would buy a roll of nickels, throw them in that damn machine, and soon get another one to throw in.

When spring came, Irene's mom was getting anxious to move to her own home. She was getting an allowance by that time, and felt that she could make things go. As she became more independent financially, she got more difficult to get along with. She was certainly your basic mother-in-law. She always took Irene's side of any little argument or disagreement that would arise between us.

Finally she was ready to go back home and try it on her own. We took them and their belongings to the little home, and they got along fine. When she wanted to go see Paw, a neighbour would take her. She would always pay her share. She was a kind, generous lady, and I loved her dearly in spite of the hell she sometimes put me through. Irene's father spent the next eight years in that old sanatorium. They discovered that he was also suffering from diabetes and would need injections of insulin two or three times a day for the rest of his life. By now, hearing aids were not much good to him, he was almost totally deaf. Then they had to amputate one of his fingers. The man wasn't in very good shape, considering everything.

Willie

Book Eighteen: The Gambler

As the summer of 1951 wore on, my addiction to gambling became a real problem. Often I would go and sell $10.00 worth of Ton-A-Lax, drive back and dump the 10 bucks right into that fool pinball machine, then go get some more and do the same. I wasn't fixing the house, I wasn't paying my bills, I owed Daddy over $200.00 for medicine. We were eating good and getting along, but it was very difficult. Irene didn't ask any questions, didn't suspect a thing. I guess she was too busy with the baby or something. I had talked of quitting the road for a while, maybe I needed a change. I was getting into a rut, sure enough!

It wasn't long before Billy's first birthday that I went to see my old friend, Wes Litt, at the Windsor Hotel in Stratford. He had told me that I could work for him anytime. Well, this was as good a time as any other. I met Wes in the lobby of the hotel, and he was glad to see me. One of the clerks at the hotel wanted a couple of months off to take a trip to California. Well, I told him I just wanted to work for a couple of months. I figured I could forget those pinball machines in that time. The pay wasn't much, just $37.50 a week. Of course, there would be some tips, and I could have my meal at the hotel when I worked either morning or evenings.

I started to work at the hotel in a couple of days. It was a wonderful hotel, although it had just 50 guestrooms, the same as the Seldon House. The rooms were bigger, and quite a few had private baths. There

Willie Kell

were some sample rooms and meeting rooms, a lovely dining room, and a modern kitchen. Then there were the beverage rooms: a large men's room and a room for ladies and escorts, as was the regulation then. A couple of years later the liquor lounge was added.

Wes had a manager who ran the hotel under his watchful eyes. This manager didn't care a lot for me. He kind of resented Wes hiring me over his head and expounding on my great qualifications. He was nice when Wes was around, but became a bit abrupt when Wes went away, which was quite often.

Wes had a stable of racehorses in the States and was a partner with the almost legendary Harold Wellwood, who trained and drove them. Harold had several outside horses for different owners. They raced the horses mostly at the border tracks of New York and Michigan. Wes and his wife Nora would leave Stratford about Tuesday or Wednesday in their Cadillac and travel to wherever their horses were stabled in the States. They lived in their travel trailer at the tracks. They would often arrive back on Sunday afternoon; they had a nice apartment in the hotel.

Wes didn't have very much hair on his head, and always wore a light-coloured Stetson hat. When I first knew him, he smoked cigars, but he finally gave them up. Nora had been a schoolteacher before she was married, but she didn't teach Wes much about the English language. He only had a public school education, and seemed to enjoy using words like "ain't." One of his expressions was, "I ain't educated like you fellows." Well, he might not have gone to school much, but he sure enough was educated. He was a very astute businessman, but honest and fair. We became good friends and spent many hours talking. He told me so many wonderful stories, and as time went on, I learned to love him and his wife Nora.

Willie

He was raised on a small farm, an only child. He started trading horses or anything else when he was a boy. He bought his first racehorse for $150.00, a horse called Oliver Pete. He drove him up and down the country roads, and when he realised the horse had speed, he turned him over to his cousin Gid Litt. Gid was a great driver in his day. Oliver Pete won a string of races, then Wes sold him and bought his mother a new fur coat with part of the money.

His dealings eventually got him into the hotel business when, one day in the early 1930s, he bought the Bedford Hotel in the lakeshore town of Goderich. He bought the hotel and the seven stores that went with it, along with the finest house in Goderich. The price for the entire package was just $7500.00. The very next morning, he and Nora were in the hotel business. He didn't know how to run a cash register or anything else, but he soon learned. He learned a lot of other things as well. He learned how to deal with politicians.

When Mitch Hepburn was campaigning to become the Premier of Ontario in 1934, his campaign trail took him to Goderich. At that time, Huron, Perth, and Bruce counties were under the Canada Temperance Act and were all dry, including the town of Goderich. The city of Stratford was the only exception. Hepburn promised Wes that if he became Premier, Goderich would be a wet town and that Wes would be able to sell beer in the Bedford Hotel. Well, Mitch Hepburn won the election and became Premier in July 1934. When no word came to say that Wes could sell beer, he went to visit Hepburn at Queen's Park in Toronto. Hepburn gave him the go-ahead, and Wes was in the beer business. He later sold the Bedford and bought the Windsor in Stratford, and was on his way to becoming a wealthy man.

Gid Litt went on to drive the great racehorse Gratton Bars to a world's record for a half-mile race.

Willie Kell

He also won the Canadian Pacing Derby at New Hamburg twice. I was proud to meet this interesting fellow, when cousin Wes introduced him to me.

Things went along well at the Windsor, folks checking in, checking out, and I was meeting lots of interesting people. I really liked Wes and Nora's daughter, Marjorie. Marjorie was the bookkeeper, and we worked closely together; she was about four or five years younger than I.

After a few months, I started to work the night shift all the time. I liked it better. I was never very good at getting up before 6 in the morning, and if I did, I was never really awake until about 9. The evening shift was 3.30 PM until midnight. That was fine with me, because I have always been a night person. It gave me lots of time to spend with Irene and Billy and to work around home during the day. If we were having some fixing done on the house, I could spend the day helping Johnny Bellar. By this time we had the phone, so if Irene wanted to call me at work, she could. I called her every night and talked to her.

In the evening after the dinner hour, when the rush was over, I would have a little time to sit and talk with the hotel guests, people from all walks of life and from different countries. It was a good way to further my education. Although there were always interruptions, with people coming and going, the switchboard buzzing, reservations coming in from all over North America and Europe, and there wasn't much room for error. Being busy wasn't an excuse; it had to be done right. It would be very embarrassing if someone showed up for their room on a busy evening and you hadn't marked the reservation in the book, and had no room in the inn.

The two months that I was supposed to work at the hotel lasted four and a half years. When the other clerk came back after the two months, Wes asked me to stay

Willie

on for a while. I worked part-time in the beverage room, thought I should learn something about that part of the hotel business. Wes had visions of me becoming manager, but I didn't. It wasn't very long, I was back on the desk full time.

The manager that didn't like me was fired—not because he didn't like me, but because Wes didn't like him. We had a couple of different managers after that; they knew my status at the hotel, and I got the same pay as they did as time went on, so the managers really didn't manage me. It was a good position to be in.

It was just a few months before the very first Festival season opened, and Wes was looking for a new manager. I recommended a young fellow I had broke in to the hotel business at the Seldon House. Wes asked me to call him; he was working in a big hotel in Windsor, Ontario at the time. He came to see us and Wes hired Perry. It turned out real good for everybody. It was great to work with Perry again and we had a lot of fun. Then, one evening, Irene and I went to our favourite Chinese restaurant and this big, handsome Chinese waiter came to our table. It was our old friend, Jimmy Yemon. It seems he had lost everything gambling, and by then his horny blonde wife had left him. He was broke and looking for a chef job. We needed a good chef at the Windsor, so I told Wes about Jimmy and he was soon working there. Now Perry, Jimmy, and I were back together again.

Perry had just got into the swing of things when the reservations started coming in for the first season of the Stratford Shakespearean Festival. A local fellow we knew, his name was Tom Patterson, dreamed up the idea to have a theater in Stratford Ontario, like the one at Stratford-on-Avon in merry old England. The idea caught on like a barbecue at a boy's school. It was soon evident that we were about to have the most exciting thing that had perhaps ever happened in theatre in Canada, right there in Stratford.

By this time we had a real good television for Irene to keep her entertained; it would be company for her in the evenings when I wasn't there. We were the first ones to have TV out our way.

Our Billy had started to walk by the time he was ten months old. We put up a nice fence around the front of the place and a white ranch fence along the back of the lawn. It was a great place for him to play. The big lawn was well shaded by the large maple trees along the front. There were a couple of apple trees spreading their branches over the board fence, and a huge chestnut tree in the backyard. We put up a swing and built a sandbox in the corner of the lawn. When we looked out the front living room window, it was like a picture, for there were the sloping fields that stretched down to the Nith River, then beyond the river the green hills climbed to the horizon. We often fished at the river. Johnny and Nancy, our Amish friends, liked fishing too; they had long bamboo poles and we would sit on the bank of that pretty old river and wait for some big fish to bite.

It was in the fall of 1952 that Irene was pregnant again. We were looking forward to having a playmate for our Billy. Our baby girl was born June 28th, 1953, and she weighed 5lbs., 4 ozs. We named her Patricia Elizabeth Florence. Irene chose the name Patricia. With all her official names, we mostly called her Pat or Patti. She had a little darker complexion than Billy, and her hair was brown like mine. We just about had everything: the two most beautiful kids in the world, healthy and bright, we had each other, didn't owe much, and the old house was looking better all the time.

I bought a small building up the road a mile or so; Johnny Bellar and his men and I brought it home and made a nice little barn. I dug a trench by hand and put water in the barn and bought a strip of land behind ours, making our back lot big enough for a small pasture or paddock.

By then—about 1952—Daddy and Mary had moved to Kitchener, where the girls lived.

Willie Kell

Book Nineteen: June 1953—Our Patti and Shakespeare

It was just at the time our Patti was born that the famous Stratford Shakespearean Theatre was also born. It opened in June 1953. It wasn't a theatre back then, it was a tent—a big top, like the circus tents. The man who set that tent up and stayed to make sure that it didn't fall down was a fellow named Skip Manley. He stayed at the Windsor Hotel the whole time he was in town. Skip had been with Ringling Bros, Barnum & Bailey Circus for years and told some great stories of his days travelling around with the Greatest Show on Earth.

The Windsor Hotel was the place to stay in Stratford. There was a line-up every night for the dining room. The rooms were full all the time, and Wes raised the rates considerably. Of course, in the summer the commercial travellers take holidays, and many of them avoided coming when the festival was open. Those that did come, we tried to take care of as usual. There was one other good hotel in town, the Queen's Hotel, which was owned and operated by Dave Pinkney.

The Queens wasn't as big or prestigious as the Windsor, but the meals were excellent and the place was clean and well-run. Dave Pinkney was also in the harness-racing business and raised some pretty good horses, but didn't have much luck racing them. He was also a great promoter of hockey and knew many NHL players. He had been a friend of the immortal Howie Morenz. Dave was a very close friend of the legendary harness-horse driver Clint Hodgins, and as time went

Willie

on, Dave and I became friends. He wanted me to work for him around the time I started at the Windsor.

The hotel job was very temporary for me; I planned to go back on the road. Although time kept going on, and Wes treated me good. He would often give Perry and me an extra $20 bill out of his pocket. He took me to the races with him, paid my hotel expenses in the States. Sometimes we would take off to a fair or small race meet in Ontario. We were good friends. And there were a lot of interesting happenings at the hotel that kept me there. Irene and I went to the races in the States with other friends we got to know, people who were also friends of Wes and Nora. We could go to shed row and meet the big-time trainers and drivers. We would bet just a few dollars, what we could afford; by this time I was over my gambling addiction. At least, I had learned how to control it.

Those first years of the Festival was very exciting, so many interesting people staying at the hotel, eating at the hotel, or visiting someone who was staying there. I got to know several of these famous people. There was Sir Alec Guinness—I had admired his acting in the classic movie, *Oliver Twist*, when he played the part of the infamous "Fagan". Then there was the wonderful British actress Irene Worth, and others of great renown, and of course the Canadian actors and actresses. William Shatner, Donald Sutherland, Chris Plummer, Brunno Geruso, and so many more. There was Barry Morse, who played for years in the TV production of *The Fugitive*, and his daughter, Barbara Chilicoot. Then there was the late legendary classical pianist Glenn Gould. He always stayed at the Windsor. He wore a coat and mitts even in the hot summer; he was quite interesting, and has become a folk hero. There was the world-renowned English director Sir Tyrone Guthrie, a nice man. The great classical violinist, Isaac Stern, stayed at the Windsor with his wife for quite a while—or it seemed quite a while. He was rather fussy and hard to satisfy, but unforgettable. I got along well with him, once I got to know him. The magnificent French mime Marcel Marceau also stayed with us, as well as so many newspaper critics from different places. Then the people involved with a movie, I even had a bit part in that. There were several visitors who went on to be authors, like Robertson Davies. At that time he was a drama critic for a newspaper in Peterborough, and didn't become famous for writing novels and plays until he was an old man. Now his work is known around the world.

Of course I will never forget meeting Faron Young. He was a big country music star at the time he came to Stratford with his band. It was in the fall, and they spent a weekend at the hotel and played the Coliseum in town. It was after he had a huge country hit called "Hello, Walls"; Willie Nelson had written it and pitched it around Nashville where he was living, or trying to make a living. Faron Young says Willie offered to sell him the song for $500.00, but Faron said he wouldn't take advantage of a struggling songwriter down on his luck. He told Willie that he would record the song, it would become a hit, and it would make Willie a lot of money. And that's what happened. That song became a #1 country hit and Willie Nelson earned thousands of dollars in royalties from it. It was about the same time that "Crazy," another Willie Nelson tune, became a big hit for Patsy Cline.

Well, Faron Young's gig in Stratford went well that Saturday night. The next day, I was working the afternoon shift at the hotel and Faron and his band were hanging around with some other locals, having liquid refreshments in their rooms close to the lobby. I said,

Willie

"Faron, how about singing 'Hello Walls'?" He said, "All right Willie, I'll get my guitar." Then he went to his room, came back carrying this guitar in the case, set it on the floor and opened it, and pulled out this guitar that had been smashed flat as a pancake the night before, as part of the act.

It seems old Faron liked to party, and I guess he and Hank Williams had some times together. Faron had been going with Billie Jean before Hank met her. She was at the Opry with Faron when old Hank first laid eyes on her. Hank took a liking to that pretty gal, and they were married in October 1952, a few short months before Hank's sad and untimely death.

It was just a few years ago that things weren't going well for Faron, and he up and shot himself to death. But I'll never forget that smile and that wonderful voice, and every once in a while I play the record "Hello Walls" and memories of happier times come back to me.

There was a lady who stayed at the Windsor for several years. She had a government job and came to the hotel quite often. Her name was Olive Palmer, and she married John Diefenbaker in 1953, not long before he became Prime Minister of Canada. Olive became a gracious First Lady.

Sometimes we had parties out at our place and these interesting people would come. They would ask me to sing, and they would tell stories and maybe sing a few songs themselves. We had some wonderful times. I thought it would be nice to include Irene, that she would get to know these intriguing people I kept telling her about. But Irene would go back to that old game of hers, grabbing onto some man, then a little kissing. Of course we would fight about it after the guests left. No, she wasn't over that; having a family wasn't the answer to her problem.

Willie Kell

Book Twenty: The Executioners

Although there were many famous people who stayed at the hotel, there was one who could be classed as infamous, I suppose. Yes, in the early spring of 1954, the Hangman, Canada's official executioner, stayed at the Windsor Hotel. He spent the weekend there in Stratford, measuring, preparing, getting his hood and rope ready to hang a young man.

This young man had shot and killed a beautiful seventeen-year-old blond girl in cold blood. It happened just half a block from the hotel one early afternoon. She had gone out with this fellow a few times, but had decided to break off the relationship. This jealous young man pumped six bullets into her body in front of the drugstore where she worked, then walked across the street to the police station and gave himself up, while she lay dying on the sidewalk. We could hear the shots; it was just a half block down the street. When we looked out, a crowd had gathered around her lifeless body.

That night when I finished my shift at midnight, I walked down to where the murder had taken place. The streets were vacant and the crowd had gone. There seemed an eerie silence until the town hall clock rang out. There were still deep, red streaks of dried blood on the cold cement sidewalk. I stood there alone on the empty street, deeply touched by this senseless deed. I had talked to this pretty girl in the drugstore just a few days before she was murdered, and we knew her family well.

Willie

When the young man's trial came up, the judge and several other officials stayed at the Windsor Hotel. He was found guilty of murder in the first degree and was sentenced to hang. The county-sheriff, who often came into the hotel, called me one night and made reservations for the hangman. He told me to book the room under the sheriff's name.

The hangman arrived in town early on a Friday by train, and a taxi brought him to the hotel. That evening, when he came down from his room for dinner, was the first I had laid eyes on him. He was a Frenchman, from the province of Quebec. He was quite fat, had a brush cut, dark grey hair, and wore horn-rimmed glasses. He had a very deep French accent. I had several interesting conversations with the fellow. He told me that he went to the races at Richelieu Park, near Montreal. We talked about the races, about politics, even about the weather, but not a word about his job of hanging people. He was in and out of the hotel several times in the next couple of days, back and forth to the jail where the young man was being held. Measuring him, weighing him, checking out every last grisly detail. He seemed to enjoy his job and took it seriously.

When Sunday night came, I was alone there behind the desk, adding up the guest's accounts. It was past 11 PM; there were just a few guests at the hotel. This fat fellow came walking down the stairs; he had a coat and hat on and a black duffel bag in his hand. He sat the bag on a chair and asked me to call a taxi. He gave me the number to call. It was the same taxi that he had used during his stay in town, the one that had brought him from the station. It was a cold, rainy, windy night in March. We talked briefly before the taxi came. Then he picked up the mysterious-looking bag and walked out, got in the cab, and was driven away to kill that young man. I said goodnight to the big fellow as he went out the door, and just as the door closed, I said in a quiet voice, "Great night for a hangin'." It was little more than an hour later and the young man was pronounced dead.

The wooden scaffold had been built by local contractors, and stood on the outside of the jail. It reached up to a door on the second storey, just outside the young man's cell. I knew some of the fellows who'd helped to build it. The young man's dead body was claimed by his family and buried that same night in a lonely hillside grave out in the country, in a small cemetery surrounded by peaceful pine trees. At the head of his grave there's a small tombstone, which gives his name, the year of his birth, the year of his death—1954—and the word "REDEEMED." It seems he had found the Lord while he was waiting for the hangman to come. I've always thought it was a shame he hadn't found the Lord before he took that beautiful girl's life.

Willie

Book Twenty-one: One Night of Cheatin'

Irene and I were mostly happy, and thankful for all we had. Our Patti learned to walk when she was ten months old. Billy loved her from the start, and she loved him. The children played on the big lawn when the weather was nice. Billy would take his little sister's hand, and they were always together. Trix was good with the children and seemed to watch over them. By the time Patti was walking, we had a nice Jersey cow. When the grass was green, we kept her tied on a long chain on the roadside in the daytime and at nights she stayed in the little pasture behind the barn. When the winter snow came, we kept her in the small barn. Irene milked her and we had plenty of good, rich milk for the children. Trix and Joe, our big black cat, were always in the barn at milk time to get their share of fresh, warm milk.

We had relatives come to visit us and stay over a day or two from time to time. By now there were several cousins for Billy and Patti to play with. My sister Elizabeth and her husband and two children lived in Woodstock, and it was only a half-hour drive to their place. We often visited back and forth, and their children and ours had great times together. By the mid 1950s, Grandma Crighton had passed away, and Jock had died in the fall of '52, just a couple of months before Hank Williams was found dead in the back seat of his Cadillac in a little town called Oak Hill, West Virginia.

For the most part, Irene and I got along real good, but for the times we went some place were there were men around. She would try her best to make a fool of herself, and me. One evening we were at a family

Willie Kell

wedding reception and she hung around this one fellow all night, dancing, holding hands, and acting like a sex-starved bitch in front of my relatives. We had so many fights over these incidents, but the problem just grew worse. At the same time, if I were to even be friendly with a lady, she would be so jealous, she would fly into a wild rage. One night we were at a neighbour's party, with a few people we knew well, and the lady of the house and I were standing talking—not touching one another, just talking. Irene came roaring between us, screaming and accusing us of having an affair, which was crazy! The woman's husband, being a bit intoxicated, grabbed the shotgun and threatened to shoot me! What a time; that ruined our friendship with the neighbours, and made a complete fool out of us both.

I had every opportunity to cheat on her; there were a lot of lonely women who stayed at the Windsor Hotel, and many temptations came my way. However, I had never seen anyone I could love more than my beautiful Irene, nor could I ever risk ruining our lives.

Finally I told her that the next time she pulled one of these silly games, I would stop being so nice and patient and would play the same game myself.

It wasn't long until she did it again. This time I didn't say anything; I figured there was no use. But it was only a week or so later that a good-looking nineteen-year-old gal checked into the hotel. She was working for a big grocery company and was working in town for the week. She was real friendly and seemed to have her eye on me. She hung around the desk and we talked in the evenings. She was quite flirtatious, and I kind of lead her on. She asked me to come up to her room on Friday night after work and we could have a couple of drinks together. I told her that I thought it was a good plan and looked forward to it; I would bring the ice and the mix.

Willie

Friday evening came, and after we had talked a while, there at the check-in desk, she started walking up the stairs and reminded me with a sexy twinkle in her eyes, "Don't forget." When the hour of midnight came and I was finished my shift, I took some ice and mix, walked to her room, and gently knocked on her door.

"Come on in, it's open," she said in a sexy voice. I went in, gave her a little hug, poured a stiff drink for each of us, and sat beside her on the bed. She had long brown hair, brown eyes, nice shapely legs, and big nipple-y breasts that seemed to stick out through the silky red dress she was wearing. We talked a while about nothing, then a little kiss, some more whiskey, and then she lay back on the bed, her dress slipping up to reveal her thighs. It was obvious why this girl had invited me to her room.

Her kisses were so warm and passionate. After more whiskey and more kissing, I unfastened the front of her dress and put my hand inside, down between her full breasts. She wiggled and squirmed and pushed herself ever closer to my body. Then she started to take off her clothes, like a strip-tease artist. First the red dress, then her slip, then slowly she pulled her brassiere straps down over her shoulders, after I had helped undo it. Then she slid out of her frilly panties. Now, if I would say that I wasn't a bit excited and greatly aroused, I would be telling a huge lie. I kissed her, I felt her warm breasts, and I gave each nipple a little kiss. I knew before I went up to her room that it would be an interesting and entertaining way to unwind after a hard day at the office. But now the situation was getting dangerous.

She was a pretty thing to look at, lying across that bed in the dim, shadowy light glimmering in through the partly open bathroom door, her long auburn hair down on her shoulders. Her sexy wet lips pouting out ... her country-girl breasts bulging ... a slim waist accentuating the fullness of her hips and thighs ... her slender legs stretched out to the edge of the bed.

All the time I knew I was leading that girl on. I knew I could never go any farther with that horny girl; not that it wasn't very tempting. But I just couldn't bring myself to do that; after all, Irene wouldn't do anything like that. What I did with that girl was little more than I knew Irene had been doing for years, and when I would tell her about it, sometime soon, maybe she would smarten up and we could go on with our lives. The girl was very disappointed when I told her that I had a beautiful wife and two lovely children at home, and as much as I enjoyed the foreplay, I could never go any farther.

It was late when I got home and Irene knew it. The next morning, when she asked me what kept me so late, I purposely gave her an awkward answer, hoping that she would be suspicious and inquisitive. She was neither, so the next time she pulled one of her little capers, I told her what had happened. Maybe she would be hurt, like I had been so many times.

It didn't work the way I thought it might. She was furious; she told her mother how terrible I was. She went to our family doctor and told him that I had been unfaithful. She would not let it rest, and wouldn't accept any blame. I had done a terrible thing, she claimed; she even became violent.

I thought that I had tried everything. I knew that I wasn't sorry for my little escapade with that gal in the hotel room, in view of all the hell Irene had put me through those past nine years. But I *was* sorry for being honest with her.

Things were going along real well at the hotel. That girl never did come back; guess she wasn't satisfied with

Willie

the service. As time went on, some motels sprang up around town, but the Windsor continued to be the place to stay and eat. The big names from Hollywood still came to town, like James Mason, and Jason Robarts and Lauren Bacall. Their son, Jason Robarts III, and I got to be buddies; he stayed at the Windsor for quite a while and we had great conversations.

It was along about this time that Wes asked me if I would like to take a day or two off and take his horse trailer and half-ton and go and bring home a black filly that a big horse breeder in Michigan had given to Harold Wellwood. I said I would, but I wanted to take my father and stay over and go to the races at Wolverine Raceway on the outskirts of Detroit. Daddy had never been to night harness races and I knew it would be a thrill for him to get to that big track. We had a wonderful trip; we had supper backstretch at the dining hall with the trainers and drivers. Daddy just loved being there, and I loved having him with me on that trip. We stayed at a motel overnight, picked up the filly the next day, and brought her home. Her name was Royal Eileen. She became a good racehorse for Harold, and when her racing days were over, she was an even better brood mare. One of her colts was Eileen's Tour; he took a race record of 1.57, which was great at the time, and he won close to half a million dollars for Harold. He raced against the world's champion, Niatross. At the time Daddy and I were hauling that black filly in that trailer, we had no idea how precious she was.

I recommended a couple of good trotting mares to Wes. I had seen them race at the small tracks and believed they had potential to be useful racehorses. He ended up buying both of them, Rosena Chips and Lady K. Brooke, and they both turned out great under Harold's training. They won many races in the States and Lady K. Brooke became the second-fastest trotting mare on a 1/2 mile track that had ever been bred in

Canada up until that time. Rosena Chips was even better as a racehorse and a brood mare.

When the races were over in late November, Harold would ship the horses home to Wes's farm, a few miles out of town. I got to know Harold quite well, and his wife, Marjorie. I often went to the farm with Wes and watched them train the horses. Harold was a quiet-talking fellow, very honest and respected by everyone who knew him. One time he and I went to the races at the old Dufferin racetrack in Toronto. When he came home from the races with a broken leg one fall, after a serious accident in a race, his young nephew Bill Wellwood took over some of the driving and training. Bill stayed on with Harold for a few years and learned the business. Harold got back driving the next year, and it was after that that he had some of his best horses. Bill started a stable of his own, and has been one of the most successful trainer drivers in North America. His own horses alone have won millions of dollars.

Harold's only son Buddy, whom I remember as a boy growing up, had some success in harness racing. He owned and trained a world champion and the winner of close to a million dollars. However, sad to say, Buddy died in his mid-forties.

Those days, Irene and I got to the races at Buffalo Raceway and Batavia Downs at nearby Hamburg, New York. One time we took Daddy and Mary; we stayed a few nights at a motel and enjoyed the races. It was there at those tracks I heard the great race announcer Dr. Harrison V. Baker call the races. He also called the famous Hambletonian at Goshen, New York. I was intrigued with the way this man described those races. A veterinarian by day, he helped to keep the horses healthy, but when night came, he was on that microphone, calling the races. Wes knew him well, but I never got to meet him. At that time, I was having ideas

Willie

about becoming a race caller myself. Everybody said that I had a good voice, and with my photographic memory and love for the sport of harness racing, maybe I could do it.

Things went along well with Irene and I and our little family for the most part. When Irene was good, she was very good; when she was bad, she was something else. There was never a harsh word between us, except for the horny things she did around strange men. And the times she would bring up my adventure with the gal at the hotel that one fateful night. In the summer, we used to take the kids and go to the beach for a week or so. We rented a small cabin; Irene liked to swim and the children enjoyed the water too.

In the summer of 1955, Daddy took a heart attack and was in the hospital for a while. He had to quit smoking for a time. After they moved to Kitchener, Mary did some things that drove him crazy. I used to go see him once a week or call him on the phone. He always liked to talk. Before he had the heart attack, he would often come to our place, and sometimes stay overnight. But he was ordered by the doctor not to drive for almost a year. I got him a good deal on a TV, and he enjoyed watching it. There were times when he'd get a letter for medicine, so I would go and deliver it for him and spend the day selling Ton-A-Lax in the area. He could use the money, and I was always proud to help him in any way I knew how.

Mary treated us okay when we went there, but I couldn't forget some of the things she had done. Like when I owed Daddy $200.00 the time I started working at the hotel, when I was hooked on gambling. She wrote me at the Windsor Hotel and told me to either pay my father what I owed him or she would write Wes Litt and have my wages garnisheed. I didn't answer her letter.

Book Twenty-two: The Great Betrayal

It was in the spring of '56 that I left the hotel and went back to selling Ton-A-Lax. I was also busy putting together a new herbal remedy. Actually, it was an old formula that my uncle Jock had got hold of years before and given to me, a combination of dry herbs. I planned to sell it in packages and have the customers make a tea from it. I had it passed by the Department Of Food and Drugs, and had little green boxes made with the directions and other necessary information on them. I would be ready to start selling it in early July, along with Ton-A-Lax. It was called "Your Friend."

It was just before I left the hotel, in March, that Irene was bothered with her back and hip. She'd had this trouble from time to time since she was a kid. It seems when she took the Ton-A-Lax she didn't have much trouble. Now she hadn't been taking it for a while. I heard about a chiropractor in Stratford, and asked her if she wanted to make an appointment, he might help her. She agreed to try a few treatments and I went with her the first time.

He seemed a nice old fellow, and he said he could do something for her. It was only a few times after she started with him that she was calling him by his first name, and I could smell liquor on her breath when she came home from her treatments. She talked about him a lot; I could feel that she was quite taken with this old fellow. She told me that his wife had died and the poor fellow was lonesome. Well, he wasn't lonesome long, Irene saw to that. She kept going to him, usually twice a week, until I found out what was happening behind those curtains.

I would take the kids to the park, over to the hotel, or some place while we waited for Mom to have her "treatment"! I became more suspicious as the weeks passed, and told her my feelings. But Irene assured me she wouldn't think of having an affair with him, or anyone else, though all the signs told a different story. I never acted jealous, petty, or possessive with Irene. Always tried to trust her, hoping she would learn to earn my trust. I tried and wanted to believe that, although she was flirtatious, she would never cross that line.

One night this chiropractor came to visit us; he had been drinking. You could always see Irene's big blue eyes light up when he came over. Irene and I had a beer or two while he had some more whiskey. The next thing, Irene was on his knee, wiggling around and acting like a horny, sex-starved high school girl. It was obvious there was something very funny going on, but how would I know for sure? If I found out that she had been untrue, I would divorce her, as much as I loved her and needed her. But I couldn't divorce her for just sitting on his knee.

I was getting tired, tired of watching Irene teasing around with that old man and just plain tired. I thought if I went to bed, he would go home. Irene's mother and young brother were there, and Mom and the kids were already in bed. I said good night and headed to bed, hoping Irene would soon join me.

I heard the kitchen door open and close quietly. I came back down, went out the front door of the house, and walked around to his car parked in our drive. There was this son of a bitch and Irene in the front seat. Her dress was up around her thighs, and they were kissing. My inner instinct was to get a club and kill both of them. But my plan was to just find out what my sweet,

Willie Kell

innocent Irene was really like and what had she been doing with this old home-wrecking whoremaster for the past four months. What they had been doing was what they were doing right there on the front seat of that car. I had to see it with my own eyes.

I went in the house, heartbroken, walked up the stairs, woke up her mother and told her what was happening out in the car. Her mother didn't seem all that surprised or disappointed. I went and looked at my beautiful, sleeping children, there in their beds. Billy was 5 and Patti was just 3. I was confused; my world was crumbling around me. When Irene came in to bed, I was wide awake. She took off all her clothes and got into bed naked, then curled tightly up to my back, put her arm around me, and held me close. I ignored her and had a restless night.

The next morning I confronted her with what I had seen. She lied, as usual. She tried to deny everything, said nothing happened. She was just trying to get even with me, for what I had done with that girl in the hotel room. Her mother sided with her, and blamed me, as usual. I got in my car and started driving. I really didn't know where I wanted to go or what I wanted to do. But I ended up at Daddy's house in Kitchener. He was alone, Mary was at work.

I didn't tell him my troubles; I just sat around kind of staring into space. I fell asleep for a while on Daddy's couch and was awakened by a loud clap of thunder from a summer storm. I told him I had been up late the night before. He asked me to stay for supper, came out to the car when I left, still wanting me to stay. I didn't want to be there when Mary got home, I just didn't need her that day. So I left, went downtown, and had supper in a restaurant. It was the LAST time I saw Daddy alive! He died in the early morning hours, in bed, just a week and a day later.

Willie

When I got back home that Saturday night, they told me that Irene's mother had to go to the hospital in Owen Sound for an operation the next day, and we drove her there. It was a hundred miles, so we stayed a day or two in a motel until she was on the mend. It was just a few days after we got home that Daddy died. Mary made arrangements to have the funeral in Owen Sound. He was lying in his coffin in the funeral home and Irene's mother was on the other side of town in the hospital. Daddy was not buried in the family plot; Mary bought a new plot for her and Daddy in the same cemetery. It was a bad couple of weeks.

Now I could never trust Irene, couldn't count on her as a friend. It took a few weeks of all-night fights and hard questions until she finally admitted that she had been unfaithful since she had started going to that chiropractor. I went and confronted him, and he admitted it too, but said he would deny it if I tried to name him in a divorce. Irene would not hear tell of a divorce. She talked of suicide if I mentioned it. As for my feelings, I hated her, and yet I still loved her. What was I going to do? I knew that I couldn't give up the children, and at that time the only grounds for a divorce was adultery, and I couldn't prove it. I had always told her that if she wanted someone else, if that's what she was trying to say, just leave me, I'd take care of the kids. Just get out of my life and leave me alone.

I tried to forget the whole thing, but then I would remember it all and the fight would start again. We would make up, make love, get along for a little while, then it would start again. It seemed we were either fighting or making love. I couldn't get over this awful betrayal, but Lord knows I tried. It was difficult to go out and sell medicine; I would end up driving around the roads talking to myself. But we had to eat, so I just kept going on. Sometimes we would fight half the night. It was hell.

When Billy started to school in September, instead of happiness in our home there was unhappiness and terrible fights. I couldn't help think that whore-master of a chiropractor was probably screwing around with somebody else's wife while we were going through this hell. Irene was easy to get along with as long as I didn't mention what she had done. If I brought up the subject, she would go crazy. One day we had a big fight, and she was going to take the car and go away. She was sitting in the car, the motor running, I walked in front; she stepped on the gas and just about ran over me. She smashed into the woodshed just as I jumped out of the way. Smashed a big hole in it, and then I had to fix the damn woodshed.

Another time we had a big fight and she threw a bunch of my medicine boxes in the burning stove and just about kicked the TV in. I caught her leg and wrestled her to the floor. Then, when I did let her up, she took off with my car. She went to London and got a job. Left me with the kids, no money, I didn't know where she was, and I had no car to drive to sell medicine.

After about a week she wrote and let me know where she was. It was a rainy afternoon in late fall when I hitchhiked to London to get my car. I remember standing at the outskirts of Stratford, my thumb out, waiting for a ride, with about one dollar in my pocket. I walked miles in London to get to the nursing home where she was working. She cried to come home, said how much she loved me and missed me and the kids. She was so sorry and wouldn't do anything bad again. I left her there, but after another week I gave in and brought her home. Truth is, I never really figured out a way to live without her, I still loved her so much. When we were

Willie

leaving the nursing home and saying her good-byes, her supervisor told me rather sternly, "You be nice to her." It was easy to see that she had lied to them and blamed me. That should have been a big red flag! I should have left her there. But I didn't; I brought her home, and she seemed glad to see the kids, but she would talk about her job there at the nursing home, not about how we could solve our problems. She never really faced reality. She didn't ever plan to change; maybe she didn't know how.

Billy, Patti & Jimmy

Willie Kell

Book Twenty-three: The Big Race

It was that fall, after Daddy died and just after Billy started to school, that I announced my first race. It was at a fall fair at Ridgetown, Ontario. Irene went with me; we stayed in a hotel and had a big fight in the middle of the night. We didn't get much sleep, but by morning things got back to peace and quiet and we journeyed on to the racetrack at Ridgetown. Of course, the judges, timers, and other locals didn't know me and were rather unfriendly. To say that I was nervous would be putting it very mildly. I was downright scared, but determined to succeed. There were four horses in the first race and three of them collided and fell down on the first turn. It was hard to think of something to say while those horses and drivers were tangled up among bits of harness and broken sulkies there on the racetrack.

I called the races at a few fairs that fall and Irene went with me. It helped to get my mind on something else, although I never had my mind off Irene and what she had done. When we were away, Nancy Bellar, our good Amish neighbour, looked after our children, Billy would go there when he came from school; it was a second home for them.

I was still selling medicine and bought Ton-A-Lax from Mary by the case. She knew how to make it, but wouldn't tell me or sell me the formula, although it wasn't much good to her.

It was later that fall that I bought a standardbred mare and a set of harness for $150.00. We bought an old

Willie

high-wheel cart and drove her on the road. Irene helped me with her. She liked being outside doing things, rather than housework. The mare was a trotter and had raced some but had never won any money. We planned to enter her in The F.S. Scott Memorial Trot at New Hamburg. But when March came, I sold her for $400.00 to a show horseman, who showed her at all the big fairs for years. She got a wonderful home and we made a good profit on the deal. Having this horse to drive, keeping her there in our little barn had helped heal the wounds and gave me something else to think about.

The very next day after we sold the mare we bought a bay gelding from my old friend, Wes Litt, for $200.00. A fine-looking horse, his name was The Last Chip. Wes had bought him the year before. He showed great promise, but he and Harold Wellwood didn't get along. They couldn't get him to trot; he was nervous and just danced, would do this for miles. Then he would trot a little, but if you spoke cross or the cart hit a bump, he would start dancing again. They were training 18 horses at the farm that spring, and they led Chip. I hitched him at Wes's farm and drove him down the road; he danced most of the way, but when he did trot he trotted great. Irene urged me to buy him, save him from being slaughtered, and I did.

I borrowed Wes's truck and trailer to take him home. We started driving him on the road, hitched to the big road cart. I bought an old set of harness for $8.00 and later a jogging cart with wire wheels. He gradually improved, more every day. We treated him kind and tried to settle him down. We also filled his big ears with cotton when we drove him, then he wouldn't hear the sounds that bothered him. It worked wonders.

So we entered him in the F.S. Scott Memorial Trot at New Hamburg, and paid our first entry fee in May. It was in July that we took him to the fairgrounds at

Willie Kell

Milverton, left him in the barn there, and went every day to drive him on the dirt track. Irene started driving him too. She mostly worked him his fast miles. We paid the balance of the entry fee for the race and hoped our horse would go well; we could sure use a break, and the money.

When the big day came, we borrowed a trailer to take Chip to the races, loaded the wire-wheel cart on top of the car, and headed out for New Hamburg. It was so exciting—driving along the road, heading for our first big race, Billy and Patti in the backseat, Irene and I in the front, and Chip in the borrowed trailer behind. We invited Irene's mom to come along, but she didn't. It was 20 miles to New Hamburg, but it seemed farther that day—we couldn't wait to get there.

When we got to the track, there was a stall waiting for our horse in one of the big barns with all the other great horses. While we looked after the horse, the children played on the swings under the shade of the maple trees and kept away from the barn. Irene went to check on them often and gave them their lunch. We took sandwiches and cookies and something to drink. Billy was 6 and Patti was only 4.

I had asked the well-known driver Wib Hopkins to drive our horse. He had other horses there, and was one of the good drivers up from Greenwood Raceway in Toronto. There were 14 horses in The Scott Trot that day, and because of the large field, Katzy, the secretary, split the class into two divisions. There were nine in our race and five in the other division. We had no race cart, so I asked the driver if we could borrow his, and he said we could. I explained that we didn't bring ours. I didn't tell him that we didn't have one, or couldn't afford one.

There were two heats in each race; the winner would be the horse standing best in the combined heats. Irene had friven Chip in his warm-up miles prior to the race.

Willie

Many were surprised at this good-looking girl with the long blond hair blowing in the breeze, driving this horse that had been a problem in the famous Wellwood stables.

Finally it was *post time*. Billy and Patti stood up on benches and listened to Tory Greg, the announcer, call the race. Irene and I stood in the paddock by the barns, holding hands. Wib Hopkins was a pretty good driver, he kept Chip in the middle of the pack, then brought him out at the top of the stretch and won it handily. The next heat, he sat in the three spot until the stretch, then Chip and Wib with his bright red driving colours came blazing through the stretch to win again. Wib Hopkins drove in the other division of The Scott Trot, but only managed to win one heat with a horse owned by the famous NHL Hall of Fame goalie, Harry Lumley, who by coincidence was also born in Owen Sound. He had been a goalie for The Detroit Red Wings and the Toronto Maple Leafs.

We received most of the purse money, about $600.00, and a couple of silver trophies. One of the trophies was a huge silver cup donated by the Scott-McCale Shoe Company. It was a perpetual trophy and had been in the homes of many big owners, including the Lieutenant Governor of Ontario, The Honourable Earle Rowe. The presentation of the silver cups was made to Irene and me, and the ceremony took place out on the track in front of the huge crowd, by a famous countess from Australia. A couple of radio stations were there to broadcast the races and the presentations in front of the grandstand. It was all on radio, and thousands of people were listening while our horse won that big race and when the presentations were being made. We could hardly believe that our Cinderella horse, which we had bought in March for just $200.00, was such a celebrity there at the big Derby Day Races in August. There were

Willie Kell

articles and pictures in all the papers about this great horse. Yes, our friend Wes was there to congratulate us. He sent a newspaper article to Harold, who was racing in the States. We were so proud of our horse and the beautiful big silver trophy that had been in the home of so many famous owners and drivers through the years.

Mary and Son and Irene were there, and I was wishing Daddy could have been there too. But, somehow, I often thought he had a better seat for that race than any of us had; I believe he was watching that day.

After the races were over, a well-known owner of fine race horses wanted to buy our horse for $2000.00 We felt that the horse was just beginning to show what he could do, and we said he wasn't for sale. We planned to take him to Toronto and try our luck. Our winnings that day were just over $600.00. That was a lot of money to us. We would gamble some of it by taking our great horse to the big track. Wib Hopkins had a stall for him in his stable at Greenwood.

Our gamble didn't pay off. We took him to the big track, but with all the excitement and changes, our poor horse got excited and went back to his dance. We kept him there for more than a week and stayed at the racetrack. It was a wonderful experience. He never won another race, and we finally sold him for $400.00.

That was the last Derby Day at New Hamburg, although the races continued there each civic holiday for years. The next year, the Canadian Pacing Derby was raced at Greenwood Raceway in Toronto, and has been at the big Toronto tracks ever since, billed as Canada's oldest race for pacers. The purses are over $200,000 these days. Our horse had won the last F.S. Scott Trot, and we got to keep the big silver perpetual trophy. Wib

Willie

Hopkins was killed in a race at Mohawk Raceway, near Toronto, a few years later. But we will always remember him and his red suit blazing through the stretch in the prestigious F.S. Scott Memorial Trot at New Hamburg, behind our Cinderella trotter, The Last Chip, on Derby Day, August 5th 1957.

After I sold Chip, I bought horses and sold them to the Mennonites for road horses. Then I bought and sold some ponies; I was getting to be quite a horse trader. The kids were getting big enough to enjoy the ponies. I had always wanted a pony when I was a kid, and I thought all kids were like me. Billy and Jim never got interested in them, but Patti sure did. I couldn't blame Billy. One Christmas I borrowed a pony and Billy was riding it, I was walking along beside. The fool pony slammed poor Billy into a telephone pole! He had to have a couple of stitches in his lip. I felt very sorry and foolish; it seemed I wanted Billy to be able to do the things I never had a chance to do. That time it proved to be a big mistake!

The summer of '58, we borrowed Elizabeth and Johnny's tent and went camping for a couple of weeks close to Wasaga Beach. We camped near a river, I sold medicine in the mornings, then we would go to the beach in the afternoons, fish at the river in the evening.

When we got home from our holidays, I went on selling medicine. By now I had figured out how to make the Ton-A-Lax myself. I knew what was in it and I knew the amount of each ingredient. I finally got it together and called it Tone-O-Lax, had it registered that way, and most people didn't notice the name change.

Between selling medicine, buying and selling horses and ponies, announcing some races at one-day meets, and acting as MC for fairs, we were making a living.

Book Twenty-four: Jimmy, From Whence He Came

Irene discovered she was pregnant again, and blamed it on the good times we had when we were camping, back about the middle of August. Come to think of it, we did have some pretty good times in that tent. We hadn't planned on having any more kids, but if it was going to happen, that tent was as good as any place. The next spring, May 1st, 1959, our Jimmy was born. Another bald-headed, beautiful, healthy boy. He was bigger than the other two, even though he was supposedly three weeks premature.

We had a horse all that winter before Jimmy was born; Irene and I drove him every day in the cutter. She had lots of fresh air and exercise. I trained that horse and sold him for a nice profit in the spring. He wasn't much of a horse, but he did win a couple of races.

It was around the time that Jimmy was born that I met a wonderful Amish man named Johnny Kuepfer (Kipfer). He was short and stout, with a round face and a big, bushy red beard. He looked like a young Santa Claus. We had so many deals—horses, cattle, ponies, implements, and just about anything that could be bought sold or traded

It was about the same time that I met another great fellow; his name was Burt Graham. Burt lived in a homemade plywood horse trailer at the racetrack in Stratford when I first met him. He kept some horses there. This trailer had a bed across the one end, and his clothes hung on hangers from an iron rod above the bed.

Willie

He heated the trailer with a small oil space heater, cooked on a two-burner hot plate, and there was a small table and a couple of chairs. Burt had been overseas in World War II, all through Europe in the front lines. When the war was over, he went to work for several different horse trainers and became an expert horseman himself. He never made any big money. He was content with life the way it was, it seemed.

During these years, Wes would call me from the hotel and ask me to come into work when someone would want a day or two off. Sometimes he would just call me and we would talk about things. By this time Perry had left the hotel and so had Jimmy Yemon. Jimmy's body was later found floating in a river. He took his own life, they say, but he could have been murdered for a gambling debt. Gambling and cheating women had finally brought him down.

One day I was in Stratford, it was about noon, and I stopped in at the Windsor Hotel. Wes and Nora were just going to the dining room for lunch and asked me to join them. As we sat having lunch, he told me that he had sold the Windsor Hotel. He asked me to come and work the desk the last day he had the hotel, before the new owners took over. He wanted to introduce me to them. They were three brothers from the west who had come into some money. I got to know them and worked for them once in a while. They were interesting, and a bit wild. Two out of the three were serious drunks. Running a hotel was the last thing they should have been doing. They didn't last long; the second-mortgage people, headed by a young, rich, Jewish fellow who specialised in such things, soon took over, and the playboys were gone.

Willie Kell

Book Twenty-five: Our Own Farm

It was the early fall of 1963 that we started to negotiate for a 50-acre farm on the highway, just 5 miles away. The place was in awful shape. It had a good-sized brick house that had been plastered over with white stucco, a bank barn, and a driving shed, all needing repairs. Some boards were falling off the barn, and the windows were all broken out. The house was a mess, there was electricity in all the buildings, and although the land was good, the whole place was growing up in weeds and grass.

Someone had bought it through the Veteran's Land Act and didn't make the payments or look after it. They had been evicted, and the place was vacant. I offered $8000.00 for it, and they finally took it. We couldn't afford anything more expensive. We liked the location— 8 miles north of Stratford on Highway #19. It was just a couple of days later that I sold our little place for a pretty good price, $4500.00. I paid a good down payment on the farm and took a mortgage for the balance. The payments of $275.00 were every six months, spring and fall, for 20 years, with interest at 5%. Including taxes, it cost us about $700.00 a year to live there, but sometimes, back then, it seemed enough.

We spent $2000.00, mostly on the house, before we moved in. We put in a new bathroom, new ceilings, ripped out walls, and put a new window in the kitchen. The house had an oil furnace, and we also kept our wood-burning cookstove to heat the big kitchen. It was a short drive to the farm from where we lived; I would take a load of things every day and go work there, either by myself or with the people I had hired. One day I was there by myself, fixing a window in the old house, and I had the radio on. A news report came on saying that President Kennedy had been assassinated in Dallas, Texas. That was November 22nd, 1963.

I bought a truckload of good used planks and lumber for $60.00, delivered. All they could pile on a big dump truck. It was enough to put all new box stalls in the stable. I had the windows in by the first of December when we moved in. Then Billy and I kept building the stalls after we moved there. We just had one horse at the time. We had sold the cow a couple of years earlier, but now we bought a couple of more cows and a couple of not-fast-enough racehorses to sell to the Mennonites, to drive in buggies. I was always looking for a way to make a few extra dollars. The first winter on the farm, I bought a big trotter called Good Product for $125.00 from a bailiff. He had been a pretty good racehorse. I sold him in a few weeks for $250.00. That horse was a great bargain, for he raced well for that fellow for several years.

Billy was 13, just starting high school, when we moved to the farm, Patti was 10 and Jimmy, 4. Irene was 34 and I was 37. I wanted the farm so we could have more horses and cattle, and felt that the place would grow into money as we improved it. I also wanted it so the children would have something to do after school and holidays—some work, something to keep them occupied. Billy wasn't much of a farmer, neither was I, but it would be exercise, fresh air, and hopefully fun. It became all of those things and more.

By the time we moved to the farm, Irene's father had been home from the sanatorium for a few years and they were living on a disability allowance. But for the hearing problem and the fact that he had to stick the insulin needle in his arm a couple of times a day, he was getting along fine, and the TB was gone.

Christmas came just three and a half weeks after we moved to the farm. Irene's parents and David were at our place, as usual. By now David had a car, he had finished high school, and was working in an office. We always had a nice Christmas together. Mom liked a little drink, we would have one or two while they prepared the Christmas dinner. She would giggle and have a wonderful time. The old man didn't drink, though he smoked cigarettes like a chimney. Santa Claus brought Irene and the children new skates. They made good use of them on the big patches of ice that lay in the fields.

Our farm was quite flat and there were several good- sized places in the fields where small lakes of water would lie. When it froze over, these places were great to skate on. If there was snow on the ice, the kids and I would shovel it off, and 'though I didn't skate myself I enjoyed being out there with them. I skated a little when I was a small boy on Maw's farm, with oversized skates, but had somehow forgotten. Irene and the children would be out there most Sunday afternoons and the children often skated when they came from school. We had wonderful, happy times as a family.

The hills near our first place were great for tobogganing. Sunday afternoons, we would take the kids and have fun on those big hills in the winter. The children would go there after school and play until suppertime, then come home, change into dry clothes, and hang the wet ones by the warm stove to dry.

We seemed to keep busy, and got the first winter in at the farm. I continued selling medicine, mostly in the Amish and Mennonite districts. I bought and sold some horses and ponies, I worked at the hotel once in a while, when they were shorthanded. And of course there were

Willie

always stalls to build and things to fix. Although Johnny Bellar was getting older by now, he still helped me once in a while.

When spring came, we planted some oats to feed our livestock and seeded down some hay with it. Then we sowed 21 acres of flax to sell as a cash crop. We had the land ploughed the fall before. We still had a field for pasture, and my Amish friend, Johnny Keupfer, brought 19 small Hereford cattle to pasture. Well, when fall came, after he paid me for the summer's pasture, I traded him the 21 acres of flax for the 19 cattle. I built a big pen in one side of the barn and put a wide door in the end for cleaning out with a tractor.

That first summer that we were on the farm, Hanover Raceway opened and raced a few twilight evenings, and hired me as announcer. By this time I was announcing at several fairs and one-day race meets all over south-western Ontario, including the races and the fair at New Hamburg.

Willie Kell

The Farm

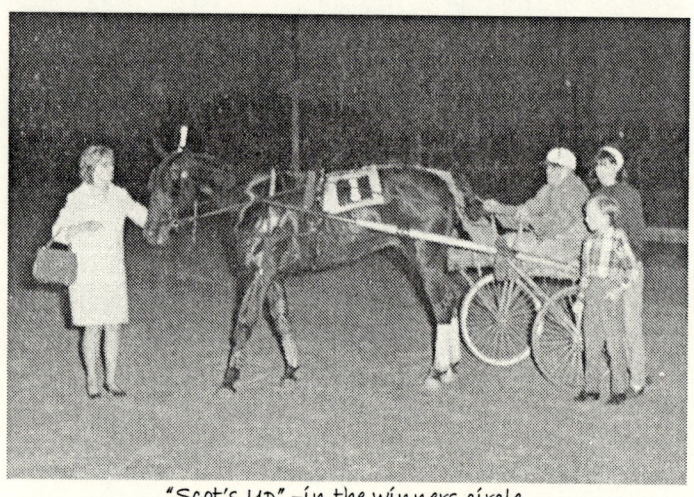

"Scot's Up" – in the winners circle.
Irene holding horse, Burt driving, Patti and Jim

Book Twenty-six: The Cardboard Guitars

It was along about this time that our kids were becoming quite interested in music. Irene and I had always sung, driving along in the car, and I sang to them when I rocked them on my knee when they were babies. When the children got old enough, they would sing along. They knew every song that we did, but now they were being influenced by the Beatles, Bob Dylan, Ian and Sylvia Tyson, Roger Miller, and the other folk, rock, and country singers coming along at the time. They made guitars out of sticks and pieces of cardboard, painted strings on them, and mouthed the words the Beatles were singing as they strummed those imaginary guitars. They had a stage set up in the upper part of the barn and spent a lot of happy times out there, especially if some of their cousins were visiting. They made a drum out of a cardboard box; the drumsticks were rungs out of an old chair. Young Jimmy was the drummer. Billy wanted an acoustic guitar, and kept asking me to buy him one. He was always patient and never demanding. Our kids were so good, unspoiled from the time they were babies. I loved them too much to spoil them.

It seemed to me, when the kids were growing up, that money was often scarce, especially those first couple of years on the farm. There was a tractor and other farm implements to buy, and even though everything was secondhand, expenses kept cropping up and money wasn't all that plentiful. When I would come home off the road from selling medicine, Billy would look in the car to see if that guitar was there. It took a while, but

Willie Kell

one day when he looked on the backseat of the car, sure enough, that $20.00 guitar was there. I bought it in a music store in Elmira. He learned a few chords from his uncle, David Grenfell, who didn't play much but knew some chord patterns, and it wasn't very long until that kid could play the guitar real good. When I wanted to find Billy to help with something, he would be in his room, working on the guitar.

By the time we had been living at the farm a year, we had 23 head of cattle, although cattle weren't worth very much at the time. We had a couple of sows with little pigs, and always a few horses and ponies around. We never got very far in debt, and everything was paid for but the mortgage, which at first was $6400.00, but kept getting smaller.

The kids soon learned to drive the tractor, and as time went on we all could plough, cultivate, and of course hitch the tractor to the manure spreader and take a stinky, steamy load from the pile in the barnyard and spread it on the fields. Irene always enjoyed driving the tractor, and she was good with the livestock.

Patti and Jimmy went to a one-room school about a mile away. Billy caught the bus at the farm gate and went to high school in Milverton. It wasn't long until he was taking his guitar to school and playing and singing for special events. Then the teachers invited him to sing at the Rotary Club dinners, and soon he was becoming a celebrity at school. It was only a little while and he had Patti singing harmony with him.

Book Twenty-seven: The Race Announcer

In the spring of 1965, Hanover Raceway installed lights and held races every Saturday night from the middle of May until October. People came from all around. They were the first so-called "B track" to have night racing in Western Ontario. I soon coined the phrase and always referred to it as "Western Ontario's Pioneer B Track." I did a live broadcast of the races on the popular radio station, CKNX. I was also the master of ceremonies for their fall fair. At the end of the first season, the mayor of Hanover, in closing ceremonies, came to the microphone and read a wonderful letter of citation to me, praising my colourful contributions to the success of the track as the voice of Hanover Raceway and their fair. It seemed that I had come a long way from the time I attended that old school house at Campell's Corner a mile and a quarter down the road as a boy. Although, by now, I lived about 50 miles south of Hanover and we drove there on Saturday evening. When I climbed the stairs to my room at the top of the grandstand and strapped the microphone around my neck to call the races, I was back home and everybody knew me. I was no longer that boy in the shabby clothes. I was a celebrity!!

The following year, Owen Sound Raceway installed lights at their fairgrounds and had races every Wednesday night from June into October. They also had a big four-day fair at Owen Sound and I was the MC for the grandstand show, both the afternoon and evening shows. Their local radio station, CFOS, also broadcast the races. I was becoming well-known as the voice of harness racing and the fall fair circuit.

I continued to MC fairs and exhibitions as long as they were in a radius of those tracks. Newspapers, including Toronto's *Globe and Mail*, wrote about me. My pictures and stories on my life as a track announcer and master of ceremonies for fairs and exhibitions were in several papers. Of course, Irene travelled with me; we stayed in hotels and ate at fancy places. When we went into a restaurant, people would recognise me and stare at me every time I took a bite. Others would come over and ask me about the races, who did I think would win.

Most of the fairs were on Saturdays, which meant travelling to a fair, then introducing politicians and local celebrities, and I got to know several prominent members of parliament, met at least two premiers of Ontario, and a prime minister. I also kept the horse shows and other events moving along on an interesting and entertaining schedule. Introducing each exhibitor, every Queen-of-the-fair contestant, learning new names, trying to remember the names of those I had learned the year before, and talking on the microphone all afternoon. Trying my best to get out of that town in time to get to Hanover Raceway for the first race at 7:30. Driving sometimes at breakneck speed or caught behind someone out for a leisure drive. Often arriving after the horses were on the track for the first race, then running up to my announcer's room at the top of the grandstand, strapping the microphone around my neck, and saying, "Good evening, ladies and gentlemen, and welcome to Hanover Raceway." Then getting the scratches and changes from the judges, announcing them to the public and telling them, "ONE MINUTE TO POST." Of course, looking out onto the track through binoculars, memorising the horses' names so I would know every one of them when I said "THEY'RE AT THE POST." It was a nerve-wracking schedule, but I enjoyed the excitement and the challenge. It was never boring, like school was. And it seemed a long way from the times when I was a kid and I forgot to water that thirsty bull, back on Maw's farm.

Irene would bring me a hamburger or hot dog and some pop to drink, then she would enjoy the races or whatever else she did. It was sometimes close to midnight when we would get away from the track and then drive more than 50 miles home to the farm. It was a long day, but with all the exciting challenges, I loved it. When we got home, it was time to party, throw back a few drinks of whiskey, kind of unravel. Sometimes we had to drive from Hanover or Owen Sound after the races back to a motel at Barrie or Collingwood, where we were working a fair. Burt and the children looked after the farm chores while we were away.

My in-laws by now just lived a couple of miles out of Hanover. They had sold their little place and David bought a small farm where he and his parents lived. David started working in the mutual department at the track, and before long he bought some computers and did all the calculating. Not only for Hanover Raceway, but for all the other tracks that had sprung up around the circuit. Irene's mother enjoyed the races; she went every Saturday night and bet every race.

The children were singing more all the time and improving with every gig. It wasn't very long until I bought Jimmy a snare drum and a cymbal and some real drum sticks. He had wonderful rhythm, and it didn't take much practice until our three kids were a trio. I got Patti a bass guitar and Billy taught her to play it. Billy mostly sang lead vocals and the other two did harmony. They started entering contests, and won everywhere they went. They called themselves The

Willie Kell

Badgers. In the spring of 1967, there was a big event held in Stratford, put on by the city officials and businessmen. They had blocked off the street and put a covered stage on the steps of the city hall, and invited all the local bands in the area to compete. The prize was a trip to Expo in Montreal or a full set of drums. I felt that our kids weren't quite ready for this, and urged them not to enter. They insisted they wanted to try. I had some work to do at the farm, then I had to go to work at the hotel starting at 3:30 that day. Irene took the kids into Stratford and helped them set up their equipment. They not only competed, they won the hearts of everybody—and the set of drums. Just what they needed.

Patti, riding one of our horses at the farm

Book Twenty-eight: Irene and her Racehorses

It was about two years after we moved to the farm that my friend Burt Graham needed a place to live and keep his horses. I invited him to bring his horses and stay at our farm. He set his little homemade house trailer up in the yard and put his two horses in the barn. He had raced a big trotter he had raised a few times; he called him "Doug Peters." He also had a well-bred brood mare he had bought in the States. She was in foal, and had a nice chestnut foal in our barn in the spring of '66. We named him Darn-U-Jim.

Burt trained his horse on the gravel shoulder of the road. We marked out a mile by quarters, half, and three-quarters—this way he could rate the horse. We used to keep it level with a drag behind our tractor.

Burt was very good to help around the farm; he knew how to plough and gave us good advice on many things. He also watched over the children when we were away. Sometimes Irene and I would be away for several days at fairs and races. Burt would help the kids do the chores, and even took them places where they were singing. He was honest, and a good friend.

During that winter, I got a secondhand trotter on a deal. His name was Scott's Up, and he cost me $165.00. A well-known trainer driver had bought him in Chicago the year before, but had no luck with him. At first I had planned to sell him to the Mennonites for a road horse, but with Burt and Irene's encouragement, we started to train him. I bought him a secondhand set of race harness and borrowed one of Burt's jogging carts. We trained the two trotters on the side of the highway, by the farm; I trained my horse and Burt trained his.

When Hanover Raceway opened in May 1967, we took both horses and entered them in separate races. They raced well and were in the money; Burt drove them both, and Irene and Billy helped with them. Of course, I was the announcer. It was interesting for me, announcing my own horse and trying to watch everything he did. We raced the horses in Irene's name; I thought she deserved some notoriety. The children had their busy and exciting world, and so did I. It sounded good to announce her name as the owner.

It was in his third race that year that Scot's Up broke the track record for trotters at Hanover Raceway. Irene, her mom, and the kids were in the winner's circle for the picture following the race. He raced consistently all summer; the purses were small, but he soon paid for himself and his expenses. We took him to the big track at Mohawk Raceway, and though he had bad racing luck, he was in the money. Shortly after, we sold him for $1000.00. Someone else bought him, raced him for a while, and then kept him for a pet the rest of his life.

It was along about this time that the Windsor Hotel was owned by a Jewish family from Toronto—two brothers, both successful lawyers, along with their sister and her husband. The sister and her husband took over the hotel and lived there with their two little girls. This sister—her name was Annette—and I became special friends. She had such a warm, outgoing personality, it was difficult to keep from falling in love with her. She was also one of the most attractive ladies I had ever seen, and ten years younger than I. Her flashing, dark brown eyes seemed to radiate an aura of passion, innocence,

Willie

and intelligence all at the same time. Her high cheekbones gave her countenance an almost Asian-like look. Her coal-black hair hung down in curls and ringlets. Her voice had a special quality. It could sound like that of a criminal lawyer, and at other times it could purr like a contented kitten.

Annette and I became friends. We had wonderful conversations and could talk about anything. We revealed deep, dark secrets to one another. After some of Irene's great romantic escapades, especially the one with that old chiropractor, I felt a much greater sense of freedom from my matrimonial chains. Yes, although I was still very much in love with Irene, I didn't feel the same sense of loyalty. I was quite attracted to this sensuous, dark eyed beauty, and I knew that she was attracted to me. We became close, but didn't get involved in lovemaking. She was so intelligent, so charming, and yet so very down to earth and folksy.

She got all of these qualities from her wonderful parents. They arrived in Canada from Poland during the Depression with little more than the clothes on their backs. Through hard work and a lot of good savvy, they became successful. They sold a property in Toronto and bought a little hotel at Lucan, Ontario; that's were the kids were raised. The two boys, Paul and Sydney, went through for lawyers and both became very successful while still in their thirties. Annette was just as smart as her brothers, and would have made a great lawyer, had she wanted to. But with all their good fortune and wealth, these fine people never forgot where they came from. Annette's parents lived in Miami, Florida when I knew them, but came north and stayed with her at the hotel in the summer. At that time, I often worked at the hotel a couple of days a week, mostly Sunday and Monday evenings. Sometimes Annette cooked kosher meals and would bring me a plate loaded with this

Willie Kell

delicious food. Then she would take my fork and steal a bite from my plate. I worked part-time at the hotel for about three years and met a lot of interesting people, but none quite as interesting as Annette.

Meanwhile back in the real world of Irene, my family, and the farm, life moved along. I worked the races and the fairs, the kids kept doing the music, we raced the horses, sold some medicine, traded, bought, and sold, and kept improving the farm. By now Billy was writing some nice songs and getting to play the guitar real good.

It was in 1968 that the Salada Tea Co. put on a contest across Ontario. They were looking for songwriters to write a commercial song about Salada tea. Billy had written a couple of songs by this time, and he entered the contest. They taped the song and sent it in and became finalists. The prize was an all-expense-paid trip to Toronto to stay at the Lord Simcoe Hotel and attend a banquet there, in which Bobby Gimby a well-known Canadian songwriter, singer, and musician, was our host. Irene and I were also invited. Then the next day, the kids performed their Salada tea song and a couple of other songs at the famous Toronto Exhibition, along with the other finalists from across Ontario.

Our kids, The Badgers, did great; they were the youngest performers there and were the overwhelming favourites with the large crowd, but they were judged second best. A professional group from Toronto were the winners. It was a wonderful experience for them and they showed their great natural ability to write and perform. When they got home, they continued their music and were guests on a couple of local TV programs and did well. Uncle David Grenfell had put together a good sound system for them.

Willie

We were a busy family, what with my travelling around, announcing races and fairs, having racehorses, a farm, selling medicine, working evenings at the hotel part-time, and being very much involved with the children and their music. We didn't have a lot of extra money; if the children wanted money for school or something, they just helped themselves. I trusted them. We lived comfortable, never went without anything that we really wanted.

We were never very good at budgeting. Irene had never learned to be a thrifty shopper, and neither had I. It seemed we were always running to the expensive store down the road to buy things at the last minute. We had a big freezer, but most of the time there was very little in it.

In the fall of '67 Irene and I went to the standardbred sale in Toronto and bought a chestnut gelding called Noral Royal out of the Ken Galbraith stable. He was a pacer and had raced a couple of times, but had not won any money. We gave $150.00 for him; Irene liked him, and she had the last bid on him. We started to drive him during the winter. He had some problems with his hind legs, but Burt had a remedy for that.

In the past, that horse had a habit of running off the track when he felt like it. We soon ran into this same thing, when he dashed in the lane at the farm when I was driving him one day. I quickly turned the matter over to Burt. He had a remedy for this as well. After a few lessons from Burt, he behaved much better, but every once in a while, he needed another lesson. He trained wonderfully, and when spring came he was ready for the races. We took him to Hanover Raceway and soon Irene had another nice racehorse. Burt's trotter was also racing well, and both horses won a few

Willie Kell

races during the summer. We also took them to Mohawk Raceway, where they were in the money. Irene's horse was 1st, 2nd, or 3rd in every start but one that year at Hanover.

Irene had been going to her mother's doctor in Walkerton, and he gave her a pap test. It apparently revealed that she needed a partial hysterectomy. She was admitted into the Walkerton hospital and had the operation in the winter of '69. They had to operate a second time; for a while it looked as if she wouldn't pull through. She was in the hospital for over a month. How could I go on without her? I was there when they brought her out of the operating room both times, and although it was 60 miles away, I went to see her as often as I could. We had the pastor lay hands on her and pray over her, and I believe it helped.

By this time Billy was spending a lot of time with his girlfriend, and often didn't live at home, although he and the other two were still playing music together. One night they had a gig up Walkerton way, and it gave us all a chance to go see Irene in the hospital for a while before the show. Of course, her parents and David lived close and they went to see her often. She had other friends go to see her too, including one of her boyfriends.

While Irene was in the hospital, I made appointments with a talent co-ordinator at the CBC television network and a recording executive in Toronto. The day went well, and Billy was offered a contract at Arc Records, which we didn't accept. We went for dinner and had a nice time. However, when we got home, Patti had bad pains; we took her into the Stratford hospital, where she was operated on for appendicitis.

Willie

At last Irene was able to come home from that hospital. She gained strength every day and soon was her old self again, but for the fact that she could never have any more children.

When spring came, our horses seemed ready for the races. We took them to Hanover for opening night in May, and they both won. By now, Burt couldn't get a license to drive the horses, because of a heart condition. Irene and I raced her horse at London Raceway twice; he raced great, was second and third in two starts, and then we sold him.

Irene wasn't much help to me; she spent the evenings with one of her boyfriends in the clubhouse. Again I was very disappointed; instead of helping with the horse, she was doing what she always did best—cheating! That's when I decided to sell the horse. I was tired of being her fool. We didn't get enough for that horse, although he had been a good investment. He was just getting great when we sold him. He got hurt in an accident after I sold him and never reached his potential. But, in spite of this, he managed to win over $6000.00 in one season racing at the big track in Toronto. Again Irene's frivolous ways cost us financially.

The summer went by in the usual way. The time seemed to fly by, what with all of our activities. Mom Grenfell was planning on going to England for a few weeks in September, and Irene wanted to go with her. They would stay with relatives.

The mood was very quiet and subdued on the way to the airport at Toronto. I was ticked off with Irene for an escapade the Saturday night before. I didn't kiss her good-bye when she got on the plane. I was getting tired of her foolish ways; she was becoming the talk of the backstretch while I was trying to make something better for all of us. But I still loved her so much, and kept hoping she would change.

Although we were busy, our lifestyle was expensive; it cost money to stay in nice hotels and eat in fancy places. The kids didn't make much money, but anything they made was their own, although they bought most of their clothes. We were famous, but we weren't rich. Irene and I went to bars where there was entertainment, then we would go to eat and live the good life. So when she went to England, I not only had the expense of her trip, I also had bills to pay.

While Irene was in England, I missed her; it seemed I couldn't live without her, and it was hell living with her sometimes. I couldn't wait for her to get home, although I was still quiet with her when she did. But, as usual, things got back to normal. Normal was loving, and fighting, and then going for long periods when we got along great. We got along great when she wasn't fooling around, or when I didn't know she was. Our life was a big roller-coaster ride, sometimes heaven, sometimes hell, sometimes something between, but interesting.

Although our boys didn't care much about horses and ponies, Patti did. She got a couple of ponies ready and showed them at the Milverton fair. I bought a nice western saddle and she trained the ponies and won first prize. She also won the pony race. She had her pony well broke, and when the others ran off the track, Patti and her pony kept right on going and, like the hare and the tortoise story, she won. I was the announcer, and it was a big thrill for me.

During these years I didn't sing very much, or write any poetry. I had planned a career in show business, but that part of my life ran off the tracks when I got married. Getting into the announcing business was the next best thing. That way I could be close to home with my family. But I tried to teach the children some of what I knew about showmanship and stage presentation. They responded well, and became fine performers. I got great satisfaction from watching and listening and helping them.

When Billy got through high school, The Badgers were a thing of the past. He and Jimmy played and sang in a country band for a couple of years, playing for local dances, while Billy was still in school and after. When Billy graduated from high school, he moved to Kitchener and worked in the advertisement department of the newspaper. It was about this time that he started playing and singing folk songs in clubs and coffee houses and gaining quite a following. When he came home weekends, they would sing and play and sounded great.

Life at the farm kept going along. We had a standardbred brood mare and a couple of nice colts. Burt was training his horses. The first one, "Darn-U-Jim," turned out great. Burt took him to Hanover Raceway and he won his first two starts, and then he sold him. That horse went on to break several track records and win close to $100,000, racing in Canada and the U.S.A., We were proud to say that he was foaled in our barn. We had made a half-mile training track at the farm, although we still trained them often on the roadside.

Willie Kell

Book Twenty-nine: The Creamcheeze Good-Time Band

It was New Year's Day, 1971, and we were all together at Irene's parents' place near Hanover. Billy had his guitar, by this time Patti was playing the auto-harp, and Jimmy was playing bass guitar. We had a wonderful dinner and enjoyed the kids singing and playing. We decided that day they should be back together again, the three of them. Billy asked me to take an active part in their career and manage them.

It was soon after that New Year's Day that we added a couple of more members to the band. A friend of Billy's, a year younger, was a good bass guitar player; his name was Dave Harwood. Soon we found a 15-year old girl who played the classical violin; her name was Barb Payne. She and her family were from North Carolina, but were transferred to Stratford. Her father was an executive in a big American corporation. It wasn't long before these two young people were playing country, folk, rock, and gospel together with our three kids. Barb was as cute as she could be—honey-blond hair, dimpled cheeks, and quite talented. Billy was writing some nice songs, and they worked this original material into great stage productions along with other old songs, new songs, sad songs, and funny songs. Our kids and Dave couldn't read music notes, they all played by ear. They soon were playing some nice gigs around the area of Stratford and Kitchener.

Uncle Dave Grenfell recorded some tapes of their music during the winter and it sounded real professional. By this time, he had put together a fine sound system for them. When those five young people were on the stage with the coloured lights beaming down, the two girls in long dresses, the boys in jeans and nice shirts, it gave you goose bumps just to see them. Then when they played and sang, it was some kind of magic. Billy came up with a name for them, said he dreamed it. Their name would be:

"THE CREAMCHEEZE GOOD-TIME BAND"

In the spring, Billy and I took the train to Toronto. I had called three recording companies and made appointments. We took the big old tape player and a tape of several songs with us. We rode the subways, streetcars. and buses to the recording places. The first one we talked with was ready to sign them to a one-record deal. He was a veteran in the business, his name was St. Claire Lowe, and he owned his own recording company, Dominion Records. He liked what he heard on that tape. He had signed Hank Snow, Stompin' Tom Connors, and several more well-known singers and entertainers through the years. We told Mr. Lowe that we would call him in a day or two and let him know. Billy and I were ecstatic when we walked out of that man's office; we liked what he said and planned to sign with him. We went to the others I had called, and although we didn't get another offer, they sounded encouraging too. Just imagine—we were going to cut a record at the famous RCA Studios in Toronto. When we got home the next day, the other kids were quite excited with what we had been able to do in such a short time. Although Barb's father, being the educated executive that he was, got a lawyer and we had a meeting with him. He used all kinds of lawyer words, but I said we are

Willie Kell

going to do the deal. I could read the contract as well as that lawyer.

We cut the record, with several of Billy's original songs on it, a few weeks later, about the first of May, near Jimmy's 12th birthday. What an exciting thing for all of us to be in that studio in Toronto, cutting our first record. It turned out great.

This was before the time of cassette tapes or CDs. The album and the singles were released on vinyl. Billy had a friend who did the artwork for the album cover, with a nice picture of the five members of the band on the front. We had the picture taken among the old horse-drawn implements at Johnny Kuepfer's farm. Soon they were playing the songs on radio stations all across Canada. The local stores in Stratford had huge displays of their albums all over the walls and they sold like snow shovels in Saskatchewan. One song got on the pop charts, and one was on the country charts.

Book Thirty: Cutting Records, National TV, The Forum

They were soon playing in places as far away as Toronto. Finally they got a gig at The Forum at Ontario Place in Toronto, as guests with several other performers. But it soon was established that The Creamcheeze Good-Time Band was a real favourite with the crowd. They got a standing ovation at The Forum, followed by a nice write-up in Canada's biggest paper, the *Toronto Star*, and several more prominent papers. Then they were invited to appear on the prestigious *Tommy Hunter Show* on the CBC TV Network. It was a thrill for the kids to meet those people on the *Tommy Hunter Show*, some big names from Nashville. Gordie Tapp, who was on the big TV show, *Hee Haw*, was nice to the kids, and everybody was impressed with them. Irene and I drove them to Toronto and I stayed until they had taped part of the show on Friday, then I left for home Friday night. There were horses to look after and other things to do at the farm. Then, the next evening being Saturday, I was in Hanover to call the races. Irene stayed with the band in a fancy hotel paid for by CBC TV. On Sunday they came directly from taping the *Tommy Hunter Show* in Toronto to headline the evening grandstand show at the Paris Ontario Fair. I drove to Paris and introduced them onstage at the fair on Sunday evening. Our life was exciting as usual, and becoming more so all the time.

It wasn't long after that they did a TV special on CKCO TV. A producer and crew of cameramen came to the farm and showed The Creamcheeze Good-Time Band in their home. There were several pictures and stories about them in papers, and it was interesting to meet so many nice people who genuinely loved them. They were asked to play at a party in Toronto for Prime Minister John Dieffenbaker. The notoriety didn't seem to change them; they went about their schoolwork and Billy still worked at the newspaper by day, but had to take a lot of time off for the music. Irene and I went with them all the time, unless I was at fairs or races, then she went with the kids and I went to the races and fairs alone. Of course we had racehorses to train, pigs were having pigs, mares were foaling, there were crops to plant, and all the other things that a normal family does.

We had a wonderful experience when they had an opportunity to play with Doug Kershaw, the Louisiana Man. It was at Waterloo University. The Creamcheeze Good-Time Band had recorded his big song, "Louisiana Man" and it got in the top 30 on the country charts across the country. He called the band on stage with him and they played up a storm. Doug Kershaw had appeared on all the big TV shows, even the *Tonight Show* with Johnny Carson, in Hollywood.

As time went on, we lost our beautiful fiddle player; Barb and her family moved back to North Carolina. It was difficult to replace that sweet little girl from North Carolina with the honey-blond hair and the big blue eyes. We finally found a real talented fellow a year older than Billy, living in Stratford, who could make a fiddle sing; his name was Doug McNaughton. He not only played the fiddle, but he played the guitar, mandolin, and the piano.

Billy had been going with a nice girl who lived with her family in Stratford, and things were getting serious between them. Annie was quite clever, but terribly quiet. It was hard to get a word out of her. Patti had left home and was going with a tall blond-haired fellow by the name of Dave Burns. She got to know him when they both hung around with the Perth County Conspiracy. The Conspiracy was group of songwriters, singers, and musicians that possessed huge amounts of talent mixed with a generous portion of far-out feelings of frustrations spilled over from the radical mid-sixties. This was a time of sharing. People of this era shared their love, their money, and their dope. I found the people of this generation very interesting, though I didn't always agree with their politics, and I didn't share their dope.

The Creamcheeze Good-Time Band
Billy, Dave, Patti, Jimmy, Doug
Taken at the farm

Willie Kell

Book Thirty-one: Record Deal With MCA, World's Largest

In the spring of 1972, I called MCA records in Toronto and talked to a fellow named Richard Bibbey, I'm not sure of his status at the time. I called him, but he asked me to send the Creamcheeze album to him in Toronto and he would have a listen.

It was a week or so later, I was in the barn doing something with the horses, and the phone in the barn rang (yes, we had a phone in the barn). It was Richard; he called to say that he liked the album and would be interested in hearing the band in person. We arranged a gig in Kitchener, at a coffee- house where the kids played sometimes. Richard and his pretty wife Pam came and enjoyed the music and fell in love with the group. The place was packed and it was a nice concert. It wasn't long after that we signed a deal with MCA, the world's largest record company and part of Universal Pictures, the world's largest movie producers, based in Hollywood, California. Richard Bibbey soon became vice-president and head of Canadian operations. He came to the farm several times, played ball with the kids, had supper with us, and was a friend.

Richard brought producers with him to the farm. They listened to the band, Irene made nice suppers, and soon we were preparing for our next album.

It seems that, at the same time, Billy and Annie were preparing to get married. Although Billy was 21, Annie was three years younger. Knowing what I had gone

Willie

through, marrying Irene when she was so young, I tried to get them to put it off for a while. I also felt the timing wasn't the best, in view of Billy's career being very promising then. When it was evident that I couldn't persuade them to wait a while, I suggested that we get some publicity from it, and Billy and Anne agreed. They decided to get married on the front lawn at the farm, under our big weeping willow tree.

The Wedding

Willie Kell

Book Thirty-two: The Wedding by The Willow —and Other Interesting Things

The big wedding day came, a Sunday in July. The weather was beautiful and there were newspaper reporters, television cameras, friends, and relatives from everywhere. The huge lawn at the farm seemed full of people, and chairs were scattered all over the place. There were musicians, singers, and of course Richard and Pam Bibbey and the people from Duchess Publishing, who would be publishing Billy's songs. The yard was filled with cars and they were parked all along the highway in front of the farm.

The wedding was on several local TV specials and news programs. The local paper had it all over the front page. The Creemcheeze Good-time Band played on the veranda. Anne looked beautiful; her white wedding dress seemed to bring even more beauty to her dark brown eyes. She wore a strand of roses in her auburn hair; Billy had written a song, and in the lines said, "Annie's got roses in her hair," so, the roses. Billy seemed so happy and he always looked so nice, he had that wonderful smile.

After the wedding, Billy and Anne headed out on a little honeymoon to Cinncinnatti. I bought them an old car and fixed it up for them. Looking back, I have often thought that it wasn't much of a car to take on a honeymoon, but it was the best I could afford. However, it lasted them a while; it was their first car, and they never were without one after.

Willie

The day went real well, and everyone seemed to have a good time, although I wasn't very happy with Irene. She had pulled off another silly caper just a day or two before at a dinner party we were invited to in a little town. I had gone to that little town to announce the harness races. After the races, the judges and their wives and Irene and I were invited to a dinner and cocktail party at this big racehorse owner-promoter's house. After she had a couple of drinks, Irene got friendly with one of the judges and went and sat on his knee and wiggled around like she'd wet her pants. Thank goodness his wife wasn't there with him. We had known this fellow for some time and I worked with him quite often. It was very embarrassing and a real put-down for me, but that was Irene. Take her with me, treat her well, and she would mostly screw up.

Irene's mom was going to England in August and Irene was planning on going with her again. They had been to Britain three years before, and she didn't think her mother should go alone. Jimmy would have to go with them; he couldn't be with me all the time, when I travelled to fairs, and I couldn't leave him alone at the farm. He was just thirteen at the time, but had some money from all his playing with the band and could buy his own ticket. It would be a good experience for him.

There was something else playing on my mind. Irene had been writing and receiving letters from a fellow in England she had met when she was there three years before. In the meantime, this man's wife had died, and she felt sorry for him. Somehow this all sounded so familiar ... hadn't I heard that song before?

Jimmy was 13, and the other kids were out on their own. I didn't mention my suspicions, but I made up my mind that if I found out that Irene fooled around in England, this time would be the last time. I made sure

Willie Kell

she had enough money for the trip, drove them to the airport, and watched them fly away.

While they were away, I kept busy at the fairs, the races, and the farm and paid some bills that had somehow got overdue. The Creamcheeze Good-Time Band played an evening grandstand show at Woodstock Fair. We got a drummer to take Jimmy's place. I couldn't be there because I was a hundred and fifty miles away, working the grandstand shows at Barrie Fair at the same time, and had to be there for several days. Then, of course, there was the races at Hanover and Owen Sound as well. I missed Irene and Jimmy a lot while they were away, but I had made up my mind that I could live without her. I knew that whatever she might have done while she was away, giving her up would be difficult. But give her up I would, if I found one more reason.

When she got home, she told me about her time in England, about her relatives and a lot of things, but I sensed that she hadn't told me everything. But I didn't show a sign; I told her how I loved her and missed her, and it was true. Jimmy enjoyed his first trip to England, but wasn't as excited about it as his Mom.

The following Saturday, I had to MC the New Hamburg Fair grandstand show. It was always big and busy. The kids had a grandstand show at another fair; Irene would go with the band and I would go by myself. When I was getting dressed for the fair, I happened to look in my desk drawer and found a partly written letter to this fellow in England. I was devastated, but didn't say anything. Irene came out and kissed me good-bye at the car when I left and told me to have a good day. How could I have a good day, knowing that she was going to go in and finish writing that secret love letter?

I drove to the fair with a heavy heart. It was a busy day, running three rings from 11 o'clock in the morning

Willie

until near 6 o'clock in the evening. Then drive like a fire truck to get to Hanover for the races, without supper. The races were over, as usual, after 11 at night. I'd had a busy day, trying to entertain the big crowd at the fair, then the roaring crowd at the races at night. I drove Irene's mom home, as I always did after the races. She told me, unknowingly that Irene had been to this fellow's place while she was in England, and that he had been to the relatives' place where they stayed.

I headed for home after that hectic day at the office, arriving after 1 AM. Everybody was in bed. I went to our bedroom on the ground floor to see Irene; she had just gone to bed, she said. She didn't bother to get up and come to see me when I got home, tell me about how the kids' show had gone, or ask me how I managed to get through the long day and night or the miles of driving. But the Saturday night before that, she could stay out half the night with that guy in England. It's the way she always was—couldn't keep her pretty eyes open at home. But if we were out somewhere and I suggested it was time to go home, she would make some cruel remark in front of everybody, like, "You're always tired; I like to boogie." Well, she didn't seem ready to boogie right then, *she* was the one that was tired. I wanted to get drunk!

I hadn't had much to eat all day, my mind was filled with people, ponies, Clydesdales, and carriage horses that I'd had to deal with at the fair, then the night at the track calling the ten races and going crazy. Through it all, my mind was on Irene, and how she had lied again. Damn that woman! I brought out a bottle of whiskey, sat it on the kitchen table, and planned to drink that sucker dry in world's-record time. After I had a few drinks of that whiskey and got to thinking of what a fool I had been the past twenty-six years, I went into the bedroom, woke up Irene, and told her what I knew.

Willie Kell

Book Thirty-three: Sometimes It's Hell

All hell broke out, as usual, when I confronted Irene. She got out of bed, called her mother on the phone, and told her what I said. Of course, her mother didn't really know she had told me, because I didn't ask her directly. I'd only said that Irene had been to this fellow's apartment and she agreed she had been. It may have been a sneaky way to find out, but somebody told me that all is fair in love and war, and this sure enough was both!

Well, Irene came to the kitchen and poured herself a stiff double drink of rye, then started screaming, lying, crying and denying, perhaps not in that exact order. Then I mentioned the letter; she had finished writing it and it was in a sealed envelope. She got it out of the desk drawer, ripped it in little pieces, and threw it in the unlit stove. I later retrieved it and put it together. She had signed it, "With Love, Forever." Yes, over the years I had become somewhat of a Sherlock Holmes.

After threatening me with a huge butcher knife (her favourite weapon), which I took out of her hand at great risk to life and limb, she grabbed the keys to my car (another favourite trick of hers) and took off into the night. I went to bed, but hardly slept.

Irene finally came back about daylight and things settled down some. But it was mostly hell for the weeks and months ahead. She would talk of suicide when I talked of divorce. She would come after me with sharp objects in the middle of the night when we fought about her frivolous ways.

Willie

Over the years I had become somewhat of an expert in disarming her. Sometimes it meant grabbing her arms and twisting until she dropped the knife. Other times a flying tackle and other quick-footed calisthenics to avoid disaster. Oh, I didn't always come away unscathed, and neither did she. One time she tried to carve a memory into my bare chest with a set of car keys. I have several battle scars from sharp fingernails. Then there was the huge battle, the time we had some unkind words and she threw a bottle of liniment at me in the dark while I lay in bed, then ran upstairs. I didn't see that bottle coming, but I felt it when it ripped my eyebrow wide open. The warm blood washed down in my eye and over my face. I ran upstairs and started yelling at her, calling her some uncomplimentary names. When she ran into a darkened bedroom, I could hardly see her, but I felt another smash to my head. She had picked up a little musical powder box that I had bought for her in more pleasant and romantic times and smashed it into my already bloody eyebrow. When I brushed it away and knocked it out of her hand, it landed over in the darkest corner of the bedroom, playing ever so sweetly the love song, "You Belong to My Heart." It sure wasn't funny at the time, but I have often chuckled since about it.

Oh, she wasn't through with her hell-bent damage on my body; she was just getting warmed up. We went downstairs, where the battle continued. The big, dirty iron frying pan was sitting on the stove, as usual. She picked it up and crashed it against the side of my head. Now I had another three-corner rip of quite a dimension about halfway between my right ear and the already damaged eyebrow. Through all of this one-sided battle I didn't hit Irene even once, just tried to hold her arms and defend myself. But I called her some choice names, let me tell you.

Willie Kell

This was about 3 in the morning. Jimmy had got up and came downstairs by this time. He suggested that we quit fighting, and that I go to the hospital for repairs. He called Patti; she came and we all went to the hospital, as a family—yes, Irene too. She waited in the car while the doctor sewed 12 stitches into my head and eyebrow. The doctor asked me what happened, I told him I fell.

Looking back, I have often wondered if there might have been some better way to handle this whole situation, but at the time I couldn't think of any and still haven't figured out a better way to deal with her.

The fights went on. Oh, we did make up, make love ... and then fight again. I told myself that I hated her, that I could never love her again, but I was lying to myself. I still loved her. I guess deep down inside of me I just wanted to believe that she would change, that we could somehow go on with our lives. But more and more I realised that this was impossible; our dream had ended long ago. It was just that I didn't want to believe it, and I still tried to believe in her.

These all-night wrestling matches were hard on Jimmy; he had to get up and go to school and play gigs all over the country. It was hard for me to think, I couldn't do the things that I should be doing. Lord knows the price we all had to pay. It's hard to say what real damage it did to our children and what it did to their career, or what the cost was in dollars.

I had left the hotel a year or two earlier. I regretted some of the things I had passed up for Irene, I regretted ever having loved her so. We had to part or we would not survive. We could not go on this way; one of us would be killed, the other one would be in prison.

Willie

Book Thirty-four: Cutting The MCA Album and Cutting Irene Loose

Through all of this turmoil we somehow negotiated a deal with MCA and recorded our album at the RCA Studios in Toronto. Billy wrote a little song called "Home Cookin'"—it was to be the title song. He also wrote a great song called "Living Without You." It was released as a single and got a bunch of airplay all across Canada. It climbed to 18 on the pop charts.

Gordon Lightfoot was quite popular at the time, and had written some great tunes. The Creamcheeze Good-Time Band recorded one of his tunes, called "Redwood Hill," and it became a country hit for the band.

We went to Montreal and did a guest spot on a TV show called *Musical Friends* on the CTV Network. The kids did some interviews and played a nice show in the Laurentians at a maple sugar festival. The president of MCA was there, from Hollywood, to meet the band. After that it was a guest appearance on the Ronnie Prophet show on CBC TV. Jimmy had to be signed as a child star with MCA because of his age; they were used to those things out in Hollywood.

The band played concerts with many famous stars. One time, at a big country show, they played with David Houston, a big Nashville star with a bunch of hit records. He came from Nashville with his custom-made bus. He had a Japanese fiddler in his band called Shoji Tabuchi; this fellow has gone on to great things at

Branson, Missouri, where he has one of the finest theaters there.

The Creamcheeze Good-Time Band played the famous Royal Winter Fair in Toronto, the world's largest fair. They played that fair 3 or 4 years in a row, several shows a day and a couple in the evening; we'd be in Toronto for a week. It was at the Royal Winter Fair in November 1972 that I saw my long-lost cousin Isabelle. She came to the Royal to hear my kids. I hadn't seen her in 20 years. She was born and lived in Toronto her whole life. She was my Aunt Lizzie's girl. She enjoyed the concert and came back to the dressing room with us and talked a little while, but with all the confusion, people getting autographs and taking pictures, we didn't have much time to talk. I was so happy she had come. I called her the next day from the Lord Simcoe Hotel, where we were staying, and we talked for while. That was a few months after Irene got back from England.

We had a nice time in Toronto that week, and Irene and I seemed to get along during our stay there, but when we got back to the farm, the fights started again. By this time her mother was mad at me; she said I lied, that she hadn't told me about Irene and that Englishman. She'd told me, but she didn't realise she had. That's the way it always had been—she took Irene's side. It was okay what Irene did, but it wasn't right the way I found out. I went to her house to talk to her, but she wouldn't let me come in.

Irene got a job in Stratford at a department store and soon bought herself a car. It was good that she did, it made our break-up that much easier. I went to the races by myself, or sometimes took Jimmy or Burt. I said that I would never take Irene with me to the races and fairs again, and I didn't.

Willie

By the next fall, she left home, just after our 27th wedding anniversary. I purposely was in Toronto; I went the day before and stayed over at the Westbury Hotel. I booked the Good-Time Band in a couple of gigs in Toronto, and I called Isabelle and she took me to some places to see people. She knew every inch of the city. Then we went out for supper and talked about some things before she drove me to catch the train at Union Station to come home. When I got home, Irene had been drinking wine and was raging mad. We fought, I received a few bangs and bruises, and she ended up with a bit of a fat lip. The following night the fight went on again, and after smashing glasses, ornaments, and anything else she could get her hands on, she loaded some things in her car and left in the early morning darkness. It seems she had a place to stay.

The whole thing was very traumatic and it tore me up. But the children seemed relieved to see her go, and wouldn't hear tell of me taking her back. By this time Patti was married; she and Dave lived just a mile away in a rented house, and we saw them quite often.

Willie Kell

Book Thirty-five: Good Night, Irene—I'll See You in My Dreams

Those months after Irene left were terrible. I missed her so much, I wondered how I could live without her. I couldn't do business, I sat at the kitchen table staring at the wall, talking to myself, drinking whiskey, and kind of wasting. I was heartbroken, I cried and walked the floor ... such torture and turmoil. Many times I wished she would come home, but somehow I had enough strength to fight my inner craving. Yes, giving up that woman seemed like trying to kick a heroin habit, but give her up I must.

Jimmy went to school and helped me around the place. When I knew he was coming home from school, I would put the bottle away, wash my face, get the tears out of my eyes, and try to be normal, whatever that was. He became more a friend than a child. He chastised me for drinking so much, until I was ashamed of myself. He saved the empty whiskey bottles and put them one on top of the other in his room, then he would show me. He cried, Burt cried, and my heart felt like it had been torn from my body.

I was getting very short of cash as time went on, and I finally went to work in a furniture factory, gluing furniture together. It was great therapy, although I hated it, but it brought in enough money to live on, and it didn't require any great amount of brainpower. I took time off when I had to go with the band. I also took Burt's horses to the races a few times when he wasn't

Willie

able to go. The foreman at the furniture factory treated me good.

During that winter, the band played the Horseshoe Tavern in Toronto for a week, the place that helped to make Stompin' Tom Connors something of a legend. They moved the stage into the dining lounge, because of Jimmy's age. My kids stayed at Isabelle's place, and I went to Toronto a couple of times that week, but I had to be home to look after the farm chores and things.

The week went well, and the crowds came to see them, although maybe not in as large a number as we would have liked. Richard and all the other VIPs from MCA showed up. The trade magazines wrote them up, but the band was not a smash hit by any means. That was the last time I saw Norm Dafoe, the great CBC news reporter. He spent one evening at The Horseshoe Tavern, enjoying the band, I sat and talked to him for quite a while. He was an interesting fellow, had travelled the world reporting the news for CBC Television Network. He didn't seem to be suffering any pain when I walked with him to the door and waited until he hailed a cab, it was about a year later that he died.

Willie Kell

Book Thirty-six: The Cousins

It was in the early spring that I set up a deal with the officials of The Stratford United Way for the Creamcheeze Band to play a benefit concert at Stratford's famous Avon Theater. It turned out to be a huge success. The theatre was sold out, all eleven hundred seats, and the concert was wonderful. The band got an encore and a long, loud standing ovation. It was a touching tribute from the city where all five members of the band were born. The Festival directors were bringing in people from all over the United States, even Europe, and they often didn't fill the theatre. We didn't get much money for the gig and very little help. We never got any help from the musicians' union either. If you did something that didn't suit them, they would fine you. They were a real dictatorial pain in the ass.

As time went on I had several talks with my cousin Isabelle. She said she would like to get out of the *Globe and Mail*, where she worked the phones, taking advertisements. She also planned to sell her house in Toronto and move to a smaller town. Isabelle said she would like to come to the farm, to live. She had been to the farm a couple of times and seemed to like it. I guess it took her back to when she used to go to Maw's farm when she was a girl. It would be nice to have a woman around the house. She had a car and could go where she liked. She could visit her children, have them come to the farm for a visit, and make it her home.

Willie

It was in July of 1974 when Isabelle sold her house in Toronto and came to live at the farm. She brought her furniture and everything she owned. She could have the big bedroom upstairs; Jimmy had moved into Pat's bedroom, and I slept in the bedroom downstairs, where I had always slept. Things were changing in our lives. Burt was married and moved to a small farm a few miles away.

Isabelle was quite organised, a good cook, and ran a tight ship. We had never been used to that, with Irene—mealtime was anytime. But now Isabelle had set up new rules.

We had quite a few clashes about almost everything. If one of my kids happened to come by around mealtime, I would invite them to stay. Isabelle would about take a spell; she wasn't used to people dropping by. If the band came to practice, things would be scattered around the front room, and they would get something out of the fridge to eat or drink. This is the way it had always been. I guess some changes were necessary, but they came a bit sudden.

It was during my time alone—a time when I was lonesome and hurt by all the things that Irene had put me through—that I started getting back to my poetry. I began to put some feelings down, and then a melody with it. I couldn't play an instrument, but Jimmy got me started on the mandolin, and I was able to put a few chords together. Mostly I would sing the song and Jimmy would play it on the acoustic guitar. I wrote the lyrics down and kept the melody in my head; I became obsessed with writing. Those lonesome heartbreak feelings were being crafted into songs. I had always had words and melodies coming into my mind, but with all the other pressures of life, I never took time to listen to them.

Willie Kell

Book Thirty-seven: Guitar Pickin', Songwritin' Son of a Gun

Jimmy kept after me to learn to play the guitar. He insisted that I try some chords. He would stretch my fingers onto those strings, and sometimes I thought that I would never be able to learn. He and Patti heard about a music store that was having an auction of new and used instruments. The three of us went and I came home with a nice secondhand acoustic guitar from that bankrupt sale. I was proud of that old box and I practised every day. Isabelle didn't seem that impressed at me buying the guitar, but Jimmy kept teaching me, and before long I could play a few chords on that darn thing. Now I spent more time at my song-writing and was turning out country, folk, and gospel songs. It was during this time that I wrote one of my best songs, "Daddy's Rollin' Home Tonight," a song about my Daddy and Mama and that old covered wagon. It soon was a favourite among some of those in our family, and then the band, and then everybody that heard the song could feel that warm, folksy feeling that was living in it. I had always been proud of my Daddy and his gypsy way of life, and now, in this song, I could tell the world about him and my dear old mother, and that legendary covered wagon.

As time went on, The Creamcheeze Good-Time Band was playing fewer dates. I just wasn't working as hard at getting them gigs. Billy and Patti were married, Irene was no longer in the picture, and with all the other

Willie

happenings and the changes, there just wasn't a good enough reason any longer. Although they played the Avon and Festival Theatres, some fairs, special events, and nice hotel lounges during those years. The second year that they played the Avon Theatre, our regular fiddle player was unable to be there, so I called our old friend, Al Cherney, who was a regular on the famous *Tommy Hunter Show*. He said he would be happy to play the gig with The Creamcheeze Good-Time Band, and it turned out great.

The children didn't see Irene for a while after she left; I saw her a few times. We met for a drink and talked about things. She talked about wanting to come home, but I told her it was too late, it was over, we had danced the last waltz. Some of the things she did after she left home made it easier to give up on her.

It was the spring of 1977 that we were divorced. I got me a city lawyer, we made a deal to give Irene a considerable amount of cash and a quiet, no-fault divorce, which I paid for. She didn't have to appear in court, and she didn't. Jimmy and I were there; it was good to get it all behind me, although deep inside I still loved her. By this time Patti and Dave were living in Stratford, then Jimmy left home and went to live with them. He was eighteen by this time. Isabelle often acted like the typical stepmother, and we had several hot arguments about it.

Soon after my divorce, I sold the farm, the livestock, and the few implements. Then I bought back my first little house just 5 miles away. It was strange, living there in that little house again after being at the farm for 14 years, and all the things that had happened.

I had sold the farm through a real estate agent on condition that the man who bought my farm sold his

Willie Kell

house to someone from a place called Putnam, a small hamlet 20 miles east of London, Ontario, on the 401. I had never heard tell of it. Some problems came up somewhere along the line and the whole deal was coming unravelled. There was only one thing for me to do—buy the house in Putnam. That's what I did, and it worked out great. Isabelle and I moved from the farm into the little house in Perth County, where Irene and I lived when our children were born. I did some minor repairs, and after living there for 7 months, I sold it and we moved to the big house in the village of Putnam.

It was a 2-storey brick with an attic, on a nice double lot with lovely trees, flowers, and shrubs around. The neighbourhood was friendly and quiet. It was a wonderful place for writing songs. By this time I had written several pretty good gospel songs, and was asked to sing and play my guitar at the local church several times. I had my own sound system by then. The people seemed to like my songs wherever I sang.

That first year we were there at the big house, after we had planted a little garden, Isabelle suggested that we take a trip. She didn't only suggest it; she threatened that if I didn't want to go, she would go by herself. Well, come to think of it, maybe it was a good time for a trip. Isabelle had been quite a traveller before she came to live with me, and now she was anxious to get on the road again. We made reservations at hotels and motels, and we had maps and brochures.

Book Thirty-eight: Nashville, New Orleans, and Texas

We headed out, crossed the border at Detroit, and went on down to Nashville. We stayed in Nashville a day or so and toured the place, then we headed south down through Alabama. Then on down to Pensacola, Florida—they claim it's the oldest city in the U.S.A. We toured the old town and found it very interesting. We had a place on the beach where the sand is as white as snow, washing up from the Gulf of Mexico. Then we drove across the top of the Gulf, stopping in Mobile, Alabama and Biloxi, Mississippi, and then New Orleans, Louisiana.

Now, there is no way you can go past New Orleans without stopping and seeing all the sights of that fascinating place. We got a hotel on Canal Street. It was a beautiful, older place, and we could walk from our hotel to the famous French Quarter that reaches out to the Mississippi River. We went into every bar and fancy restaurant in the French Quarter. We sat in Jackson Square and watched artists at work, and listened to the street singers. It was there in Jackson Square on a warm April morning that I met the Fiddler. I later wrote the song, "New Orleans Fiddler," one of the first songs I ever had published.

After several wonderful days, including a tour of the mansions in the Garden District, the above-ground cemeteries, Lake Ponchertrain, and almost every inch of that fairy-tale city, we left New Orleans and started out for Houston, Texas, stopping for lunch in Baton Rouge,

Willie Kell

Louisiana. We got a nice motel in Houston, stayed overnight and toured the city the next day. It is a wonderful city, but we moved on, down into the Rio Grande Valley. You can travel for many miles and not see much but some longhorned cattle in them badlands.

After stopping for a bite on the west coast of the Gulf of Mexico, a place called Corpus Christi, we headed on down to the South Padre Islands, a few miles from the border city of Matamoros, Mexico. The weather became very hot and humid, and the temperature climbed past 100 degrees. The hotel where we stayed was also home to many Mexicans there for a holiday. They cooked in their rooms, and the aroma of that Mexican food mixed with the humidity in the air gave the whole place a special atmosphere. We left that semi-tropical island in the Gulf of Mexico and headed northwest past the famous King Ranch, headed for San Antonio.

Now there is a real nice place. Isabelle and I loved it in San Antonio. We ate at the sidewalk cafes on the river walk, and we were serenaded by the Spanish table singers and their guitars. We stayed for days, toured the city, and visited the historic old missions. We went to the famous Alamo and remembered Davy Crockett. We did it all and loved every bit of that beautiful place. There was a sad moment for Isabelle and I there in San Antonio as well, when some poor and unfortunate fellow with too much wine in his belly fell under the wheels of a bus we were about to board and was killed there on the street.

After a few interesting days in San Antonio, we headed out early in the morning for the Arkansas border. It was a beautiful drive through the state capital of Austin, then up through Waco. We kept driving northeast to Texarkana and stayed at a motel right on the state line. We walked across the freeway and ate our

Willie

supper in a nice place in Arkansas. There wasn't much to keep us in Texarkana, so we left the next morning and started on a journey that would take us back to Music City, U.S.A. It was a good day's drive, up through Memphis.

When we got back to Nashville, we stayed a day or two. Went to the Grand Ole Opry and heard Roy Acuff singing "Wabash Cannon Ball" and Bill Monroe singing "Blue Moon of Kentucky." We spent a day at Opryland, and then it was time to go back to Putnam, to our big old beautiful house.

Isabelle and Me
Book 38 "Nashville, New Orleans, and Texas"

Book Thirty-nine: I'm Published

That summer went by as usual, what with the races at the two tracks, Owen Sound and Hanover, then the fairs and exhibitions starting in August. I continued to write some pretty good songs, and in the fall we decided to go into the studio and record some of them on a demo. We recorded nine songs, including "Daddy's Rollin' Home Tonight," and "New Orleans Fiddler." Billy sang some, Patti sang one or two, and I did a couple. Jimmy played drums, with Dave on bass and Doug on fiddle and piano. The tape turned out pretty good. It seemed that everybody was saying nice things about my songs, so maybe it would be a good time to find out what music publishers thought about them. That would be a real test of my song writing. I called four publishers in Toronto and made appointments for them to listen to my songs. Isabelle and I went to Toronto, spent a day or two calling on these people with the big ears. I was fortunate to have three out of the four offer a publisher's contract for all nine songs, including Quality Records, the same label that distributed all of Hank Williams' records in Canada. I didn't sign with any of them; I signed with a small independent publisher. But it felt good to know that my songs had been accepted by those big-city publishers.

The next spring Isabelle became restless again, so we decided to take a trip to California. This time we crossed at Detroit, went west to Indianapolis, stayed overnight, then on down to West Memphis and into Arkansas. We

Willie

bedded down in Little Rock, the town that President Bill Clinton would later make famous for the things he did there. We didn't tour any of these towns, just rested overnight. After Little Rock, it was the cowboy town of Abilene, Texas, by way of Dallas. Texas is a beautiful state, it has just about everything—the beaches on the west coast of the Gulf of Mexico, the Rio Grande Valley, mountains, deserts, and some interesting things like oil wells, sagebrush, sidewinders, rattlesnakes, horses, and longhorn cattle.

Our journey took us southwest from old Abilene and on through the Sierra Mountains to the legendary city that Marty Robbins sang about, El Paso. It's right on the Mexican border. There are more Spanish people in El Paso than there are in San Antonio. Just about everywhere they serve Mexican food, and, as usual, we tried just about everything. We walked across the bridge that spans the Rio Grande River and spent hours talking, trying, bargaining, and buying in the Mexican shops in the town of Juarez. We stayed in El Paso for days, soaking up the warm sun and the friendly hacienda feelings of the place.

When we said good-bye to El Paso, we headed out of Texas and into southern New Mexico. All along the highway you could look out onto the hills in Mexico and see the sad state of poverty that lived among the shacks on the hillsides. We stopped at Lordsburg, New Mexico for lunch, and I thought it must have been the loneliest place in the whole U.S.A. Our destination was Tucson, Arizona, where we'd stay for a few days. When we got there we toured the city, walked out in the country among the stovepipe cactus, always keeping an eye open for sidewinders and rattlesnakes. Then we visited the famous missions, and went to Old Tucson, where they make a lot of cowboy movies.

Willie Kell

Our next stop was Phoenix. I sang some songs in a bar there and met a few nice people. After a day or two we headed out for the golden state of California. We drove miles through the desert, past mountains, and stopped in Yuma, Arizona for lunch. We travelled west through some real pretty mountains and on down to the Pacific Ocean to San Diego. This beautiful city is everything I ever dreamed it would be and more. It is on the very southwestern tip of the U.S.A., and seems to reach out into the Pacific Ocean. Very pretty, built on a hundred hills. We toured the city, went to their famous zoo, and enjoyed all of it.

After San Diego, it was on to Los Angeles and Hollywood. Yes, it took a long time, but I finally got to Hollywood! When we got to L.A., we booked into a nice older hotel downtown, across from the famous Biltmore. We toured the town, went to the movie studios, ate at fancy restaurants, went to Dodger Stadium, and anything else we could think of. After L.A., our journey took us to Capistrano, to see if there were any swallows hanging around, for every year on March 19th, Isabelle's birthday, that's where they come, to an old mission there. We drove on through that beautiful part of California and stopped overnight in Santa Maria.

The next morning we started out early, driving along the side of the mountain on that winding highway, looking down into the raging waters of the Pacific Ocean on our way to San Francisco. It was late afternoon when we arrived in that intriguing city. Our hotel was downtown. Now, here was a town I had always wanted to experience. We rode miles on those old trolley cars, mostly in the rush time; I like to mingle with the locals, it's a good way to get the feel of a place. We walked, went to bars, ate at their famous Chinese restaurants, and toured almost every part of that fairy-tale city. We drove across the Golden Gate Bridge to Oakland, where

Willie

we spent an evening that was unforgettable. Yes, Isabelle and me even took a boat out into San Francisco Bay to Alcatraz Prison, the place where so many infamous prisoners lived—Al Capone, the Birdman of Alcatraz, and so many others. The place seemed to be filled with ghosts from the past.

When we left San Francisco, we drove through the Redwood forest and saw those huge trees. Then on down to Bakersfield for overnight, before starting out across the great Mojave Desert to Las Vegas, Nevada. Vegas is great, if you are into gambling or a raving Wayne Newton fan. It's billed as the city that never sleeps; the lights are so bright on the strip you need your shades on at midnight.

I think I really enjoyed the drive out of town over to Hoover Dam and looking down into the Colorado River more than I did Vegas. And I know that I enjoyed the beauty of the Grand Canyon even more. The sun was hanging in the western sky when we stopped at the rim of the canyon. It was a sight one never forgets. We stayed in a nice motel at the canyon, and the next morning the ground was white with snow. We hung around that beautiful place a while, looking down into that wonder of the world from different angles and places, and then we moved on.

It was near noon when we got away from the canyon and headed east to Gallup and Tucumcari, New Mexico, through the Painted Desert and the Petrified Forest. Driving around in that desert for days, we didn't see a tree. This is Billy The Kid country; that famous outlaw was killed back in 1881 by Sheriff Pat Garrett and is buried at Ft. Sumner, New Mexico.

We drove on to Alberqurque and stopped at a quaint little Spanish restaurant and had lunch and toured the old missions. Then we headed into the Texas Panhandle and on through Amarillo, heading east into

Oklahoma. We spent half of a morning visiting the Will Rogers Museum in Oklahoma I had always been a fan of this interesting cowboy philosopher. Oklahoma is a nice state, but we didn't spend much time there. We drove through Oklahoma City and on to Tulsa for overnight. Then it was on to St. Louis, Missouri, and in just a day or two we'd be back home. We had been away about a month and enjoyed every day of it. But now it was time to get back to watching those horses going around the tracks and writing some more songs.

My family, by this, time was playing bars under the name "KELL," and they had others playing with them from time to time. Jimmy joined a rock & roll band and toured eastern Canada for a while. Billy and Patti hired a bass player and continued playing the bars. Then Jimmy came back to the KELL band, and with another young fellow they toured western Canada a couple of times, all the way to British Columbia. They cut another record, which turned out pretty good.

Billy and Patti each had two beautiful children, and it was difficult being on the road so much. Billy was a wonderful father and delighted in his children. Patti loved her children, and though she enjoyed the music business, it was becoming a burden to leave her children behind and head out on that lonesome old road.

For me it was time to be restless again and try to find an interesting change of scenery. So we sold the big old house in Putnam and ended up with a cute little bungalow in Woodstock. We went to Florida for a while in the winter, toured some nice towns, including Savannah, Georgia, took in the usual sights in Florida, including Mickey Mouse. We had seen him in California as well, and he hadn't changed any.

Due to government regulations, I no longer sold medicine. In order to go on with it, I would have needed

Willie

a laboratory, even though my name was registered along with all of the big drug manufacturers in the book. But with the announcing, the music, and some money I had gathered around, I lived quite well. Isabelle kept our home sailing on a steady course, it seemed. My closets were filled with nice clothes, I had more pairs of shoes than I ever could wear. Of course, I could still lounge around home in my wonderful raggy clothes that I could never throw away; some would go to the thrift shops or garbage bags at the hands of Isabelle.

The racetrack at Owen Sound closed, but Hanover picked up their night. Then I was hired to announce at two other tracks, Goderich and Clinton. This gave me four nights a week at the tracks, just at a time when I should have been concentrating more on my music and songs. I was interviewed and asked to talk about some historical moments in my life regarding the harness racing industry. This interview was taped and, along with my announcing style, found its way into the Canadian Trotting Archives in Toronto.

I never pushed myself in with people, or begged for any favours; any recognition I got came from my ability. I never tried to become friends with judges, racetrack managers, or others because of their position. In my opinion, some that I worked with got their jobs by being on the inside, knowing the right people, not for any special talent they had. It wasn't my intention to be more than I already was, said by most to be one of the best race announcers in the business. Reliable and honest, I was well known for speaking out. This did not endear me to the officials sometimes, but the public loved me, and the feeling was mutual. I always believed my job was to make the public happy and bring excitement into the races, not to suck up to the officials or the management.

Willie Kell

Now that we had no horses, no farm, the kids were grown up and away, life was kind of easy. I worked the races from May through September, then I had the fairs starting in August until around mid-October. After that would be some concerts to play, keep writing songs, then, when the cold winds of winter started to blow, head off to the warmer climates.

It seemed after Irene and I broke up and the kids were gone I couldn't really feel at home in one place. It was in the early '80s that I sold that little bungalow and moved out to the quiet little village of Innerkip, a few miles away. I bought an older house sitting on about an acre of land that ran back to the Thames River. The house was big and open, with a quaint little upstairs. I bought a wood-burning cookstove for the big kitchen and another wood-burning stove for the large family room just off the kitchen. Maybe that's what was missing in my life—those stoves and the feel of home from the warm fire. I had the place remodelled and soon settled in. It became a nice place to lay back, live, and write.

The Siblings
Elizabeth, Willie, Jim, Son, Sweet, Toots
Book 39 "I'm Published"

Willie

Book Forty: Pitching Songs In Nashville and Loving Her

Although we enjoyed living in the old farmhouse, when winter came it was time to head south. We continued our travels, touring cities in the U.S.A., places like Washington, D.C., then Gettysburg, and Wheeling, West Virginia. It was early in 1980 that Isabelle and I flew to Nashville, taking some songs we had recorded on a demo. It was an interesting time. We got a hotel near Music Row, where most of the publishers are. We stayed for about a week and talked to several publishers. Some kept my songs, and I got a good positive feeling about being there. I met Maggie Cavender, and she insisted that I join Nashville Songwriters International. Most people there said I should move to Nashville and pitch my songs. Mel Tillis had a publishing house there at the time, and they kept one of my songs to send to M-M-Mel. It was a song called "Getting Used To Missing You." They thought Mel might record that song; well, if he did, I never heard about it.

However, I met some nice people and had a few unforgettable experiences. I was sitting in a tall building one day, talking to a young publisher who liked my songs. And in walked one of the finest songwriters in Nashville, Harland Howard, the man who wrote so many great country hits, like "I Fall to Pieces," the lovesick song that helped to make Patsy Cline a legend, "Heart Aches by The Number," and many more. I felt proud to be walking those old ghostly streets where Hank Williams, Kris Kristofferson, Mel Tillis, Roger

Willie Kell

Miller, Tammy Wynette, Dottie West and so many had walked, pitching their songs just like I was doing.

One day while we were in Nashville, I called Gail Tubb, daughter of the legendary Ernest Tubb. She invited me to her office and listened to my songs and I spent an hour or so with her. She told me that I should record them myself. She said, "You write like Kristofferson." While she was telling me these nice things, the phone rang. It was her father, the great Hall of Fame country singer-songwriter calling from Texas. They talked a while, then as she was hanging up, she said to him, "I love you too, Daddy." I thought it was touching.

She was a very down to earth person. She was sending a tape of my songs to her father, said he would listen to them while riding his bus from town to town when he was on tour. It was a while after that when Ernest Tubb got sick and died in a hospital in Nashville. But his classic songs—"Walking the Floor Over You," "Soldier's Last Letter," and many more—will always live.

When we got back from Nashville, it was time to start the racing circuit again. We had a travel trailer and we moved it to the town of Kincardine, on beautiful Lake Huron, for the summer. We spent more than half of our time in the trailer. It was closer to the tracks and a good place to lie back and dream. It was a pretty sight to see the sailboats out on Lake Huron, and we had an enjoyable time.

I was sitting by myself in a secluded place one day, looking out on the blue water of Lake Huron. I watched a mother and small boy down on the shore; the little boy was picking up pebbles. The lines of a pretty good song, "Little Boy," came to me, and I later recorded it. That

Willie

song has always been a favourite at my concerts, and is published in Nashville.

I enjoyed the life I was living, announcing the races, being somewhat of a celebrity, and meeting nice people. One of the nicest people I ever met was a sweet girl that I worked with at the racetracks. Her name was Karen, and she was a pretty, natural blonde with a great figure. Some said she looked like Dolly Parton. Come to think back on it, she did resemble Dolly in some ways, and not only for the blonde hair. We became friends, and when Saturday night rolled around, she would come to Hanover Raceway and spend the evening there with me, while I called the races.

Isabelle and I were going through a difficult period in our relationship. It was about a week after Isabelle and I had a falling-out that Karen came falling into my world, into my little "office" at the top of the grandstand. I hadn't seen her for almost a year. She told me how she missed me, that she cared for me, and of course I told her that I had always felt close to her. Karen had the kind of personality that attracted the opposite sex, not only for her natural beauty, but also for her outgoing friendly way. She was 27 at the time, about half my age, and being such an attractive gal, I was flattered. She was married and had two children. However, I couldn't wait to see her walk through that door into my private, darkened little world high above the roaring crowd, wrap her loving arms around me and put that warm kiss on my waiting lips. It certainly added to the excitement of the races. Although, at times, it was rather challenging trying to keep my mind on a fleeting field of race horses going around the far turn, doing my best to describe the action out on the track, with that pretty gal's leg wrapped around mine and feeling her body so close to me. Sometimes it seemed the action in my little "eagle's nest" was more exciting than what was happening out on the racetrack. Sometimes I wondered if the judges in the next room spent more time trying to watch Karen than they did the horses out on the track. My little room was dark but for the light that shone in from the lights out on the track.

Our seasonal relationship continued for about five years during the spring, summer, and fall, while the races and fall fairs were going. I did visit her at her home a couple of times, and she came to visit me. Our affair was more friendship, I suppose; although there was a strong feeling between us, we didn't let it develop into a sexual thing. I didn't want to get involved in an ugly divorce triangle that could perhaps damage all of us, and especially those two beautiful children of hers. And because of what Irene had put me through, I felt a sense of responsibility and guilt for doing the same thing myself. Perhaps it was a way of finding some of the inner egoistic feelings that Irene had seemingly stolen from me with her frivolous escapades there at the same place years before. I'm sure that we were the talk of the racing circuit back then, and Karen and I sure enough turned some heads during our time. As the announcer, I was the last one to leave the upstairs area. Karen would wait while I made my final announcements and said, "This is Willie Kell, saying good evening and drive carefully." Then we would walk down together into what was left of the race-going crowd.

I am not saying it was right to be involved with a married woman, but looking back on it, I am glad to have known her. Maybe I played an important part in her life, like she played in mine. Her marriage had been faltering and she later was divorced, but not because of me. However, after I left Hanover Raceway in 1985, I didn't see her more than once or twice a year at some fairs I was working. I haven't seen her for several years, although we talk on the phone once in a long while.

Willie

Book Forty-one: The Serpent of Florida

The second winter we lived in Innerkip, we decided to take our travel trailer and go to Englewood, Florida, about thirty miles south of Sarasota on the Gulf Coast. Toots, my older sister, and her husband lived there in the winter and liked it. I had a Volare wagon and we had hauled the trailer back and forth between Kincardine and Innerkip in the spring and fall for a few years. However, this was more than a hundred-mile trip; we were going to head out over the Smoky Mountains of Tennessee with the old wagon and that trailer. We took off in March and had a wonderful trip. We parked the trailer about a city block from the Gulf of Mexico in a quaint little trailer park. Our trailer was beside the beach road. We stayed six weeks and loved it. I did some singing in Florida and met wonderful people and had interesting experiences.

Often we walked along the beautiful sandy beach and gathered shells and prehistoric shark's teeth that had been in that great body of water for more than a million years. This was a relaxing way to get some sun and exercise. Someone had told us that we could find even more interesting shells at Middle Beach, a couple of miles up the road. We decided to get up the next morning a little earlier than usual and drive up there and gather some of those shells. It turned out to be quite an experience. Although as a rule we can't wait to have our breakfast in the morning, that morning we didn't take time to have breakfast, not even a coffee.

Willie Kell

We were rather excited as we jumped into the wagon, rolled the windows down, and headed up the beautiful beach road. It was a hot, sultry morning in April, the breeze off the Gulf of Mexico felt so good as it blew in the windows while we drove along the winding road. There is a place along that road where the treetops cover the road, and it is like driving through a tunnel. We always watched for snakes; what if one fell out of the trees into the open car window? There are a lot of poisonous snakes in Florida. We had heard of some scary happenings with those slimy, slinky serpents. There are several different species, like water moccasins, poisonous coral snakes, cottonmouths and a few kinds of rattlesnakes. A couple of our friends had close encounters with rattlers on their front lawns around there.

Well, that hot sultry April morning as we drove slowly along the beach road, our mind was on gathering some pretty shells, not on snakes. However, just as we got past the overhanging trees, we saw it—a huge snake in the middle of the road, likely a rattler. It was curled up with its head reaching out, as if to bite anyone that came near. I knew just what to do—run over it, kill it! Isabelle screamed, "Don't run over it!" She put her head down on the seat of the car so she wouldn't see the thing; she is terrified of snakes. "Don't worry," I told her.

Well, when I looked into the rearview mirror, the thing was still there on the road, madder than hell. I turned around and tried to run over it again, Isabelle still hollering, "Don't run over it!" The darn snake was still on the road, looking rather annoyed. "I'll get him this time."

Well, this time when I looked in the mirror, the snake had vanished. Where did it go? Didn't seem like it had got off the road. A lady on the roadside with her little dog said she thought it had jumped up under the

Willie

car as I passed over it. "Oh, no," Isabelle said, "that snake will crawl up into the car!" Maybe it would come up through where the brakes are.

We rolled up the windows tight and headed back towards our trailer, or somewhere, forgetting about the shells we started out to gather. We really didn't know what to do or where to go; we didn't stop at the trailer park, we just kept driving. We would go to the fire hall in Englewood, a few miles away on the mainland; those brave firemen would know what to do with a vicious rattlesnake. We were scared; if a bug or even a fly had landed on the back of our neck, we would surely die of fright, thinking it was the snake. When we got to the lift-bridge that spans the inland waterway, sure enough, the bridge was up and there was a long line of cars waiting. We sat there in that old wagon with the windows rolled up tight, sweating profusely in the sweltering heat of that south Florida April morning. There was no air conditioner in the wagon. We were afraid to look around; we might look right into the slimy, slinky eyes of that serpent.

At last the lift-bridge descended and we were moving again. We drove straight to the fire station on the main street. I honked the horn and one of the firemen came out, looking rather bewildered. I rolled the window down about an inch and asked him to come over to the car. When at last he did, I told him about the snake. He jumped back from the car and explained that they had never been trained in dealing with snakes, and that we should go to the sheriff's office. Well, we got lost trying to find the sheriff, so we drove around asking people where to find the sheriff and getting strange reactions from everybody. I guess it looked funny, me trying to yell, asking about the sheriff with the car window almost closed.

Willie Kell

We finally found the place, and when we drove into the Charlotte County Sheriff's parking lot, I honked the horn and a deputy came running out with a strange look on his face, his hat pulled down on his forehead and his trigger-happy hand not far from his loaded pistol. He asked rather sternly what he could do for us. Isabelle and me hunched down in the old station wagon must have looked a little weird. I rolled down the window an inch or so and told him about the snake. He looked at us like we were a little crazy, or perhaps an older version of Bonnie and Clyde. I don't know what he would have thought if he'd asked to see my driver's license or the ownership of the wagon, cause we hadn't bothered to bring a wallet, money, or anything with us when we went for the shells.

Oh, it seemed hours since we had left the trailer so happily to go to Middle Beach. We were hot, hungry, and haggled as we sat in the old wagon while that deputy sheriff got down on his hands and knees there in the parking lot, looking for that silly rattlesnake curled up and waiting to strike out at somebody. He looked under the hood as well, but didn't see the snake. He said he didn't think there ever was a snake under the car, and we got the feeling that he took us for some kind of dumb northerners who wouldn't know a rattler if one bit us. He sent us to a local garage, where they put the car on a hoist and checked it all over, but they didn't find the snake and neither did we. By this time we were getting pretty brave. Thank God they didn't charge us for looking for the snake, 'cause we had no money. They did make smartass remarks and treated us as aliens, or Yankees at best.

We finally got back to the trailer, washed up, and ate breakfast. The next morning, I overheard two wise men say that the best way to deal with snakes is to leave them alone.

Willie

Book Forty-two: The Life and Songs Of Stephen Foster

In the area around Englewood, I was soon playing, singing, and meeting people who liked my music. I started doing guest spots with a country band, the leader was Ralph Blizzard, the Tennessee Fiddler. He has gone on to do some great things in music all across the U.S.A. It was fun playing and singing with these talented people from Nashville, Ohio, Indiana, New York, North Carolina and other places. I met interesting people from all over the U.S.A

It seemed too soon and it was time to start back home, back to our farmhouse at Innerkip. Before we did go back, we bought a bigger trailer, left it in Florida, and made plans to come back to the same place the next year for 3 months.

I had always been a big fan of Stephen Foster, America's first great songwriter. I knew a lot about the fellow from stories Daddy had told me and things I had read. While I was in Florida, I did a tribute to Stephen Foster one night at a concert—told some stories about the man and sang some of his songs. The people liked it and asked me if I had recorded it.

After that I did considerable research on the life of this talented man, and during the following summer I wrote the story in my own words. I was finally ready to record

Willie Kell

"THE LIFE AND SONGS OF STEPHEN FOSTER."

It was the next year that I put it all together. On side one, I told the story while strumming my guitar, then sang the songs, putting them in as the story unfolded. In all, I sang 10 of his best songs and told his story, from his childhood in Pittsburgh, his career, his love for "Jeannie with The Light Brown Hair." Then his last tragic years and untimely death on the Bowery in lower New York City, at just 37 years of age. On side two, I sang longer versions of the songs, backed up by banjo, fiddle, guitar, and mandolin: 'Oh, Susannah," "Old Kentucky Home," "Swanee River," "Camptown Races," and several more of his classics.

It wasn't very long until we had a fine-looking, entertaining, and educational product. I sent a copy of the tape to the Library of Congress in Washington, D.C. for copyright. I sent a copy to Bob Graham, the Governor of Florida, and he wrote me a nice letter of praise. I also sent a copy to Dr. Deane Root, the curator of the Stephen Foster Memorial at the University of Pittsburgh, and received a nice letter complimenting my work and inviting me to come to Pittsburgh. That tape would remain in the Foster Hall Collection for future students to learn of America's first great songwriter.

It was a thrill to be invited to the Foster Memorial, where Dr. Root rolled out the red carpet for me. I spent the afternoon there looking over Foster's original manuscripts.

Then our friends, who have lived in Pittsburgh all of their lives, took me to Stephen's grave out at Allegheny Cemetery. It was a wonderful experience, standing there beside the simple tombstone of Stephen Foster. I couldn't help but think that this problem child of the prominent Foster family who died penniless and alone

Willie

back in 1864 had come a long way since then. People all around the world had heard his music. Several of his songs are classics, and he has remained one of America's most beloved folk-heroes. As time went on, folks from all across the U.S.A., parts of Canada, and as far away as Germany, Scotland, and Japan were enjoying that album and learning about Stephen Foster.

Meanwhile, Billy was playing solo gigs and was into music full-time, playing bars and other concerts. He did some guest spots with The Good Brothers, Ronnie Prophet, and other recording artists. He had a good following wherever he went, and people loved him. He became perhaps one of the best flattop guitar pickers anywhere. His stage presence was great, and he could sing so well.

It might have been about this time when he signed a deal with Shotgun Records. He recorded some of his songs on their label and they got him some airplay at radio stations all across the southern states, from North Carolina to California. He was on TV a few times, and they even featured Billy singing a couple of his songs in a movie called *The Cowboy*.

Jimmy was playing drums and singing with another country band, and Patti wasn't doing anything in the entertainment field, but for some guest spots with Billy and me. She was trying to raise her kids. By this time she was separated from her husband and making it on her own.

It was around the time my Stephen Foster album came out that Billy and Anne parted. They still remained friends. Anne was a nurse by this time and had a good position. Billy moved in with a girl he met at the bars where he sang; her name was Donna, and she worked in an office. The children, Erin and Travis, stayed with Billy some of the time. Donna seemed to love

Willie Kell

Billy and his music; she went with him every place he played and never seemed to take her eyes off of him. Of course, Anne couldn't follow Billy and his songs, she had the children to take care of.

In the meantime, while Billy and Patti parted from their partners, Jimmy decided to get married. He married Shirley, after they had lived together for a while.

By now Irene was married again, and she and her husband were at the wedding. I hadn't seen her for several years, but we talked a little and got along fine that day. We even had our pictures taken with our arm around each other. By this time both her mother and father had died and her brother David was married. There were many changes in all of our lives.

Willie

Dr. Deane L. Root and Willie at the Foster Hall Collection
University of Pittsburgh

Stephen Foster's grave
Allegheny Cemetary - Pittsburgh

Willie Kell

Book Forty-three: Beautiful Stoney Keppel

I had often heard of Bev Shouldice; he was a prominent businessman at Shallow Lake, in Keppel Township, just a few miles from Maw's farm and where I went to school as a boy. He was also the chairman of the Keppel Historical Society. He was co-author of a book they had out about Keppel. Well, when he showed me a school picture of me that was in the book, taken at that old Cruickshank School in Keppel back when I was a boy on Maw's farm, we made a deal. I bought a book and he bought one of my Stephen Foster tapes.

Some time later he called me on the phone, said he really enjoyed the Foster tape, and that the Keppel Historical Society would like to commission me to write a song about Keppel Township. They would like to have it completed in a couple of months. I was delighted to be asked to write a song about that beautiful part of the world. So many things had happened since I lived there on Maw's old farm, although I worked the races and fairs for a number of years in Owen Sound and the races were broadcast on the local radio station. They had also written several stories about me in the daily paper through those years. But I hadn't lived in the area since Irene and I went on the road selling medicine some forty years earlier.

When Bev Shouldice called me about writing the song, I was busy with fairs and concerts, but told him I would work on it and see him in about a month. I wrote the song and recorded it with just me and the guitar. I called it "Beautiful Stoney Keppel." I got the idea from

Willie

Billy's song, "Perth County Green." I called Bev Shouldice and told him I had the song written and would see him the next day. He invited the deputy reeve to hear my song too.

When I got to that house, it wasn't a house—it was a castle. I believe it had 24 rooms and 6 bathrooms.

We played the tape and they loved the song, it was just perfect. I said I would record it along with nine other songs and would be happy to have $1000.00 towards the cost of producing it, and he agreed. I came home and made arrangements to record the album. It would be titled "Beautiful Stoney Keppel." Billy played guitar, Jimmy played drums and some bass, and they sang harmony. We got a fiddle player, and soon we had a nice album. We recorded 8 of my own songs and a couple of gospel standards. The Keppel Historical Society ordered several hundred tapes; they soon sold those and ordered more.

It became the #1 best-selling album at the biggest record store in Owen Sound, located just a few doors down Main Street from the old Seldon House, where I used to work as a boy. The Keppel Historical Society is still sending them out all over North America, and some to Europe. I did interviews on the local radio, and there were several nice pictures and articles in the papers—this time not about my announcing races and fairs, but about my music. They wrote about me going to school in Keppel, about me herding the cows on that old winding side road when I was a boy on Maw's farm. They had me on the TV news, signing autographs at the record store. The Hanover paper did a front-page cover story about me that just about covered the front page, telling of the time I attended Campbell's Corner school east of town.

Willie Kell

Bev and Dot Shouldice became special friends. We were invited to their parties, came to know their big family, and we slept in their castle several times.

The next year the Keppel township council decided to put up signs on the roadsides in Keppel, with the title of my song along with musical notes. My name was proudly written on every sign. These are green and white signs, very colourful and attractive. Yes, it was a great feeling to have the people where I lived and went to school as a boy so touched by my song. Everybody in that part of Ontario knows the words to "Beautiful Stony Keppel."

Someone at the National Library in Ottawa called; they had heard about my songs. They requested that I send copies of my recordings to be placed in the Archives of the National Library in Ottawa. I was honoured.

When I went to Florida, the radio station in Englewood did an interview with me and played my songs. They got requests and still play my music. They have also featured my album, "The Life and Songs of Stephen Foster." Yes, the media in both Canada and the U.S.A. have been very kind to me through the years.

We were spending more time in Florida each year and getting to know some interesting people there from all over the U.S.A. I was being noticed for my songs, and playing some really nice places in the south. Isabelle bought me a keyboard and I learned to chord on it and play the guitar at the same time. I also had a tambourine under my foot that helped keep the rhythm. I learned this trick from Billy. We got invited to a preacher's house a few times to sing and started going to his little church. I was also singing in other churches around Englewood, Florida. They seemed to like my gospel songs. This preacher, Brian Lee, and his wife Elsie became good friends, and she sang with me at different

Willie

churches. Elsie soon knew all of my gospel songs. We became friends with another couple from the little church, Bea and Marlyn; they lived just up the street from the preacher. We were often invited for dinner parties where we would sing for the guests, and they showed me some good things about life.

I met Marlyn and Bea Johnson about the same time, they had moved from Wisconsin. Bea had some good stories to tell about her childhood, she later wrote a book and we became friends. She told me that the Chicago gangster AL CAPONE used to run liquor from Chicago to north Wisconsin back in probation days. He had a hideaway in the woods near a place called Draper, about five miles from where she lived as a child. Her sister's in laws had a farm near Spooner and when Capone and his boys were heading to the hideout with the booze they would stop at they're place, put the car in the barn and those folks would give them supper and put them up for the night. Capone paid good money for this special accommodation and that's how those in-laws paid for the farm.

Book Forty-four: Jesus, Fanny Crosby, and Me

These church friends encouraged me to record my gospel songs. It was during that next summer that I went to work in my music room in that nice old farmhouse by the river, and I put together "Jesus: His Life On Earth." It was the story of the Lord from the manger to the cross and beyond the resurrection. I put it in my own words, but taken from the King James Version of the Bible. In the fall Billy, Jimmy, and I went into the studio and recorded that album—the story narrated on one side and my 10 gospel songs on the other. Also, a spoken tribute to Fanny Crosby, the great blind gospel songwriter and her song "Pass Me Not."

I wrote "The Glory Train" just a day or two before we went to record the album, and it became a favourite. Along with "Thou Art The Shepherd" and "My Mother's Old Bible." Doug McNaughton from The Creamcheeze Good-Time Band played fiddle, mandolin, and piano. My two boys, Billy and Jimmy, did a great job producing, playing, and singing harmony on that album. We recorded it at the University of Waterloo and it was a wonderful experience, having my beautiful, talented boys there with me.

When it was finished, I grabbed the master and headed to Florida. I had the tapes manufactured in Orlando. We soon had a nice package and the album turned out great.

When we got to Florida, just after Christmas, I contacted some preachers and made arrangements to sing at several churches. It was a way of telling those

Willie

people about my gospel tape. We had some success selling the gospel tape, but not as much as I had hoped for. Seems a lot of those so-called Christians aren't very free with their cash. I used to tell them at churches that Billy sold more of those gospel tapes in bars than I did in church. I learned a quite a bit about preachers in dealing with them. However, it did find a way into bible studies and prisons and was enjoyed by many from Florida to California. We did get some airplay on one of the biggest gospel radio stations in the Bible Belt, in Panama City, Florida. I did an interview and they played my gospel songs on another radio station as well.

Life was going pretty good; Isabelle and I enjoyed the winters in the south. She liked swimming in the Gulf of Mexico. I kept busy with my music, playing concerts along the Sun Coast between Sarasota and Ft. Myers, Florida. We had wonderful friends. We visited, we took a cruise to the Bahamas, and it seemed that we were invited to every party and get-together that happened. We got back to Canada in early May, and it was good to see the kids.

By the mid '80s I wasn't announcing at Hanover anymore and wasn't working as many fairs. We still spent some time at the lake, and enjoyed the life there.

Willie Kell

Book Forty-five: Billy's Last Song

Our old farmhouse at Innerkip was always home to us and we liked being there. We had a vegetable garden and Isabelle had lots of flowers. We planted several nice trees when I first bought the place, and they were beginning to look great. My children and grandchildren came for Christmas several years, while Isabelle went to her kids in the Toronto area. The neighbours were always nice to us, and I developed a friendship with a couple of nice people. There was Laureen, who has remained a good friend and soulmate, and Laura, she lived in a new house across the street from us. Laura wrote some nice poetry and painted good pictures, so it was easy relating to her.

Billy had been complaining of a pain in his arm and shoulder for a while; we thought it must be some kind of arthritis. He went to the doctor and chiropractor and even took some Tone-A-Lax. The problem just seemed to get worse, and the doctor put him on painkillers.

Isabelle and I went to Florida in early November 1990; it would be our first Christmas in the south. Billy and Donna and the children came over for dinner before we left and were planning to come to Florida and would see us about February. They had been down a few years before, and we had a wonderful time. Billy sang with me at the Golden.

Now we were looking forward to them coming again. Isabelle and I had made a deal for a really nice luxury trailer, quite big and fancy, and Billy was anxious to see it. He had recorded a new album that included my song, "Daddy's Rollin' Home Tonight."

It was during that winter that I talked with the manager of the Cultural Center Theatre at Port Charlotte, Florida, to do a stage presentation of "The Life and Songs Of Stephen Foster." The manager was quite interested, but we couldn't get the chorus director into it. I had written the stage presentation and thought it would go over well.

It was disappointing when it didn't work out. I had been telling Billy about it and he was quite excited to think his father was going to do this big production in that prestigious theatre.

That winter we kept quite busy as usual, even without the Stephen Foster production. I was playing concerts along the southwest coast of Florida, at mobile home parks, condos, special events, churches, at Expo and just about any other place they play and sing music. They wrote nice things about me in the newspapers, took pictures, and treated me great.

We were looking forward to Billy and Donna coming. There would be three others with them, he said. One day late in February the phone rang, and it was Billy calling from West Palm Beach, Florida, over on the east coast. He said they would see us the next day. They were travelling in a motor home. He told me on the phone that he would have to find a doctor to get some more painkillers when he got to Englewood.

The next day they arrived. I had arranged for a place to park the motor home at a trailer park on the other side of town. We had a nice time; the first night we took them for supper at a restaurant in Venice, but Billy didn't seem to be very hungry. We were invited to our friend's home, along with several people. Billy and I would sing and play and our host, Magic Jack Smith, would do a magic show. Jack and his wife Francis were special friends. They had met Billy when they were at our place in Canada a few years before, when we went to hear him singing and playing near Kitchener.

I was looking forward to the evening, but Billy was tired when we came back after supper. When we got to Jack's place, it was full of people waiting for the show. Billy sang, I sang, we sang together, and the people liked what we did. Then Jack did his show and Billy and his friends enjoyed it. But he was ready for bed, it had been a long day.

The next day all five of them came to the trailer and we had a wonderful time. Billy put a new set of strings on my Gibson guitar; he sure liked that old box. We went to visit some more friends who had met Billy before. We stopped at the doctor's office; Billy needed painkillers.

Our friends Marlyn and Bea had a beautiful big home on the outskirts of town. That evening we were invited there for dinner, along with a big gang from the church, including the pastor and his wife. They were waiting to meet Billy and hearing him sing and play guitar.

Before we went there for supper Billy had to have a sleep, he was tired out. He rested on Isabelle's bed in the trailer and slept for a awhile.

Everybody was happy to meet Billy; they had heard me talk of him so much, they thought they knew him. We set up a couple of microphones and speakers in the family room, which was like an intimate concert hall with cathedral ceilings and a huge, friendly fireplace. When Billy started to play and sing, those people just loved to hear him, they applauded every song. Billy asked me to join in with my guitar and sing a few songs. I sang and played guitar with him, and Elsie, the preacher's wife, joined in as well. We did some gospel

Willie

songs, sang several of my songs, and we closed out with the song Billy always closed with, the great Hank Williams gospel song, "I Saw the Light." Everybody sang and clapped their hands. Though Billy seemed tired and not himself, he was great. That was his last song; he never sang or played the guitar again as long as he lived.

The next morning they drove around to our trailer on their way out of town to say good-bye. They were going to Nashville and the Grand Ole Opry and heading back home the next day. Billy had an appointment at the hospital in Kitchener for a check-up and X-ray on the following Monday, the day after they got home.

He called a week later and said he had lung cancer and was going for radiation treatment. I was devastated. I didn't know what to say, just mumbled the best things I could think of.

Isabelle hadn't been feeling well for a few days and was lying on the couch. When I got off the phone, I told her Billy had lung cancer and she started to cry. She always liked Bill.

When we took Isabelle to the doctor, we discovered she had a big bulge on the main artery in her abdomen that had to be operated on immediately. That was Good Friday, late afternoon; she had the operation on Monday morning. It was serious; they stopped her heart five times, but she had a great doctor and a lot of prayers. The preacher stayed at the hospital all day, and my brother Jim and his wife Velma were there, and everybody was so nice. Thank God she pulled through.

But the news about Billy wasn't as encouraging. They wouldn't be able to operate, his chances were not as good. I couldn't go home to him, I had to be with Isabelle. I called Billy at the hospital in London and he said he was fine, they were taking care of him. Told me to stay and take care of Isabelle, and that's what I did.

She was able to travel in a month; she was weak for a quite a while, but by the time the month was up, we were ready for home. I hated to come home and watch Billy die, but that's what we did.

The day after we got home, we went to see him in the Kitchener hospital. He looked awful and he could hardly talk. The next time we saw him he was in the cancer hospital in London, they were giving him radiation treatments there. I gave up Clinton Raceway to spend more time with him, and now just announced at Goderich Thursday nights.

Some of Billy's friends set up a couple of benefits for him. They had one benefit at the Stratford Arena, a half-dozen bands performed for free. They charged $10.00 admission and the place was full. When Donna wheeled Billy into that place in a wheelchair, he got a huge standing ovation. Irene and her husband and friends were at the head table inside the door. I went by myself, paid my $10.00, and kind of watched from the sidelines. It was a wonderful tribute to our Billy. He sat autographing his new album that people were buying.

Willie

Book Forty-six: Billy's Gone, Who's Going to Sing His Songs?

It was a couple of weeks later they had another benefit for him at Cambridge. Again the place was packed with his fans and friends. A couple of local bands played, and then his old buddies, The Good Brothers, who had been voted Canada's group of the year, were there to perform. Billy had played several shows with these talented people over the years. He and Brian Good were friends. Brian and the Good Brothers had played all over North America. I guess Brian and Gordon Lightfoot were friends too. Some say they had the same girlfriend, though not at the same time. She became more famous than they were. Her name was Cathy Smith; she gained notoriety for allegedly being the girl that was with John Belushi when he died out in Hollywood.

Our Billy just kept going downhill and it was sad to see, but he never complained, he kept his smile. Donna and he wanted to get married. Anne, his wife, came sometimes, and it was interesting to watch these two people who both loved Billy, one on each side of his bed.

His divorce from Anne came through while Billy lay dying. He and Donna got married, and Isabelle and I stood beside his bed, along with his children, as the preacher pronounced them man and wife. The next morning Donna called to say that Billy had slipped away at about 7:15 AM. Our Billy was dead at just 40 years old.

Willie Kell

When I kissed his forehead and told him I loved him the night before as we said good-bye, I wondered if I would see him alive again in this world. The last few weeks he lived, we went to see him every day but Thursday, when I was working the races. The preacher and his wife, Brian-Lee and Elsie, and our friends Marlyn and Bea, drove up from Florida to see him. The preacher asked Billy if he knew Jesus. Billy looked him in the eye and said, "I sure do, he is a friend of mine."

I got to see Irene while Billy lay dying; she came sometimes and sat with him too. When he lay at the funeral parlour, folks came from all over to pay their respects. So many knew him and loved him, not only for his music, but for what he was—a beautiful human being. They couldn't get everybody into the place for the funeral. His casket was closed, his old guitar stood beside it, and there was a picture of him on the coffin. His friends and fans came and cried for him. It was hard to lose him, there would never be one like him again.

He was laid to rest in that country cemetery beneath the tall pines, the same cemetery where that young man who was hanged back in 1954 is buried. Donna put up a nice tombstone in the likeness of a guitar. Sometimes, when we're close by, we stop and say hello.

Book Forty-seven: Playing The Big Stage

That summer wore on after Billy died. I went about my life and wrote the songs God gave me. Played some fairs, and soon it was time to go south. I had rather a busy schedule, playing gigs along the southwest coast of Florida from Sarasota to Fort Myers. It was the following year I learned that there was a new lady manager at the Port Charlotte Cultural Center Theatre. I went to see her and she was quite interested in the idea of presenting "The Life and Songs of Stephen Foster" live on the stage of the theatre.

We set a date for Sunday afternoon, March 14th, and signed a contract for a 50/50 split of the gate receipts. I would arrange for a chorus. The theatre would supply a sound and light man, have the tickets printed, and sell them at their box office. We could use their props and the grand piano. They had a publicist, but she didn't help much.

It was early in January that we signed the deal and there would be a lot of work to do before March 14th. I contacted a chorus group, and they were delighted to sing in my production. I had the music for the Foster songs I wanted them to sing. There would be about 22 voices in the mixed chorus; one of them would play the piano and another lady would play the banjo and harmonica. They had considerable experience singing at several places in the Englewood area. The leader was a lady with two degrees, one in music and one as a minister.

Willie Kell

The members of the chorus and I would be dressed in what could pass as period clothes. I would be seated on a stool at the left front of the big stage.

I was to narrate the story of Stephen Foster while strumming the guitar. I would sing part of a song, then the chorus would take over. I also sang several more obscure Foster songs; everything had to be quite precise. They had two or three soloists in the chorus, and soon everybody had their parts down great.

The tickets started selling pretty good at the box office, even though it had very little publicity, and they sold much better when a couple of newspapers did picture stories on Foster and me. Entertainment writers and photographers came up from Port Charlotte and took pictures and did nice write-ups. I also did a couple of radio interviews and commercials. We had many requests for tickets from friends and neighbours. I had decided to keep the price so that any seniors who might not have much money to spend could afford to go. There was one lady, 94 years old, from Pittsburgh originally. Her family at one time ran a funeral home at the very place where Stephen Foster was born. She called me from Port Charlotte and I arranged for her to have a complimentary ticket.

Finally the big day arrived—March 14th, 1993. We had already had one rehearsal at the theatre and had the feel of the place. Isabelle and I arrived early and got the stagehands busy setting up for our show. We were there helping and directing where things would go. The show was scheduled to start at 2.30 PM. The box office was open at 1:30. The theatre had less than 500 seats, but it is a very prestigious theater, so many famous people had performed there over the years. Isabelle had brought a lunch and we ate it there in my large dressing room backstage.

Willie

We did a sound and light check and everything was going fine. The theatre looked so ghostly in the dim lights. It was time to dress and get prepared for the big moment. Isabelle looked out the dressing room door and there was a lineup at the box-office, the theater was filling up. We knew it would be a sell-out, because most of the seats were already sold. I had recordings of Foster songs playing, so the sounds of "Swanee River" and "My Old Kentucky Home" and several more Foster classics were quietly floating through the theatre.

Then the house lights dimmed, the huge curtains swung open, and the chorus began singing "Way down upon the Swanee River, far far away ..." When they finished singing "Swanee River," I made an entrance from left stage and sat on the stool with my guitar. And as the lights dimmed on center stage and the spotlight shone down on me, I began to tell the story of America's first great songwriter. I could see that every eye was on me. I could hear the faint sounds of people softly crying in the sad parts, and I could see the happy faces as they listened to the happy songs, "Oh, Susannah" and "Camptown Races."

When the production was over, just past 4 o'clock, there was a loud, thunderous ovation, and when the announcer mentioned my name, everyone in the theatre got to their feet for a loud and long standing tribute as I humbly stood holding my old Gibson guitar. It felt good to know that several of my friends were there in the audience, including my two sisters, Toots and Elizabeth.

Isabelle and Bea were selling my Foster tapes in the lobby, and I was soon busy signing autographs. It had all been a huge success. After writing, producing, and presenting it here for the first time, this creation of mine, this dream that I had dreamed, had come true. Billy would have loved it; so would Daddy and Mother. Now I had a production, a show that I had written and

Willie Kell

created. Now it could be done anywhere—in New York, or Atlanta, or even Tokyo. But, being like my Daddy, I probably wouldn't do much with it. I had proven something to me.

The following year we did it all over again in the same theatre, and again it was a huge success. It was even better than the year before. As I was signing autographs in the lobby of the theatre after the show, a fine-looking couple from Japan came up to me. The man put his arms around me and said in his beautiful Japanese tongue, "I have waited 70 years to see Stephen Foster, and at last I have seen him." Even though I tell the story of Foster, and not from a first-person perspective, people still believe when they leave that theatre that I am Stephen Foster, perhaps because I feel a special closeness to Stephen, the man and his music. Some have said that I'm the reincarnated Stephen Foster. He was born in the summer of 1826, while I was born in the summer of 1926.

When we made plans for the first production of the Foster presentation, I wrote Dr. Root and sent him a poster, which he would proudly display at the Foster Memorial at The University of Pittsburgh. We keep in touch and write occasionally. He also has my "Beautiful Stony Keppel" tape and wrote me a nice letter complimenting me on those songs. It was a thrill for me when this great man with a degree in music, a writer, and lecturer asked me for my autograph. Moments like that can make one feel mighty humble, knowing our beginning in this world and realising how well we can be blessed. I have always believed that my songs and the things I am able to write are given to me, and I'm ever grateful.

Willie

These times, I spend a little while in Nashville, pitching my songs on my way to Florida. I suppose I should go live there, but it's hard to give up my life as I have it. One of my albums is titled along those lines; it's called "WILLIE KELL IN NASHVILLE." There's 10 of my songs on that tape, and when I pitched it in Nashville, the publishers kept six of those songs. Now, the chances of somebody recording them isn't all that great, but at least somebody likes them in Music City, U.S.A. The people in Nashville want me to record my songs there; perhaps I will do more recording there.

It could be that I'm like my Daddy, more content than I should be.

Beautiful Stoney Keppel
These signs commemorating Willie's song are part of the landscape in the Keppel area of Ontario

Willie Kell

Book Forty-eight: The Big One That Got Away—

In the summer of 1994 I wrote several pretty good songs, and we recorded six of my tunes on a demo tape. On our annual migration to Englewood, Florida in November, we went by way of Nashville, as we had done the year before. We booked into a nice place at Brentwood, Tennessee, about eight miles south of Nashville, as we did the year before. Many of the big country stars live in and around Brentwood.

I had a few dozen tapes made in Nashville from the master I had taken with me. Then, every morning, I would get busy on the phone and call small publishers; the big ones don't talk to strangers. I always try to get appointments with publishers and have them listen to my songs. Well, I pitched that tape on Music Row in Nashville for a few days and didn't have as good a reaction as I got the year before. Things were changing in Music City. The smaller publishers were finding it harder to get their songs cut.

The songs on the demo were a variety. One of the songs everyone seemed excited about when we recorded it was called "If You Should See Her." I left about 10 tapes with different publishers, hoping against all odds of getting something cut. Nothing happened.

Or so it seemed. Actually, a lot happened. Just three and a half years later, I heard this song on the radio (I hardly ever listen to the radio). Brooks & Dunn—voted the best country duo in music—and Reba McIntyre were singing what was left of my song, "If You Should See Her." It was # 4 on the country charts at the time.

I couldn't believe my ears. I heard the very lines and phrases that I had written; the melody was somewhat different, but the whole idea of my song and over 60 percent of the words were the same. Three so-called writers—none had ever had a song as big before or since—got credit for the song.

I wrote: "If you should see her, tell her I'm doing fine."
They wrote and B&D sang: "If you see her, tell her I'm doing fine."

I wrote: "Give her my very best and wish her well,
How long will this hurt go on only TIME will TELL"
They wrote and Reba sang: "If you see him, tell him I wish him well,
How am I doing? Well, sometimes it's hard to tell."

Then there were some exact phrases, and all in all it was obvious that if someone hadn't copied my song, it would have to be the biggest coincidence in song-writing history.

The song got to be a #1 country hit, a #1 video hit, and the title song for both Reba's and Brooks & Dunn's album. It went platinum for Brooks & Dunn, and Reba's did real well too. The song generated millions of $$$$$, but not a penny for Willie. MCA, Arista, several publishers, and the above recording artists all went to the bank big time, as well as those writers.

They say Nashville is famous for such things. However, I looked into it with a lawyer and a musicologist, and although they agreed it was my song, I haven't lost a minute's sleep over it and I hope they all

Willie Kell

sleep well too. I wrote Reba and her husband Narvel, but they didn't take the time to answer. I read that she said it was her best song ever. I'm sure she told Brooks & Dunn, so they all know that Willie wrote that big million-dollar hit!

Willie as Hank Williams - playing the big stage

Book Forty-nine: Willie Kell Presents "HANK WILLIAMS—HIS LIFE AND HIS SONGS" At The Port Charlotte Cultural Center Theatre, Florida

I signed the contract in early January, and the show was scheduled for March 1st. I got busy and started to write it; I prayed that God would show me what to write and tell me what to do, and He did.

I put it together something like my Stephen Foster show. However, this time I would not only tell the story of Hank's life, but would play the part. I would be sitting on a stool to one side of the big stage, with my guitar. Wearing my black stage hat and my tan leather vest. Tell Hank's story while strumming the guitar and sing parts of songs as they folded into the story. As the band played a fiddle tune, I would go behind a curtain and change into white hat and jacket and come out to center stage as Hank Williams.

The show looked good to me on paper and in my mind. The theatre printed some handbills and the tickets. Now all I had to do was get the whole thing written, get a band together, and someone to play Audrey and Cousin Minnie Pearl. But not to worry—I had all of six weeks to do these things. I knew just the gal to play Audrey and Minnie Pearl—my Patti. She would fly in and do it with one rehearsal. I found a four-piece country band, a stand-up bass player who had played with Homer and Jethro. A fine lead guitar player, a pretty good fiddle player, and a rhythm guitar player who had actually played at the Grand Ole Opry

Willie Kell

when Hank Williams last appeared there in 1952, not long before he died. This same Zack Tucker had played with the legendary Marty Robbins. They were very excited about doing the Hank Williams presentation, especially after our first rehearsal when they heard me sing those songs about as close as anyone could sing them to Hank himself.

When the time came for the show, everybody was quite excited. The theatre sold out; they even put extra seats in the back of the theatre to accommodate some that had already bought tickets. I don't know how many had to be turned away. The show was a smash! The crowd loved every minute of it and showed it with a loud, long, standing ovation. After the performance, the members of the band and several others suggested I take the show on the road. Perhaps to Branson, Misouri, billed as the music capital of the world. It was certainly something to consider.

When we got back to Canada, I decided to do "Hank Williams." We got together with Doug and Dave from the Creamcheeze Good-time Band, along with a guitar and steel player, and soon we were rehearsing for a show at the Market Center Theatre in Woodstock, Ontario.

We did two shows a Saturday night and a Sunday matinee. The shows went real well. Patti was great as both Miss Audrey and Minnie Pearl, and the band performed well. It was nice to play so close to home, just five miles from Innerkip, although the theatre was not as big as the one in Florida and it wasn't a sell-out. Of course, all my family were there, except Erin (Billy's girl) and Patti's children. Travis (Billy's boy) helped with curtains and backstage and Chuck, Patti's husband, ran the sound. It was good to have them.

Willie

For the next two years Patti came to Florida and played the parts at the Port Charlotte Theatre. The first year was another sell-out and a very good show, although Amos Shepherd, the bass player and leader of the band, was dying with lung cancer. Just a couple of months later he died at his home in Illinois.

The following year when we did the Hank Williams show, Zack the rhythm guitar player couldn't make the show, as he had moved to Georgia, and Amos was gone. Larry, the fiddle player, was sick and hardly able to play. We had a steel player and a bass player, and they did their best, but it wasn't the same without Amos and Zack. Once again Patti was great and the crowd loved it.

The first year Patti came to Florida, she brought her daughter Paula and Anne, Billy's first wife, and it was great to have them. They stayed at my friend Bea's place on the other side of town. Both Paula and Anne helped backstage; it was so good to have my family there.

Willie in Concert
Book 49 "Willie Kell Presents HANK WILLIAMS—HIS LIFE AND HIS SONGS" At The Port Charlotte Cultural Center Theatre "

Willie Kell

Book Fifty: Time's Winding Down—Still Living on Dreams

Those are some lines in a song I wrote a short while back, and I think there's a lot of truth in those very lines. I guess I have mostly lived on visions and dreams, never took myself or the world around me very serious. I think we have to do the best we can with what we have been given. Some wise person once said that money is a necessary evil, something we need to keep body and mind together. But money is certainly not what some people believe it to be. It can't buy everything. Maybe it's the challenge of being able to obtain some things that money *can* buy that makes life interesting.

I believe in the gifts that I have been given, the love that I had for my wife Irene and the children, without spoiling them. Trying to teach them what I thought was good and right, but always trying to keep a good sense of humour; sometimes, because of certain things, it was a bit difficult. I have treated Isabelle the best I know how with love, patience, and understanding, in spite of my sometimes, frivolous ways and my need to search for the love that seems so illusive.

I regret that I have not been as close to my grandchildren as I would like, but that is mostly because of the break-up of our marriage. It also could be because I have some fear of getting too close to them, then losing them, or losing their love. It has happened to me in my life so many times. First, I lost my mother when I was just six years old, then a second mother when Maw died

Willie

while I lived with her on the farm when I was ten. The trauma of losing Irene, although I divorced her because our situation became intolerable due to her infidelity. Losing the love of her mother, whom I loved dearly. Then losing Billy when he died of cancer. All of those things were very tragic to me, but I have never talked much about them or dwelt on the sorrow they brought into my life. In spite of these things, I remain an optimist, have a very positive outlook on life, and I am quite a happy person, satisfied with life's journey thus far and looking forward to more.

I believe that I have succeeded in life. Isabelle has been with me now more than 20 years. We've had some wonderful times and there have been some bumps along the road. When she came to live with me, there were no promises, it has just been a day-to-day thing. I think it is good to keep our options open; if we get restless, we can move on to greener fields.

I have never really felt settled since Irene and I broke up, but that doesn't mean I'm unhappy, it just means that I have come to see life as it really is, and God gives me the wisdom to make it work.

We have moved again. I sold the farmhouse and the big property at Innerkip and moved to the lakeshore town of Kincardine, where we used to spend time in the summer with our trailer. I bought a home, a good property in a great neighbourhood just three blocks from the beach.

I guess my greatest accomplishments are my family and the love I have for them, including my brothers and sisters. I feel very close to my dear sister Elizabeth, and I keep in close touch with Billy's widow, Anne. I believe my love for Irene helps to sustain me. Patti has two beautiful, talented children, Raurri and Paula. Paula is a gifted artist. Billy and Anne had two very talented children, and Anne is raising those kids the way Billy would have them raised. Travis has a band of his own and plays the bass guitar, and recently did some recording. Erin is planning on acting and directing movies, and with her determination and talent, she'll do it. Jimmy and Shirley have three beautiful girls—Kati and her twin sisters, Lisa and Laura. I have 7 grandchildren.

I've lived quite a while in this world, and I'm proud to have been able to meet great people from many walks of life who have come my way. Some have been hoboes and some have been kings, and after all, I don't think it matters much. It's what you are inside that really counts.

Many of my friends and loved ones have left this old world and gone to their eternal rest. Pop and Mama, Jack and Chuck from the Seldon House. Nora and Wes Litt from the Windsor. Jimmy Yemon drowned himself. My Amish friends Nancy and Johnny and Johnny Kuepfer; my race horse trainer-drivers Burt Graham and Harold Wellwood. Many of the horse judges and politicians that seemed so important in their time sleep silent now beneath the sod.

Mary died sitting in a chair, watching TV. Toots and Sweet and their husbands and Elizabeth's husband all died suddenly. My Florida friend, Marylyn, helped me get the car ready for our trip north in April a few years ago. Then he died of cancer on my birthday, August 3rd. Bea called me and asked if I would send a tape of a few gospel songs. I put together a eulogy and some songs. Bea and I have remained good friends.

Son and Irene stayed together and lived on Maw's old farm in Stony Keppel for almost sixty years. Son died rather suddenly a few years ago, just a few months after they moved to Owen Sound. My brother Jim lives there as well with his second wife. My sister Elizabeth has married again and seems quite happy; she married a good man she had gone to high school with. Billy's gone and so is Alex McDonald, Daddy's hobo friend. Alex was riding a freight train out of Stratford one cold winter night a few years back. They put him off at the little station at Brunner, near our farm in Perth County. He went to sleep and he never woke up.

My other kissing cousin, Betty, is buried out in Phoenix, Arizona. Ironically, her husband had run off with another woman and divorced her; she moved to Arizona and died there

In my life I have been blessed abundantly; many wonderful and interesting people have come my way, and some have remained friends. I am proud of my family, for who they are and what they've done. Billy is gone, but his name and the name of Patti and Jim, along with the other members of our musical family, are forever proudly written on the pages of the Encyclopedia of Canadian Rock, Pop, & Folk Music. I like to think I had a part in that happening.

My songs and Billy's songs are in the archives of Canada's National Library.

Yes, although I have seen quite a few summers come and go I feel forever youthful. I hope to remain that romantic, loving human being who has brought me this far. I'm always finding new and adventurous things to do. Life has taught me that we never really know what's around the next bend or over the winding hill that lies before us. Sometimes, beyond those hard old hills, we may find a valley filled with sunshine. Many times, in that peaceful green valley there's abundant pasture and plenty of fresh, cool water. I've climbed some of those hills and they were often paved with stone, and I've spent a share of my time in the peaceful valley filled with lush, green pastures, and plenty of cool, fresh water.

Printed in the United States
1059900001B